THE VIKINGS

By the same author
VIKING AGE DENMARK (1982)

ELSE ROESDAHL

THE VIKINGS

TRANSLATED BY SUSAN M. MARGESON
AND KIRSTEN WILLIAMS

ALLEN LANE
THE PENGUIN PRESS

ALLEN LANE
THE PENGUIN PRESS
Published by the Penguin Group
Penguin Books Ltd, 27 Wrights Lane, London W8 5TZ, England
Penguin Books Inc., 375 Hudson Street, New York, New York 10014, USA
Penguin Books Australia Ltd, Ringwood, Victoria, Australia
Penguin Books Canada Ltd, 10 Alcorn Avenue, Toronto, Ontario, Canada M4V 3B2
Penguin Books (NZ) Ltd, 182–190 Wairau Road, Auckland 10, New Zealand

Penguin Books Ltd, Registered Offices: Harmondsworth, Middlesex, England

First published in Denmark as *Vikingernes Verden* by Gyldendal, Copenhagen, 1987
First published in Great Britain by Allen Lane The Penguin Press 1991
3 5 7 9 10 8 6 4 2

Filmset in Monophoto Bembo
Printed in Great Britain by Butler & Tanner Ltd, Frome and London

A CIP catalogue record for this book is available from the British Library
LCCN 86–51203
ISBN 0–713–99048–1

TO MY FRIENDS

Contents

═══

CONCLUSION

LIST OF FIGURES AND MAPS

LIST OF PLATES

═

PICTURE CREDITS

FIGURES

All the maps and some other drawings were made for the Danish edition of this book in 1987 by Orla Svendsen, Moesgård Museum, Denmark. Place-names on maps were revised in 1990 for the English edition.

Age in the Isle of Man, 1974, p. 6, and on P. H. Sawyer, *Kings and Vikings*, 1982, p. 112

37 After D. M. Wilson and O. Klindt-Jensen, *Viking Art*, 1966, 1980, p. 113. Drawing Eva Wilson, London

38 Orla Svendsen, 1987

39 Patrick Wallace, National Museum of Ireland, reconstruction drawing 1986

40 Orla Svendsen, 1987, based on N. P. Brooks and J. A. Graham-Campbell, 'Reflections on the Viking-Age Silver Hoard from Croydon, Surrey', *Anglo-Saxon Monetary History* (ed. M. A. S. Blackburn), 1986, p. 108

41 Orla Svendsen, 1987

42 After P. H. Sawyer, *The Age of the Vikings*, 2nd ed. 1971, p. 161 (the map was first published by H. Smith in 1956)

43 Orla Svendsen, 1987

44 Orla Svendsen, 1987, based on B. Linderoth Wallace, 'Resultaten av de senare grävningarna vid l'Anse aux Meadows', *Hus, gård och bebyggelse* (ed. G. Ólafsson), 1983

45 Orla Svendsen, 1989, after a photograph

46 Left and right: Orla Svendsen, 1989, after photographs in *Duisburg und die Wikinger* (ed. Niederrheinisches Museum der Stadt Duisburg), 1983, pp. 74, 81. Centre: Orla Svendsen, 1987, after J. Herrmann, ed., *Wikinger und Slawen*, 1982, p. 287

47 After D. M. Wilson and O. Klindt-Jensen, *Viking Art*, 1966, 1980, p. 152. Drawing Eva Wilson

PLATES

2–3, 6–8, 11, 19, 23   University Museum of National Antiquities, Oslo

4, 15–16   Antikvarisk-Topografiska Arkivet, Stockholm

12, 14, 18, 20–21   National Museum of Denmark, Copenhagen

1   Statens Lantmäteriverk, Gävle, Sweden

5   York Archaeological Trust. Photo A. K. G. Jones

9   Riksantikvarieämbetet, Stockholm. Photo Jan Norrman. Drawing Orla Svendsen

10   Lars Bergström, Stockholm

ACKNOWLEDGEMENTS

The publishers are grateful for permission to reprint the following copyright material:

Boydell & Brewer Ltd for *Encomium Emmae Reginae*, edited and translated by Alastair Campbell, in Camden Third Series, Volume LXXII (Royal Historical Society, London, 1949).

David Campbell Publishers and Professor John Lucas for *Egil's Saga*, edited and translated by Christine Fell; poems translated by J. Lucas (Everyman edition, London, 1975).

Faber & Faber Ltd. for *The Elder Edda: A Selection*, translated by P. B. Taylor and W. H. Auden (London, 1969).

Hermann Palsson and Paul Edwards (translators) for *Knytlinga Saga* (Odense, 1986).

Medieval Academy Books for *The Russian Primary Chronicle: Laurentian Text*, edited and translated by S. H. Cross and O. P. Sherbowitz-Wetzov (Medieval Academy of America Publication no. 60, 1953).

Thorlac Turville-Petre for *Harald the Hard Ruler* by E. O. G. Turville-Petre (Dorothea Coke Memorial Lecture, 1966; London, 1968).

Every effort has been made to contact copyright holders. The publishers regret any errors or omissions and would be grateful to hear from any copyright holders not fully acknowledged.

PREFACE

Writing this book — a survey of an important and fascinating period of Scandinavia's past — has been exciting. It has also been fascinating to trace the activities of the Vikings in Europe and to assess their significance. The book covers what I believe to be the most important aspects of the Viking Age, where interpretations and problems are reasonably clear. The period is still being actively researched in many countries and in many scholarly disciplines, and it would have been impossible for me to write the book without help and encouragement from many valued colleagues and friends. I would like to extend my warm thanks to all of them, and especially to Hans Bekker-Nielsen, Ole Crumlin-Pedersen, Gillian Fellows-Jensen, Steen Hvass, Niels Lund and Preben Meulengracht Sørensen in Denmark; to Charlotte Blindheim, Signe Horn Fuglesang, Olav Sverre Johansen, Heid Resi and Gerd Stamsø Munch in Norway; to Björn Ambrosiani, Birgit Arrhenius, Inga Hägg, Ingmar Jansson and Peter Sawyer in Sweden; to Frans Verhaeghe in Belgium; to Thomas Fanning and Patrick Wallace in Ireland; to James Graham-Campbell and Raymond Page in England. Also to Lene Larsen and Sigrid Fallingborg for typing the final manuscript, to Mogens Kristensen of the publishers Gyldendal for his co-operation on the Danish edition of the book, *Vikingernes Verden*, to Daphne Tagg for her careful editing, and to Sue Margeson and Kirsten Williams for their translation into English and their useful comments.

But my greatest thanks go to David Wilson, who read the Danish manuscript and suggested many improvements. And to Erich, who both read and commented on the whole book, and made sure that Styrbjørn was kept happy, while his mother spent much of her time at the typewriter instead of playing with him.

Else Roesdahl
Århus, August 1990

Europe and neighbouring regions

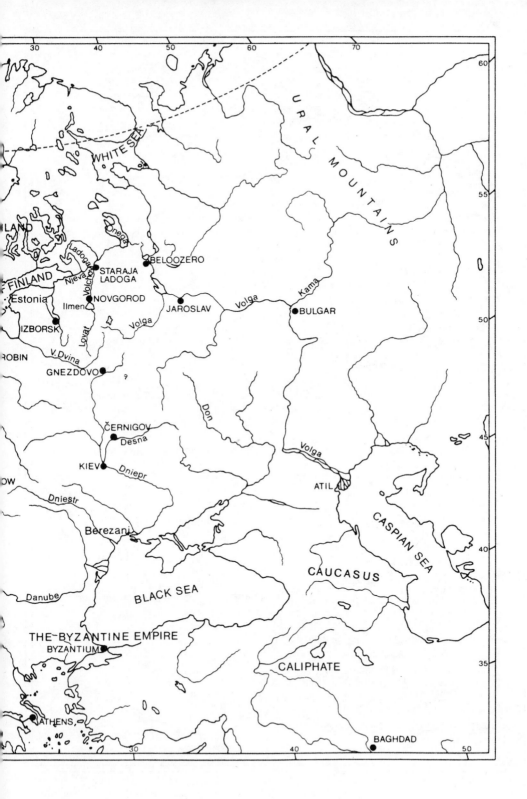

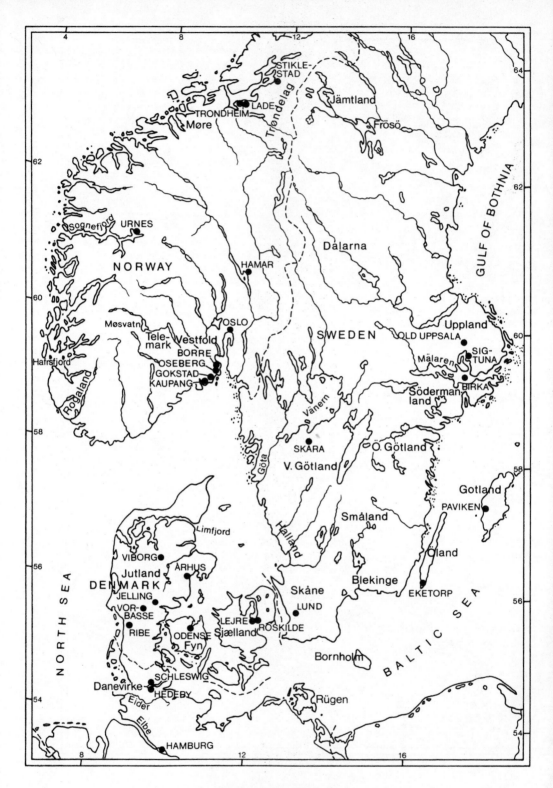

Southern Scandinavia

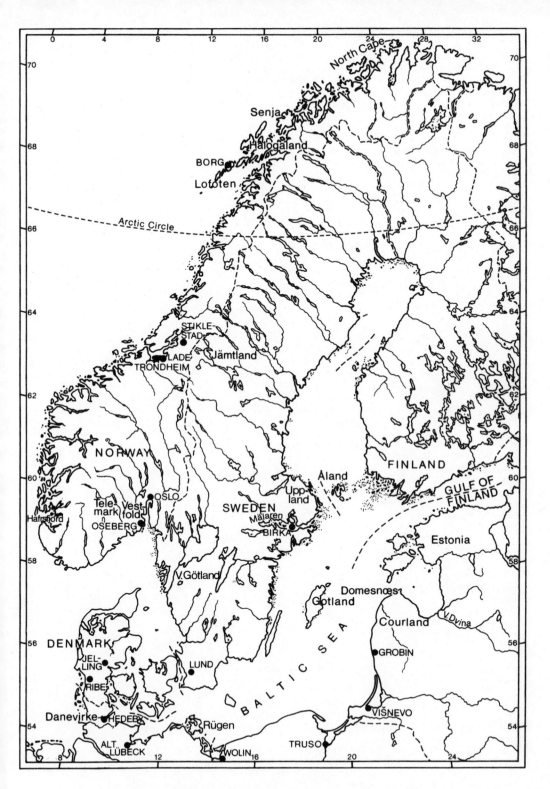

Scandinavia and the Baltic Region

INTRODUCTION

Ship, dog and hart incised on a plank in the Oseberg ship, Vestfold, Norway. University Museum of National Antiquities, Oslo.

THE ALLURE OF THE VIKINGS

The Viking Age is shot through with the spirit of adventure. For 300 years, from just before AD 800 until well into the eleventh century, Scandinavians from the modern countries of Denmark, Norway and Sweden played a decisive role in many parts of Europe. The Vikings affected almost every region accessible to their ships, and left traces that are still part of life today, such as loan-words in the English language, and many place-names in Normandy; they founded Ireland's major towns and were the first settlers on Iceland.

The modern fascination with the Vikings has inspired many books, exhibitions, museums and reconstructed monuments. The Vikings have become a kind of Scandinavian trademark and people in many parts of the world, from the Shetlands to Normandy and the United States, celebrate their Nordic roots by remembering the Vikings. Scandinavia looks upon the Viking Age as a golden age, when noble deeds were performed abroad and there were great developments at home – the modern kingdoms of Denmark, Norway and Sweden took shape, Christianity was introduced and the first towns were established, forming the basis of modern Scandinavia.

The classic image of the Vikings, appearing on foreign shores in their ships, sword in hand, performing bloody deeds, plundering churches, extorting money, engaging in battle, murder and abductions, is a one-sided picture, created originally by contemporary clerics in Western Europe, who tended to record only violent events, and elaborated by medieval story-tellers and historians, among them the Icelandic saga writers, in their search for a dramatic national identity. But the Vikings were not just warlords. Their kings were engaged in complicated international politics, engineers built fortresses and bridges, merchants traded over vast distances – from northern Norway to Hedeby in southernmost Denmark, from the town of Birka in Sweden (near Stockholm) to Russia, from Iceland to Dublin. They were explorers who colonized hitherto uninhabited lands in the North Atlantic – The Faroes, Iceland and Greenland – and they were the first Europeans to reach America (around AD 1000). Large groups of Vikings settled in areas they had conquered, cultivated the land, and became integrated with the native population, as in England; they established themselves in trading colonies, as in Dublin, or as an economic and political élite, as in certain parts of Russia.

Scandinavians were employed as imperial guards in Byzantium and as regular mercenaries. Elsewhere Viking chieftains were granted an area of land at the mouth of a great river by the local king or emperor in return for preventing other Vikings from sailing into their kingdom. Around AD 911, for instance, the French king gave the Viking chieftain Rollo the land around the mouth of the Seine. Rollo and his successors consolidated their power and in time dominated what later became Normandy. In 1066, Rollo's great-great-great grandson William conquered England, and his descendants have occupied the throne ever since.

The activities of the Vikings have an almost kaleidoscopic character, and often the same person appears in different roles and in different places. The world of the Vikings was large and offered the individual many opportunities. Most Scandinavians, however, lived peacefully and comparatively unaffected by the dramas of the age. They concentrated on winning a livelihood for themselves and their families, and from time to time they heard exciting tales of the conquest of Paris, journeys to Baghdad or a shipwreck in the North Atlantic. Many owned a few objects imported from the great world outside, perhaps a quern for grinding flour, or some beads.

Scandinavia had its own culture, with strong traditions. During the three centuries of the Viking Age that culture developed through extensive contact with other countries, assimilating and transforming many foreign influences. It is largely through the study of the Viking homelands, with their astonishingly high level of technical and organizational achievement, that our picture of the period has been altered. It used to be thought that Vikings were just energetic, robust, straight-forward people or that they were wild, barbaric, axe-wielding pirates; and that they lived in a fairly democratic society. The Viking Age is now seen as having been altogether more complex, with a strong class system, diverse social conditions and far more radical achievements. In an era of rapid change, the Vikings took every advantage of their unusual ability to re-adjust, and their gift for enterprise produced quite exceptional results and innovations.

THE VIKING AGE
AND ITS SOURCES

Ornament and inscription on a rune stone from Tullstorp in Skåne,
Sweden, *c.*AD 1000. The inscription reads: 'Kleppe and Åse set up this
monument in memory of Ulv.'

THE STUDY OF THE VIKING AGE

The generally accepted terms 'Viking Age' and 'Vikings' will often be used in this book, although they reflect concepts no longer current. The linguistic origin of the word 'Viking' is uncertain and has been much discussed, but by the end of the Viking Age, it was used both for one who fights at sea – a pirate or a robber (West Norse *víkingr*) – and for warfare at sea or harrying (West Norse *víking*). Outside Scandinavia, however, other names for the 'Vikings' were commonly used, such as heathens, northmen, the people from the North, the Danes, *rus,* the foreigners. Foreign writers clearly did not always know from which area in Scandinavia a group came, even though they gave them a name such as 'the Danes', which implies they came from Denmark. A band of Vikings was also often made up of people from different regions.

Our knowledge of the Viking Age in Scandinavia and abroad is based on a wide variety of sources: written evidence (including runic inscriptions on stones) that is either contemporary with, or dates from soon after, the events described; poetry; place-names and personal names; archaeological finds (both evidence of human activity and remains of animals and plants); landscape and climate. Each source poses its own problems and many disciplines – history, literature, linguistics, place-name studies, archaeology, numismatics, zoology, botany, geology – help cast light on many aspects of the Viking Age; a comprehensive survey is only possible through interdisciplinary research and international co-operation.

With the current influx of new information and research, our perception of the period is under constant revision. The start of the Viking Age can no longer be fixed categorically at AD 793, the earliest recorded raid in Western Europe, on Lindisfarne monastery in Northumberland, because there is indirect evidence of slightly earlier Viking attacks in the west. Also, the people from present-day Sweden had already engaged in an eastward expansion, and, most importantly, many essential characteristics of the social structure, economy and art of the Viking Age go far back into the eighth century. Today it seems more reasonable to date the beginning of the Viking Age within Scandinavia to the mid eighth century, and the Viking Age abroad to whenever the Scandinavians arrived in the various regions, whether to settle, to rob or to trade.

The end of the Viking Age is also often linked with a particular year in the English calendar: 1042, when Harthacnut, the last Scandinavian king of England, died. But all Scandinavians did not disappear from the land at this date, and in some places, such as Dublin, their presence continued to be felt until the late twelfth century. In the Orkneys and Shetlands, the Hebrides and the Isle of Man, it lasted even longer, whereas in the Rhineland it had ceased far earlier than in England. However, aggressive military activity had stopped almost entirely by the second half of the eleventh century, so it is reasonable to take that as the end of the period.

If the perception of the Viking Age's chronological boundaries has become more complex, the view of its technological and other capabilities has been revolutionized. The tub-like Viking ships of nineteenth-century pictures were painted without any archaeological information, on the assumption that Scandinavians were barbarians at a primitive stage of technological development. But during the last 100 years remains of many ships have been excavated, revealing that they were extremely elegant and efficient sailing vessels (Plate 2). The towns, fortresses and bridges that have been unearthed also bear witness to great technological and organizational abilities.

The picture of a barbaric North is no longer valid. It was created partly on the basis of written sources, and partly on the ideological grounds that European culture, classically inspired and Christian, was 'superior'. The emphasis has shifted to understanding all aspects of past cultures on their own terms. Most of what we know about Viking Age conditions, however, relates to the upper classes, as traces of their activities, deeds and ideals tend to be better preserved and more thoroughly studied than those of their inferiors.

A more complex view of the period also recognizes that the extensive Scandinavian region, while having important features in common, consisted of very different areas, and that it went through important internal changes, so a knowledge of life on a small farm in the north of Norway in the ninth century is not of great help in understanding the lifestyle of people buried in the tenth century at Birka, the great cosmopolitan trading centre in eastern Sweden. Without taking local factors into account, the great exploits abroad would be reduced to disjointed and incomprehensible events and stories.

WRITTEN SOURCES

In the past, the study of the Viking Age was based chiefly on written evidence. Since the early twentieth century, however, extensive studies have shown that many of the exciting stories about the Viking Age are more like 'historical novels' than accurate accounts; they were composed a long time after the events they describe, perhaps with the deliberate intention of glorifying a particular family in order to legitimize its rights to land, or to a kingdom, or to endorse a certain policy.

This is the case with many of the Icelandic sagas, written down mainly between about 1200 and 1400, including Snorri Sturluson's great work *Heimskringla*, 'The Circle of the World', a history of the Norwegian kings from the earliest saga age to 1177, which dates from around 1230. It is also true of the account of the first Scandinavian rulers in Normandy written by the cleric Dudo, *c.* 1020, *De moribus et actis primorum Normanniae Ducum*, and of Saxo's work on the deeds of the Danes, *Gesta Danorum*, written around 1200. Historical events and their interpretation, which had been passed on by word of mouth, often acquired a deliberate bias when they were eventually written down, or a new episode might be added to the life of a well-known person. Very few writers had reliable knowledge of what had happened and what things were like a hundred or more years ago. In addition, many of the stories are only preserved in copies of copies, which gives further scope for errors and improvements on the original manuscript.

It is often impossible, therefore, to distinguish pure fiction from an embellished version of an event, and improvements and additions to make the story more coherent from what was once objective reality. The writers themselves were clearly not always sure which was the most accurate version and in any case their perception of 'historical truth' was quite different from the one most people have today. They wrote for their own age and their work was often dedicated to a person of high rank and social standing. Their works must be seen against this background, and not as attempts to reproduce historical reality in the modern sense. Sometimes it seems that everything in a story is fiction, with the possible exception of the main characters' names, for as time went on, Vikings and the Viking Age became a literary motif. However, the stories are often works of exceptional literary merit, expressing a deep fascination with the Viking Age.

The saga of the Jomsvikings, for example, written down in Iceland around 1200, tells the story of a group of professional warriors who spent the winters in a fortress, Jomsborg, on the south coast of the Baltic, and went on expeditions during the summer. They were subject to strong discipline, performed great exploits and were closely involved in Danish politics. In the end, they suffered a crushing defeat at Hjørungavåg in Norway. Many of the protagonists, among them Norwegian earls and Danish kings, are historical figures from the end of the tenth century, but most of the rest is probably just a good yarn. Works of this kind have been instrumental in creating stereotypes of the Viking period.

Not all later written sources on the Vikings have to be rejected or used so cautiously, however. The fifteenth-century Irish Annals, for example, contain a reliable version of the original Viking Age annals which related much about the activities of the Vikings. Many scaldic poems, composed by Scandinavian poets, or scalds, whose names we know, in public eulogy of Viking princes, are thought to have been quite faithfully handed down from generation to generation, even though they were not written down until after the Viking Age, mostly at the end of the twelfth century, or in the thirteenth century, as part of the Icelandic sagas.

Many are preserved in Snorri Sturluson's *Heimskringla*, and Snorri, himself a scald, argues for the authenticity of the poems in his preface. He singles out the old scaldic poems and the historical writing of his compatriot Ari Þorgilsson as his most important sources but ends by saying that even though Ari had learnt from 'old intelligent persons' and was himself 'anxious for information, intelligent, and of excellent memory', the most accurate information came from the poems 'if the metrical rules are observed in them and if they are sensibly interpreted'. Snorri also relates that there were scalds at the court of the Norwegian king Harald Finehair around 900 '. . . whose poems people know by heart even at the present day, together with all the sagas about the kings who have ruled in Norway since his time'. He goes on:

although it be the fashion with scalds to praise most those in whose presence they are standing, yet no one would dare to relate to a chief what he, and all those who heard it, knew to be false and imaginary, not a true account of his deeds; because that would be mockery, not praise.

Some of the poems about gods and the great heroes of the past, known as eddaic poems, also go back to the Viking Age, though their date is often debatable. The eddaic poems are known mainly from a manuscript called *Codex Regius*, which is a copy made in Iceland at the end of the thirteenth century from a slightly earlier manuscript. This collection of poems is often called *The Elder Edda*, in contrast to Snorri Sturluson's book on the art of poetry, which he himself called *Edda*, and which is often referred to as *The Younger Edda*, or *Snorri's Edda*.

Many Scandinavian poems thus give information about people, events and the cultural history of the Viking Age, as well as being a distinctive, exciting and often complicated form of poetry. It is fortunate, too, that most of the surviving scaldic poems tell of the situation in Norway, as hardly any other contemporary written sources about that country have survived.

Another source of information are laws written down in the Middle Ages containing provisions which go back to the Viking Age, or provisions which prohibit certain activities customary in former pagan times. It is often difficult, however, to distinguish the earlier provisions, since the laws in general reflect social conditions of the time when they were written down. Much had changed since the Viking Age, not least because of the influence of Christianity.

Whatever the problems with such sources, an account of the Viking Age would be meagre indeed if all the later prose accounts, the eddaic poems and legal provisions were dismissed out of hand. This is particularly true of the major works of Norse literature which dramatize the fact and fiction of the Viking Age, chronicling events such as Harald Finehair's struggle to unite Norway, the colonization of Iceland, the conversion of Greenland, and the expeditions to America. Although the historical framework and the chronology may be distorted or wrong, and although additions may have been made for literary or other reasons, many sagas, if read as the literary works they are, undoubtedly contain as much of the reality of the Viking Age as anything that can be reconstructed today. The sagas were closer to the events, and were produced in an age whose ideals and outlook on life were in many ways akin to those of the Viking Age.

The most reliable written information about the Viking Age is of course contemporary, but there are very few sources dealing with Scandinavia, and there are many gaps, both chronologically and geographically. Furthermore, many contemporary sources are difficult to understand today, and they can sometimes give misleading information, either intentionally, or because the writer was badly informed.

The alphabet of Viking Age Scandinavia consisted of sixteen symbols, runes, which were used mostly for messages on wooden sticks (of which very few survive), to indicate ownership of an object, for scribbles on all sorts of objects, and most importantly, on stone memorials or rune stones. There are around forty-five Viking Age and early medieval rune stones in Norway, about 180 in modern Denmark, and around 2,500 in modern Sweden, of which about half are in Uppland in central Sweden. In addition, a number of inscriptions with Scandinavian runes have been found in the Viking colonies.

Much less research has been done into the information on rune stones than into traditional records written on parchment and kept in libraries, but, in particular, the large, late Viking Age group of rune stones from central Sweden gives a good insight into matters of cultural history, politics and social organization. A large stone at Runby (between Stockholm and Uppsala) records:

Ingrid had the *laðbro* made and the stone cut in memory of Ingemar, her husband, and of Dan and of Banke, her sons. They lived in Runby and owned a farm. Christ help their souls. It shall stand in memory of the men as long as mankind lives.

The *laðbro* is presumably a quay or jetty for the loading and unloading of ships, very useful at Runby, which lay on an important Uppland waterway. In Sjusta in the same district there is a splendidly ornamented stone which commemorates Spiallbuði, among others. He lost his life in a church in Novgorod (*Hólmgarð*) in Russia which was dedicated to St Olaf, the Norwegian king who was killed in 1030. The inscription reads:

Runa had this memorial made to Spiallbuði and to Svein and to Andvett and to Ragnar, her sons and Helgi's [?], and Sigrið to Spiallbuði, her husband. He met death in Hólmgarð in Olav's church. Öpir cut the runes.

Apart from rune stones, contemporary written information about the Viking homelands is almost exclusively the work of foreign clerics, few of whom had visited Scandinavia. Nearly all these texts are in Latin and they were usually written because of political or military confrontations on Denmark's southern border, or attempts to convert the pagan northmen to the true Christian faith. Particular light is shed on Denmark as most missionary and political activity was directed towards this country. The Frankish Annals, for example, record that in 808 Godfred, King of the Danes, wished to fortify his southern border with a wall stretching from the North Sea to the Baltic. This arose because of a dispute with Charlemagne.

A few foreign sources mention the situation in other Scandinavian countries. When the Norwegian chieftan Ohthere visited the court of King Alfred the Great in England he described his life and wealth in northern Norway, and his sea journey to Hedeby in southern Denmark c. 890; Alfred's account of his tales still survives (cf. p. 105). The experiences of Ansgar, Archbishop of Hamburg-Bremen, and other missionaries in Sweden and

Denmark in the mid-ninth century were recorded by Rimbert, Ansgar's successor, who describes life in Birka in central Sweden. There is also a fairly comprehensive description of all the Scandinavian countries written *c.* 1075 by the German cleric Adam of Bremen. The account is part of his great work about the history of the Archbishops of Hamburg-Bremen, *Gesta Hammaburgensis Ecclesiae Pontificum*. It contains many interesting pieces of information, including the only contemporary description of a pagan Scandinavian temple, the main shrine of the Svear in Uppsala in Sweden.

Far more written evidence exists of Viking activities outside Scandinavia, but here too there are gaps. It is largely a matter of chance what has survived in a reliable form and what has been lost; only those regions which were Christian or Islamic early on – Western Europe, the British Isles, Byzantium and the Middle East – had a literary tradition; and the evidence is of a very varied nature. The Christians mention Scandinavia and the Vikings chiefly in annals and in some histories, while the Muslims refer to them in geographical works, but both see the Vikings as pagan barbarians.

In the Baltic countries and in Russia Christianity did not gain a foothold until the second half of the tenth century at the earliest, and large parts of these areas remained pagan, and hence virtually undocumented, until well into the twelfth century. But a number of Swedish rune stones, such as that from Sjusta mentioned above, tell of journeys to these areas and to lands further south, and Arabs or travellers from Byzantium who encountered or heard tell of the exotic northmen in Eastern Europe mention them in their writings.

The Faroes, Iceland and Greenland were converted to Christianity around AD 1000. As they were remote from literate Europe, there is virtually no written evidence about them dating from the Viking Age itself. There is also very little about Scotland and the Scottish islands. Adam of Bremen gives us a few glimpses, but otherwise we must look to other sources, especially place-names and archaeological finds, or try to extract information about the Viking Age from later literature.

Another problem in understanding the Viking expansion is that the written accounts of events and impressions are so one-sided. The Vikings' settlements abroad, their way of life, trade and other peaceful pursuits rarely interested Western European writers. Contemporary sources recorded dramatic events such as plunder, extortion of money, slaughter and killing, battle and conquest, peace treaties and political alliances. For example, in Regino's Chronicle (Regino was abbot of the monastery at Prüm, between the rivers Maas and Mosel), the entry for the year 892 records the following:

But when the Normans [the Vikings] went into the monastery [in Prüm] they destroyed everything, killed some of the monks, slew most of the servants and led the rest away prisoners. When departing they entered the Ardennes, where they attack and without difficulty take a newly built fortress on a prominent mountain top in which an innumerable amount of people had taken refuge; after having killed them all they return with immense booty to their fleet and sail with heavily laden ships and all their crew to the regions beyond the sea.

The problem of interpreting the meaning of any thousand-year-old word, whether in Old Norse, Old English, Latin or Arabic, is often disregarded, yet the meaning of many words has altered so fundamentally that today we cannot be sure what they originally signified. Viking Age people naturally knew what the Old Norse *konungr* (king) meant and what the title represented, but it is clear that the role of a *konungr* was very different to that of a modern European king, and we only have an incomplete picture of the duties, rights and resources of Viking kings. Some words may also have had different meanings in different parts of Scandinavia, or may have undergone a semantic change during the three centuries of the Viking Age.

Despite the reservations discussed above, there are quite a few reliable written sources on the Viking Age, though most of those dealing with Scandinavia are about the later rather than the early Viking Age. For the first time in Scandinavian history these sources become numerous enough in the Viking Age to give us a framework of events and to contribute to our understanding of the development of the period and its culture, as well as recording the deeds of specific people and contemporary attitudes.

PLACE-NAMES

Many place-names established during the Viking Age are still in use both in Scandinavia and in Scandinavian settlements abroad. The name types which were common in the homelands can generally be identified on the basis of the linguistic analysis of the names' form and meaning, by analysing the status and geographical locations which are associated with settlements of various name types, and by comparing place-names at home with place-names in the colonies. In many areas, new names arose after the Scandinavian conquests and settlements, such as Stearsby in northern England, where both the prefix Stear-, derived from the Scandinavian personal name Styrr, and the suffix -*by* (settlement) are Scandinavian, or Toqueville in Normandy with the Scandinavian personal name Toke as prefix and a French suffix: *ville*. An analysis of place-names also makes it possible to distinguish between areas settled mainly by Norwegians and those settled mainly by Danes.

As well as supplying evidence of Viking settlements abroad and of the geographical distribution of settlements within Scandinavia, place-names obviously provide information about naming customs (both with regard to personal and place-names) and about language. They can also shed some light on such matters as religion. For example, place-names compounded with the name of the god Odin (such as Odense, in Denmark) are evidence of the worship of this chief god, and the number of place-names based on the names of various gods reflects their popularity in different parts of Scandinavia.

In the colonies the number and character of Scandinavian or partly Scandinavian names depended both on how many settlers arrived and on their status in the community, and also on how much influence their language came to have on the local dialect. The latter was partly determined by how closely the original language was related to Scandinavian, and perhaps also by the character of the Scandinavian settlement: whether it was peaceful co-existence or total domination. Danish and English, for example, were not very different, and people soon learnt to live peacefully together in England, so here a kind of mixed language came into being. Swedish and Slav, however, belonged to two completely different language groups, so in Russia no mixed language arose. The local language prevailed, with a number of Scandinavian loan-words, and Scandinavian names given to rapids in the river Dniepr, which many had to pass in order to reach Byzantium, were presumably used only by the Scandinavians themselves.

In the Orkneys and Shetlands, however, the local language was completely replaced by Scandinavian and developed into the dialect Norn, which has survived almost to this day. Virtually all place-names here are Scandinavian, but a number were obviously created long after the Viking Age. In England, too, not all the Scandinavian place-names are the result of name-giving and acquisition of property immediately after the ninth-century conquests. Those containing Scandinavian nature words borrowed by the English language, such as beck (Old Norse *bekkr*: brook) and fell (Old Norse *fell*: fell, mountain), are especially likely to have been created long afterwards.

ARCHAEOLOGICAL FINDS

The major advances made in our understanding of the Viking Age are due to archaeology and to interdisciplinary research based on recent archaeological finds, which have done much to stimulate popular and academic interest in the subject.

If archaeological remains are reasonably intact, they can be understood to a certain extent without specialist knowledge: a complete ceramic cooking-pot gives immediate information about the form of cooking-pots, and a silver arm-ring about fashion, aesthetics and wealth. But further research into contemporary ceramic vessels may identify a pottery sherd found in Scandinavia as an English import, and weighing large numbers of silver arm-rings may reveal that they represent units of weight in systems of Oriental origin.

Objects and structures rarely survive intact, however. A hinge may be all that remains of a casket, the lower ends of the supporting timbers all that is left of a bridge, and dark traces in the soil from posts which have completely rotted away the only sign of a house. Many iron objects, such as swords, and all wooden objects, even if the entire form has survived, usually bear scant resemblance to the original.

A model or a drawing can give a good impression of the original appearance of structures and objects, how they functioned, and what technology and labour were used in their manufacture. A full-scale reconstruction made in the original materials, using the original technology, is best of all. Such reconstructions have been made of ships and houses, not just small objects, fulfilling both scholarly and popular demands.

Unlike written sources and place-names, archaeological sources increase constantly. New material is added almost daily and occasionally sensational finds turn traditional interpretations upside down. The discovery of the circular Viking fortresses in Denmark in the 1930s and the excavations of Scandinavian Dublin and York between the 1960s and 1980s took the world by storm.

Apart from grave-goods and valuable items hidden for safe-keeping, most excavated objects tend to be discarded possessions and rubbish, which can make it difficult to draw a coherent picture of, for instance, the development of crafts in a particular town. Comparisons and generalizations about burial customs are also often problematic, since local circumstances affected what the dead were given to accompany them in their graves in pagan times. As with nearly all archaeological remains, it is mere chance which graves are known today and to what extent their contents have survived.

Recent advances in archaeology are largely due to systematic research into subjects such as the role of iron in the economy, the significance of the town of Hedeby in southern Denmark, coins and other means of payment, ships, or the relationship between Scandinavian and Lappish settlements in northern Scandinavia. New excavation methods and scientific analysis have also played an important part, raising new questions about the period and solving some of them. Perhaps the most revolutionary of the new excavation methods has been the use of machines to uncover large areas quickly and cheaply. As a result, a whole Viking Age village, Vorbasse, in central Jutland, has been discovered. When spades and manual labour were the only tools in rural excavations, hardly more than a handful of houses were uncovered. Underwater archaeology is also relatively new. Divers can now examine

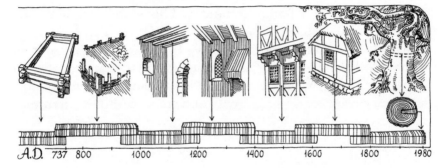

The principles of dendrochronology. The date 737 corresponds to the felling of timber for the earliest phase of the border wall, Danevirke.

wrecks in fairly deep water, while in shallow water several conventional excavations have been carried out after isolating the area with sheet piles and pumping out the sea water. The harbour area at Hedeby was investigated in this way. The water-logged conditions there were exceptionally good for the preservation of items which normally rarely survive, such as clothes.

Technological and scientific analysis has been used to determine the hardness of the cutting edges of knives and axes, which is essential for understanding the properties and effectiveness of these tools. Previously only their shape was noted. Examination of beetles, vermin and plant remains in and around houses reveal details of hygiene and people's living conditions, and an analysis of bones and plants provides evidence of diet and basic economic conditions. Thanks to geological and topographical research, we now know that in Sweden's central lake district, where the town of Birka was situated, the land has risen about 5 m since the Viking Age. This is obviously a decisive factor in our understanding of traffic and settlement conditions in that period.

Scientific dating methods, primarily dendrochronology, are also responsible for new advances. Dendrochronology allows the precise year of felling of timber to be determined by comparing the width of the year-rings with those in another piece of timber of known age, provided that the outer year-rings have not been cut away or damaged. Important structures, such as remains of fortifications, can now sometimes be dated precisely and thus linked with other structures of a similar age in a larger area, and perhaps placed in a political context. This is the case with one phase of the Danish border wall known as Danevirke, now dated to AD 968. Harald Bluetooth is known from documentary sources to have ruled Denmark at that time, and that year there was a political crisis between Denmark and Germany. The two complementary sources produce a new and more complex picture of the situation.

SCANDINAVIA

Scene on an eighth-century picture stone from Tjängvide in Alskog,
Gotland, Sweden. A woman welcomes a rider on an eight-legged
horse, perhaps the god Odin on his horse Sleipnir. Behind her is a dog,
and several people and a house. Schematic drawing. National
Antiquities Museum, Stockholm.

Geography, Nature and Culture

The Viking homelands of Denmark, Norway and Sweden were not distinct, well-defined political units in the Viking Age, but they began to take shape during this period. Their common borders, established a little later, have since changed several times, although Scandinavia's southern border along the river Eider remained in place right up to 1864. The present border lies about 60 km further north.

Travelling in Scandinavia today, the great distances and varied landscape are still very striking. Stretching from the North Cape at the northernmost tip of Norway to Denmark's southern border, it constitutes half the length of Europe measured north to south. Northern Scandinavia is crossed by the Arctic Circle and lies on the same latitude as Greenland; in mid-summer darkness never falls, while no light penetrates in mid-winter. Denmark and southern Sweden, on the other hand, are on the same latitude as northern England and southern Scotland in the west, and Estonia, Latvia, Lithuania and northernmost Poland in the east.

There have obviously been changes in the physical appearance of Scandinavia since the Viking Age. The land has risen considerably above sea-level in some places, large wetland areas, especially in Denmark, have been drained, and many forests have been cleared for agricultural use. The basic physical conditions of Viking times are, however, recognizable today and they naturally affected living conditions fundamentally (Plate 1).

NORWAY

Present-day Norway is about 1,800 km long and very narrow in places, with large areas of mountain plateaux more than 1,000 m above sea-level. The highest mountains (Galdhøpiggen at 2,469 m above sea-level, is Northern Europe's highest peak) are permanently covered with ice and snow. The mountainous coast with its deep fjords is protected from the Atlantic Ocean by a line of small islands and rocks. Strips of agricultural land are found along the fjords and in the river valleys, while there are great fertile plains in the south, in the Oslo fjord region, as well as in Jæren in south-west Norway and in Trøndelag around the Trondheim fjord. The country lies in the coniferous belt, but a large part is above the tree-line. In spite of the northerly latitude, westerly winds and the warm waters of the Gulf Stream mean the west coast has cool summers and winters so mild that the harbours can be kept open all the year round.

Many wild animals thrived in Norway in Viking times (and in some places still do), including reindeer, elk, wolf, bear, wolverine, fox and marten, which were used for meat or fur. The sea teemed with fish, there were seals and whales and walrus in the far north. Iron was a major resource and there were unlimited supplies of wood. Even today, agricultural land covers only 3 per cent of the region, forest 23 per cent, while almost 70 per cent is unforested mountain areas.

Norway had a common border with Sweden, and also a short stretch with Denmark in the Viking Age, but it looked mainly westwards and southwards. Ships were the link between settlements along the Norwegian coast and with the islands in the Atlantic Ocean, the British Isles and Western Europe.

SWEDEN

Modern Sweden is about 1,600 km long and some 500 km wide. In the north a mountainous area runs along the Norwegian border, the highest parts permanently covered with ice and snow, and numerous rivers flow down into the gently sloping land to the east, where a large coastal plain faces the Gulf of Bothnia.

The central Swedish lowlands around the great lakes Mälaren, Vänern and Vättern are fertile, while the southern highlands – Småland and the adjoining parts of the districts of Halland and Blekinge – were less so. In the past this area, with many lakes and bogs and immense woodlands, was almost impassable. The provinces of Skåne and Halland in the south were part of Denmark in the Viking Age, while Blekinge probably did not become Danish until a little later. All three provinces were ceded to Sweden in 1658 together with Norwegian Bohuslän, north of Halland. Islands and skerries lie along much of Sweden's coastline, the largest being Öland and Gotland in the Baltic.

Southern Sweden has a coastal climate but the north has very cold winters with much ice and snow. Coniferous forests cover around 57 per cent of modern Sweden and in the Viking Age the north presented particularly rich opportunities for hunting and fishing. In many places there were huge deposits of iron and vast supplies of wood.

The greater part of Sweden looked eastwards but there were also westward connections; the fertile region of Västergötland, with easy access to the sea via the river Göta, near the modern city of Göteborg, had many contacts with Denmark and the West. In the sparsely populated northern parts of Sweden and Norway there were many contacts with the Lapps.

DENMARK

Compared with Norway and Sweden, Denmark is a small country, about 375 km long from Skagen in the north to the river Eider in the south. It is very flat, its highest point only 173 m above sea-level. The mainland, Jutland, has a fjord coastline in the east; the rest of the kingdom consists of islands of all sizes.

Like Sweden, Denmark has a climate mid-way between coastal and continental, but the winters are generally mild and the summers quite warm. Agriculture was the main occupation in the Viking Age, while hunting was of minimal importance. As elsewhere in Scandinavia the sea was full of fish, but Denmark lacked inexhaustible supplies of good wood. The immense consumption of oak during the Viking Age made a considerable impact on the deciduous forests.

As Scandinavia's southern gateway, Denmark had far more political and cultural contacts with its southern neighbours – Saxons, Frisians and Slavs – than Norway and Sweden, and many European influences reached it first. For sea-going traffic, Denmark was the gateway between the Baltic on one side and the North Sea on the other.

Given the great distances and the many physical differences within Scandinavia, it is hardly surprising that life varied greatly in the different regions. Not everyone worshipped the same gods, for instance, and legal provisions recorded on rune stones in central Sweden did not necessarily apply to Denmark or western Norway. In addition each country had its own cultural, political and military contacts.

Nevertheless Scandinavia was a defined cultural and geographical entity in the Viking Age. Its natural resources made it almost self-sufficient and it was remote from the political and cultural centres in the rest of Europe. In addition, it is almost entirely surrounded by sea – the Atlantic and the North Sea to the west, the Baltic and the Gulf of Bothnia to the east. The most important inhabited areas were near the coast and communication across great distances was easy in the very efficient ships of the period, while sledges and skis over firm ice and snow made travel inland easy in the winter. Naturally, routes were also found through the large open valleys across the Scandinavian peninsula in the summer. As a result there was a vigorous exchange of goods and ideas over long distances and there is much evidence of political and military contacts, peaceful as well as hostile.

The languages were very similar throughout Scandinavia, and religion, burial customs and architecture had much in common. Objects of daily use, jewellery, dress, writing, poetry and the decorative arts, were also common to the same social class over most of Scandinavia and were distinctively Scandinavian. A well-travelled person would no doubt easily distinguish a Birka merchant from a merchant from western Norway or Hedeby, but they could all understand each other's language, culture and behaviour. To other Europeans, any differences would have been trivial, overshadowed by the fact that Scandinavians remained pagans until the second half of the tenth century or later.

THE PEOPLE

The eddaic poem *Rígsþula*, thought by many to date from the tenth century, but first preserved in manuscript form four centuries later, describes three distinct social classes, slaves, free farmers and warlords. Class consciousness is prominent in the poem; the slaves are mentioned with contempt and some disgust, the others with respect and admiration. Irrespective of its age, the poem illustrates dramatically the social differences of the Viking Age, which other sources confirm.

On his journey, Ríg – really the god Heimdall – came first to a married couple in a poor hut. The son who was born after this visit was given the name Þræl (thrall, slave). 'He grew and thrived well, on his hand was wrinkled skin, gnarled knuckles, thick fingers, foul the face, stooping the back, long the heels.' He married a girl named Þír (another word for a slave), who came to the house on foot: 'dirt was on her sole, her arm sunburnt, crooked her nose'. They had many children with ugly names and a life of hard physical labour.

The next time Ríg stayed with a well-dressed and well-groomed couple who lived in a hall. Nine months later they had a son who was named Karl (farmer, free man): 'His cheek glowed, his eye twinkled. Ox he learnt to tame, plough to make, house to build and barn to raise, carts to make and turn the plough.' His bride came driving to the farm dressed in a goatskin gown. She carried keys (a symbol of wifely dignity) and was called Snør (son's wife, daughter-in-law). They had many children with good names.

Ríg's last visit was to a beautifully dressed couple in a splendid building where he was served at table. The son who was born was given the name Iarl (earl), and 'fair was his hair, bright his cheek, fierce were his eyes like young snakes'. Iarl became a great warrior. He owned much land and he rode, hunted, swam and was a great giver of gifts. His wife was 'slender-fingered, white-skinned and wise; she was called Erna'. They had many children with beautiful names. The last one was called Konr ungr (*konungr,* king).

This literary picture of people's appearance and living conditions is supported by material evidence. The examination of skeletons from different localities in Scandinavia reveals that the average height of the Vikings was a little less than that of today: men were about 5ft 7¾in. tall and women 5ft 2½in. The most extensive recent anthropological study was carried out in Denmark, but the situation must have been similar elsewhere. Skeletons of people as tall as 6ft ½in. have been found, and those in richly furnished Viking graves – belonging to high-ranking people – were on average considerably taller than those in the more ordinary graves, undoubtedly because of better living conditions. A double grave on Langeland in Denmark contained two adult males, typically, the smaller one had been decapitated, and had probably had his hands tied behind his back, while the other was interred with his spear in the normal fashion – obviously a case of a slave (measuring 5ft 7¼in.) who had to accompany his master (5ft 9¾in.) in death. However, the skeleton found in Jelling church, thought to be that of King Gorm of Denmark (later known as Gorm the Old), was only of average height. This man was 5ft 7¾in. tall, with heavy, robust features, but not heavily built. He was between forty and fifty years old when he died, and he suffered from osteo-arthritis in his back, and had problems with his teeth.

Osteo-arthritis was common among adults in the Viking Age, as in all other periods. Some people eventually lost one or more teeth, and teeth were always worn down by the coarse food, although dental caries (holes in the teeth) are seldom found, unlike today. Naturally, they suffered from many other diseases, both congenital and acquired, and infant mortality was undoubtedly high. In rare cases skeletons have been found which bear traces of cuts or blows, showing that the person had been in a fight or had died in battle. Scaldic poems, rune stones and other written sources tell of many bloody dramas and of parents who grieve over killed sons, but the cemeteries reveal a more peaceful picture. The average lifespan of those who grew to adulthood was remarkably long for both men and women, at least in Denmark, where the standard of living was generally good. Of 240 adult skeletons, 140 had reached the age group *maturus* (about thirty-five to fifty-five years old), and 100 belonged to the age group *adultus* (about twenty to thirty-five years old). Only two people could be demonstrated to have lived beyond the age of fifty-five.

After analysing large numbers of skeletons, the anthropologist Berit Sellevold has described the 'average' Viking as follows: 'Both men and women were of harmonious proportions. The craniums are of medium width and medium height in relation to their length, and the faces are of medium height in relation to their width. Similarly, the eye-sockets and noses are of medium height in relation to their width. On average the left thigh-bone and shin-bone are a little longer than the right (which is also quite normal today). There is a slight difference between the sexes in the length of the arms: men's right upper arm is a little longer than the left, while women's upper arms are of almost equal length. This may be due to men using their right arms more than their left, while women used both arms almost equally ... In general appearance, Viking Age people were hardly any different to the Scandinavian population today – apart from slightly smaller stature and considerably better teeth, as well as dress, hair styles and jewellery, of course.'

There are few contemporary pictorial representations of people, and only rarely are they naturalistic (Plate 4). Most are of men, but a few show women, and occasionally the two sexes are depicted together, as on a pictorial tapestry found in the richly furnished women's grave at Oseberg, in southern Norway, and on some picture stones in Gotland, Sweden. Small silver or bronze figures from Sweden show stately women in beautiful, trailing gowns, with long hair arranged in an elegant knot at the back of the head, possibly covered by a hair net or head-dress. Some of them proffer a drinking-horn or a cup as a welcome.

The Oseberg grave also contained a wagon with detailed, three-dimensional carvings of male heads. The hair is well groomed and they have elegant long moustaches – some almost reach the ears and are neatly plaited – as well as beards covering the lower part of the face up to the moustache but apparently not the cheeks.

Archaeological finds of toilet articles confirm this impression that the Vikings were well-groomed. Finely decorated combs were common and were clearly not just used by the nobility, who would have been the models for the pictures. Ear-scoops, tweezers and handsome washing bowls have also been found, and traces of wear on teeth show that tooth-picks were used.

A Spanish Arab who visited Hedeby in the tenth century recorded that both men and women used artificially produced eye make-up, and the English chronicler John of Wallingford who, although he lived after the Viking Age, had access to older sources, relates that the Vikings' success with women was due to their having a bath on Saturdays, combing their hair and being handsomely dressed. An anonymous Old English letter gives the impression that the Scandinavians may even have been dandies and innovators of fashion. The writer reprimands his brother Edward, saying that he should follow the customs of his Anglo-Saxon forefathers and not indulge in the 'Danish fashion with bared necks [*ableredum hneccan*] and blinded eyes'. The latter probably means wearing a very long fringe, and the former may indicate that they shaved the back of their heads – such a hair style can be seen worn by the Normans on the Bayeux Tapestry c. 1070.

The least well off, the slaves and the landless, would have looked different. They must have been worn by heavy labour, as described in *Rígsþula*, and possibly stunted by an inferior diet. They would not have dressed in stylish clothes, worn fashionable

Small figures of silver and bronze found in various places in Sweden. The women are dressed in fine gowns and their long hair is elegantly arranged. National Antiquities Museum, Stockholm.

hair styles or had a reasonable standard of cleanliness. Vikings on expeditions and long trading voyages were not always clean or well-groomed either, and an Arab emissary, Ibn Fadhlan, who met a group of Vikings by the Volga in the 920s found them perfectly revolting: 'they are the filthiest of Allah's creatures: they do not wash after shitting or peeing, nor after sexual intercourse, and do not wash after eating. They are like wayward donkeys,' he wrote. To a devout Muslim, who had to wash before each of his five daily prayers, the washing habits of these Vikings must have seemed disgusting indeed. He does go on to say that they all washed every morning, but that this was also foul, for they all used the same water!

Archaeological research in Anglo-Scandinavian York has shown that people there did live in conditions that are unhygienic by today's standards (Plate 5), but that was undoubtedly the norm in Europe at the time, and remained so for centuries. The stereotype of the Vikings as filthy barbarians is also belied by an English drawing of the Anglo-Danish King Cnut the Great dating from the 1030s (Plate 27). The portrait shows him standing proud, well-groomed and elegantly dressed in narrow shoes, close-fitting stockings with ornamental braid, and trousers. He wears a knee-length tunic with wide decorative borders and a cloak with splendid bands draped around one shoulder.

DRESS

Despite his Danish origin, King Cnut spent most of his adult life in England, but styles of dress for noblemen seem to have been similar in Western Europe and southern Scandinavia. When Cnut was in Denmark, his dress cannot have been very different to what he is wearing in the picture.

No complete items of Viking clothing have been preserved, but examples of ordinary footwear are plentiful, especially in the towns: shoes, ankle-boots and taller boots. The uppers are usually of goat-skin, and the sole is nearly always separate. Footwear was manufactured by cobblers – shoe-making was a common urban trade – and so was standardized over large areas. Shoes and boots were usually fastened with a strap. The edges of the opening might be reinforced, and the uppers, which were sometimes coloured, might have ornamental seams.

Hardly anything is known about the elegant footwear worn with magnificent garments like those of King Cnut, but the opposite is the case with dress. Far more is known about the fine clothes of the nobility than about everyday wear or the very simple garments of the poor, and we know nothing about children's clothes. Most of our information about dress comes from fragments found in richly furnished graves, especially those at Birka, in Sweden, and a man's grave in Mammen, in central Jutland. In addition, the use and function of dress buckles and brooches, deduced from their position in graves, can often reveal aspects of dress. In 1979–80, however, excavations in the harbour at Hedeby, in southern Jutland, yielded important new information, as many fragments of clothing had been used as tarring brushes and then thrown into the water, which preserved them.

Garments were usually made of wool woven in various ways, and sometimes of linen. Some cloth was imported and in rare cases garments or parts of them were made of silk, which would always have been imported. Many different furs were used, especially for cloaks and trimmings, and we learn from written sources that other countries envied Scandinavia its abundance of fur. There were also convincing imitation furs made of textiles. Knitting was probably not known but warm garments were made of needle-binding (interlocking loops of yarn 'sewn' together), as seen in a sock from Coppergate, York, and there were elegant 'spranged' textiles (a kind of loose plaiting). Besides being trimmed with fur or imitation fur, clothes might be decorated with appliqué, embroidery, metal-wire decoration, plaited borders or tablet-woven bands which might contain gold or silver threads. They were often dyed in a range of colours. Heaps of walnut shells found in Hedeby were probably imported as a source of brown dye rather than because of a partiality for walnuts.

The basic items of male dress varied in materials, cut and decoration. Pictures show narrow, ankle-length trousers, trumpet-shaped, mid-calf-length trousers (like bell-bottoms), as well as enormous plus-fours, which must have been tied below the knee. Part of a pair of plus-fours has been found in Hedeby

Male dress with trousers, tunic and cloak fastened with a brooch.
Female dress with finely pleated shift, over-dress and oval brooches.
Reconstructions.

harbour, made of finely woven wool in two colours. The shorter
types of trousers must have been worn with stockings or hose.
Long ones could be held up by bands fastened to a strap round
the waist or else had long bands wound around the legs, as is
known from examples found at Hedeby harbour and elsewhere.

According to the pictures, a man's tunic or shirt, possibly worn
over an under-shirt, could be tight or loose. Fragments in fine
wool and linen survive (the best reserved is from Viborg,
Denmark), and they sometimes had fine ornamental borders and
a belt with handsome fittings. The cloak was of heavier material,
fastened over the right shoulder by a large, heavy brooch or with
strong ties. The sword arm was thus kept free. Some large
embroidered woollen fragments in the grave at Mammen may
be from a cloak, but they were torn to bits by the men who
found the grave in the last century. A couple of padded silk

'armbands' came from the same grave. They have been worn at the bottom of the sleeves of a handsome tunic; something similar is shown in the drawing of King Cnut. A man might also have worn a cap with a pointed or rounded crown, or a head band.

Birka's rich graves have produced fragments of kaftan-like jackets of fine wool and linen, fastened with buttons or crossed over and worn with magnificent belts. These have silk borders, embroideries with silver and gold thread, and other gold-thread ornament, all of which appears to be Oriental. The jackets often have matching head-dresses and must have been a fashion amongst the highest echelons of society, not just souvenirs bought in Eastern Europe and Asia. This reflects the fact that eastern Scandinavia was strongly influenced by the East.

The idea that all Scandinavian women wore a kind of folk costume — the same style of dress with standard jewellery — is erroneous. Such a dress was worn only by the nobility and the well-to-do middle class and was presumably kept for 'best' and was nothing like as stereotyped as has been thought although an over-dress, rather like a pinafore dress, was a typical garment. Its exact cut is uncertain, since the most substantial remains, from graves at Birka and the harbour at Hedeby, are only fragments. It was a dress of wool or linen, which might be decorated with borders and bands. It was cut straight at the top and bottom and reached from the arm-pit to mid-calf or lower. It was held up by two short straps at the front and two longer straps at the back, which were fastened at the front by two large oval brooches made of bronze, one on each shoulder. A chain of coloured beads might be suspended between the brooches, and small useful articles might be hung on a chain from one of them: a small knife, a needle-case, scissors, a key.

Oval brooches have been found in wealthy women's graves all over Scandinavia (apart from in Gotland, where very stylized animal-head brooches were used instead) and in all the areas of Viking settlement, where they usually are a sign of the Scandinavian origin of the deceased. The brooches went out of fashion at the end of the tenth century. In *Rígsþula*, the woman who gave birth to Karl is described as having 'dwarves' on her shoulders (*dvergar á öxlum*), which must be a reference to these brooches. The word 'dwarf' is used in other contexts for something small which supports something large, as in buildings. In this case the dress was supported by the 'dwarves'.

A long shift was worn under the over-dress. Tenth-century fragments from Birka show that it was sometimes very finely pleated, and it was fashionable at this time to fasten it at the neck with a small round brooch. Some of the noblewomen in the Birka graves wore a tunic decorated with borders and bands underneath the over-dress. They may have worn a fine jacket, and possibly other garments on top as well as head-dresses with handsome bands to match the tunic. Like the men's jackets, the design of both tunic and jacket must have had Eastern origins.

The standard garment worn by most women was presumably a long, tight-fitting dress, fragments of which have been found in Hedeby harbour. Most Scandinavian women also wore a shawl or cloak fastened in front with a decorative brooch of gold, silver or bronze. These brooches were usually trefoil-shaped, rectangular or, especially from the tenth century onwards, round. A distinctive type of brooch shaped like a round box was used throughout the Viking Age in Gotland, and a number of shawl and cloak brooches in ninth-century Norway were made from fittings and other items collected in the British Isles. There were possibilities for choice here, in contrast to the ubiquitous oval brooches used for the over-dress. Even the ornamentation on the oval brooches was normally stereotyped, for most were mass-produced on the basis of a few designs. Nothing factual is known about men's or women's underwear, but presumably women wore stockings, given the northern climate.

Fashions among the nobility in Hedeby, and probably through-out Denmark, are likely to have been influenced by Western Europe rather than by the East. There are accounts of Danish kings, chieftains and their wives receiving magnificent garments as gifts from Western European princes, and the gold thread used to decorate costumes, for example, was produced by a different technique in Denmark than in Birka.

JEWELLERY

Like their sophisticated fashions, the Vikings' jewellery reflected
their love of splendour. Most articles of jewellery were functional,
but arm-rings, neck-rings, necklaces and pendants, sometimes
with Christian or pagan symbols, such as a cross or Thor's
hammer (Plate 16–17), were also worn. Finger-rings were rare
and ear-rings, which are characteristically Slav, were quite foreign
to the Scandinavian tradition.

Both men and women wore and displayed their wealth in the
form of arm-rings and neck-rings of precious metals, as the Arab
Ibn Fadhlan, who met Vikings on the Volga in the 920s, describes:

Round the neck they have ornaments of gold or silver. Each husband
who owns 10,000 dirhems [Arabic silver coins] has one such ornament
made for his wife; if he has 20,000, he has two made, and each 10,000
means a new ornament for the wife. Often a woman has many such
ornaments.

Most of the necklaces, neck-rings and arm-rings surviving in
Scandinavia are made of silver and many are manufactured from
Arabic silver coins. These items of jewellery were often plain and
made in standard units of weight so that their value could be
easily assessed. Since most payments were made in silver according
to weight, jewellery was a practical way of carrying one's wealth.
If a smaller sum was required, the jewellery could simply be cut
into pieces.

Gold was naturally also used for ornament. The largest piece
of gold jewellery dating from the Viking Age is a neck-ring
found close to Tissø lake on the island of Sjælland in Denmark.
One fine spring day in 1977 it came to light caught in the wheel
of a seeder. The ring is plaited from four thick gold wires (960
per cent). Today it weighs 1,830 grams; the original weight was
about 1,900 grams, but a small part is missing. It must have been
made for an idol or for a large person with a very broad chest.

Many pieces of Viking Age jewellery have survived. They
come mainly from hoards and graves; almost all were made in
Scandinavia, even though probably all metals apart from iron
had to be imported. The items most characteristic of Scandinavian
taste and the most conservative were the oval brooches which
fastened women's over-dresses. Some brooches, however, were

Scandinavian versions of foreign designs. The trefoil brooches used to fasten women's shawls and cloaks, for example, were inspired by the trefoil sword-belt mounts used in the Frankish Empire, while the penannular brooches worn by Viking men, especially in Norway and in the British Isles, on their right shoulders to fasten their cloaks were inspired by Irish or Scottish fastenings. The fashion originated in the colonies in the British Isles and then spread eastwards. Many of these brooches are made of silver and some are enormous, so they were clearly status symbols and sources of wealth, like arm- and neck-rings.

At the beginning of the thirteenth century, Snorri Sturluson recorded that some 250 years earlier the Icelandic people gave a scald who had composed a splendid national poem a shoulder brooch of silver weighing about 25 pounds. This handsome gift was no doubt a penannular brooch, which would have been quite impossible to wear on a garment. The poet, according to the story, cut it up and bought himself a farm. The largest Scandinavian penannular brooches known today weigh around 1 kilo at the most, and even they would have been extremely heavy to wear. With a pin up to 50 cm long they would have been used with very thick cloaks, possibly of fur. Pictures show that penannular brooches were worn with the long pin pointing upwards over the shoulder.

Foreign items were, however, also used. For example a number of foreign mounts were made into women's jewellery by adding a pin or an eye on the back (illustration p. 205). All over Scandinavia it was popular to decorate necklaces of coloured beads with baubles from abroad – coins, a finger-ring or small mounts. Other imported items include Russian neck-rings of standard weights from the early Viking Age; in Scandinavia they were rolled into spirals, worn as arm-rings and used as currency.

One of the popular notions about Vikings is that they loved to festoon themselves with all manner of things brought home from all over the place. But it is wrong to imagine Vikings of rank and position as international Christmas trees. The uses to which foreign ornaments could be put were limited, and they are few in number compared with the Scandinavian items.

The reason for the misconception is that Scandinavia and Scandinavians are often seen as a single entity. But Scandinavia cannot be regarded as uniform, even with regard to native jewellery, as not all items became fashionable everywhere, and fashions changed during the Viking Age. The foreign material also shows the polarization of Eastern and Western influences that is evident in the general cultural pattern, with jewellery imported from the East found mainly in eastern Sweden, notably Birka, that from Western Europe mainly in Hedeby and items from the British Isles mainly in Norway. And, naturally, only the very wealthy could afford a unique gold brooch made by a great craftsman. Most people had to content themselves with a mass-produced gilt bronze imitation, or with no brooch at all.

Through their clothes and their jewellery the Vikings expressed their cultural relations, their financial situation and their status – just as all peoples have since time immemorial.

HOUSES AND FEASTING

Life revolved around the homestead, which was large or small, grand or poor, depending on economic and social conditions. As will be seen in later chapters, town houses and farm houses differed in appearance and size, but both normally lay on a fenced-in plot, with other buildings for various purposes spread over the plot, as revealed in numerous archaeological excavations.

Building materials (wood, clay, stone or turf, or a combination of these) as well as building techniques, varied according to local resources. The first mortared stone buildings are churches of the eleventh century. As construction techniques improved, internal free-standing roof-bearing posts came to be less common and posts were placed on stones to prevent them rotting, rather than being set straight in the earth. By the late Viking Age, in southern Scandinavia the main house on large farms was often built separately from the byre but the interior arrangements and furnishings of the dwellings did not change greatly during the period.

The exterior of houses was determined by the materials and method of construction, but the houses of the nobility were distinguished by size, elegant form and good craftsmanship. They probably also had splendid carvings and painted decoration in brilliant colours on parts of the exterior like the remains of early

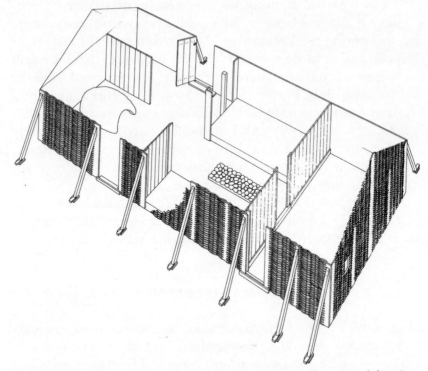

Reconstruction of a well-preserved town house from Hedeby. It
measured 5 × 12 m. The walls were of wattle and daub on a timber
frame. The weight of the roof, which was covered with reeds or straw,
was borne by sloping outer posts which supported the long walls. The
house was divided into three rooms. The central room had an open
hearth and wide platforms against the walls, and must have functioned
both as kitchen and living-room. In the larger gable-room there was
a domed baking-oven. The smaller gable-room was possibly a
workshop and had a window in the gable. The house was in use while
the Viking expeditions were at their height. Dendrochronology has
demonstrated that it was built in the year 870. A full-size replica has
been built at Moesgård Museum, Denmark.

wooden churches, sometimes re-used, such as Urnes Church in
western Norway, Hemse in Gotland, and Hørning Church in
northern Jutland. Secular buildings were no doubt just as grand
(Plates 13, 23).

The doors to the houses might be decorated with carvings or

iron fittings. Locks made of wood or iron were common for both houses and out-buildings, and theft from locked areas was regarded as a particularly serious crime, and punished accordingly. The bearer of the keys was normally the mistress of the house, and this responsibility conferred status.

Inside the houses were normally divided into several rooms, which would have been in half-darkness, as the openings in the walls were few and small; they could presumably be closed with shutters. The hearth would have shed some light, and the louvres in the roof or gables, which allowed smoke to escape, would have admitted a little more. Oil lamps, wax candles (which were expensive) and probably tallow candles could give more light for sewing and weaving. The hearth was usually in the centre of the living-room. It was a slightly raised rectangular area, used for cooking and heating. Some houses had a small domed oven against the wall, as well as, or instead of, an open hearth. There were no chimneys, so smoke must have filled the rooms, and many people must have suffered from permanent carbon-dioxide poisoning, especially in winter when they had to spend much time indoors.

Floors were made of stamped earth, sometimes spread with straw or hay. Along the walls there were often low platforms of earth faced with wood. In small houses they were as deep as a good bench, while in larger houses they could be up to 1.5 m deep. The raised areas, where cold feet and draughts could be avoided, were for living on, and the floor mostly for walking on. Some Viking Age houses had wall panels. The scaldic poem *Húsdrápa*, composed in Iceland at the end of the tenth century, describes decorated wall panels in a newly built chieftain's hall, and some decorated panels have survived at Flatatunga in Iceland; they may have come from a church.

The most important furnishings would have been rugs, tapestries, pillows and cushions, of cloth or fur, as well as lockable chests and caskets, the only storage items. Low stools were probably common too, but other furniture was rare and so little survives. People would have squatted or sat with their legs crossed when talking, eating or working. The sleeping areas were built-in alcoves or small compartments, or simply a place on the platform where rugs would be unrolled for the night. Houses would have had a large loom. Household utensils were stored on shelves and provisions must have occupied a great deal of space. Although there were certainly water-mills in Denmark, many families had a quern for grinding flour. Much time was spent on this work and on gathering, preparing and preserving food.

Viking graves and some scaldic poems give us an insight into the furnishings of wealthy households. An enormous quantity of fine items were buried with the woman in the Oseberg mound in southern Norway in the early ninth century. Most of the grave-goods were of wood, often lavishly carved and some decorated with painting and metal fittings, but there were also textiles and metal objects. These furnishings, kitchen utensils, tools for many kinds of textile work, vehicles (a ship, wagon and sledges), farm-tools, etc., came from a king's or chieftain's house. There was a narrow frieze of a tapestry decorated with narrative scenes, a chair, many chests, at least five beds (perhaps specially built for travelling, as they can be easily taken apart), bedding stuffed with feathers and down, tall oil lamps, looms, finely wrought hooks for hanging cauldrons, cauldrons, griddles, buckets, barrels, tubs, troughs, scoops, knives, ladles and much else including food (Plates 2–3).

Other finds include beds in a ship burial at Gokstad, not far from Oseberg, and the grave-chamber in the mound at Jelling in Jutland contained handsomely carved and painted pieces of wood, probably parts of furniture. There is also much evidence of down- and feather-filled bedding. Remnants of a chair were excavated in Lund in Sweden, and chairs are also known from pictures and from miniature models worn as amulets. Low stools, resembling milking stools, have been found, as well as remains of chests, caskets, kitchen utensils and fine tableware. Tables were used on festive occasions and a woman's grave in Hørning in northern Jutland contained a unique small table for a wash basin. Wash basins were commonly used among the nobility before and after meals, for they are often found in their graves. People ate with their fingers and a knife, as was customary in the rest of Europe at this time, while soup was normally drunk out of beakers or bowls. Forks were unknown, and spoons were small and rare.

Feasts were probably similar to those elsewhere in Western Europe, but the proceedings may have been rather rumbustious and wild. A royal feast would probably have looked like this: in the long hall, benches were placed on the platforms along the walls. There was a special seat for the king or his representative in the centre of one wall. The places of the other guests depended on their rank and reputation. The benches were spread with cushions and the walls were clad with hangings, which might be decorated with narrative scenes from the world of gods and heroes. In front of the benches were long narrow tables with fine tableware, and it was easy for the servants to bring in more food, either from the rooms in the gable ends, or from another building. A fire burned in the hearth in the middle of the floor, and there may have been oil lamps, candles or torches all around. People were dressed in handsome garments and wore heavy jewellery, but their weapons had probably been left outside.

There were alcoholic drinks such as beer, mead (made with honey and water), wine or *bjórr* (a highly fermented fruit wine), and many kinds of meat. Fresh meat was boiled or roasted on spits, or it was preserved by salting, smoking, drying or pickling, and the effect of castration on the quality of meat was known and exploited. Then there might be fish, bread, gruel, dairy products, vegetables, fruit, berries and nuts. The food was seasoned with salt, herbs and spices (the Oseberg grave contained cumin, mustard and horseradish).

Scalds declaimed poems, and stories were told, the flute or lyre may have been played and jugglers or acrobats may have entertained the company. A grand feast helped to establish the reputation of the host, and it might last for several days. Agreements would be struck, friendships or enmities established and marriages arranged.

Adam of Bremen relates that the Archbishop of Hamburg-Bremen was on a diplomatic mission to King Svein Estridsson in Schleswig *c.* 1050:

Finally, as is the custom among the barbarians, they feasted each other sumptuously on eight successive days to confirm the treaty of alliance. Dispositions were made there of many ecclesiastical questions; decisions were reached about peace for the Christians and about the conversion of the pagans. And so the prelate returned home full of joy and persuaded Caesar to summon the Danish king to Saxony that each might swear the other a perpetual friendship.

LANGUAGE, WRITING AND PERSONAL NAMES

The expression 'Danish tongue' (*dönsk tunga*) was used to refer to the Scandinavian languages in the Viking Age and for a couple of centuries afterwards. It is usually thought that the name originated outside Scandinavia, but that the Vikings then adopted it themselves. It implies that the differences between the Scandinavian languages were small – considerably smaller than now – and that they were clearly distinguished from other European languages with Germanic roots. The Scandinavian languages had undergone many changes in the couple of centuries before the Viking Age, making them increasingly distinct from the languages spoken by their neighbours to the south and in Anglo-Saxon England, a linguistic development which continued throughout the Viking Age.

Not much is known of how the 'Danish tongue' sounded, although something can be deduced from the scaldic poems, from Scandinavian loan-words in other languages, and from legends on coins. The runic inscriptions reveal little, for spelling is not consistent, the language is often solemn and archaic, and the alphabet of only sixteen letters gives a limited idea of the phonetic system.

It is clear, however, that linguistic differences, especially phonetic ones, did exist within Scandinavia: basically, West Norse was spoken in Norway and East Norse in Denmark and Sweden, and by the end of the Viking Age differences between Danish and Swedish had begun to develop. These developments may have contributed to a growing sense of national identity, or the opposite may have been true: the formation of the three kingdoms of Norway, Sweden and Denmark may have been partly responsible for the linguistic differences. These remained so small, however, that today Scandinavians can understand each other, and many words of runic inscriptions, once transcribed, without any great difficulty. Partly because many Old Norse words were loaned to the English language after the Viking invasions, a number of words are also familiar in English, as this inscription on a rune stone from Århus in Denmark shows: each line is translated word for word into modern Danish, Swedish and Norwegian, and into English (the words 'raised' and 'fellow' are Scandinavian loan-words).

kunulfR auk augutr auk aslakR auk rulfR risþu
Gunulf og Øgot og Aslak og Rolf rejste
Gunulf och Ögot och Aslak och Rolf reste
Gunulf og Øgot og Aslak og Rolf reiste
Gunulf and Øgot and Aslak and Rolf raised

stin þansi eftiR ful fela(k)a sin
sten denne efter Ful fælle sin
sten denne efter Ful bolagsman sin
sten denne etter Ful fellen sin
stone this after Ful fellow theirs

iaR uarþ [indecipherable runes . . .y?] *tuþr*
han var .... død
han var .... död
han var .... død
he was .... dead

þa kunukaR barþusk
da konger kæmpede
då konungar kämpade
da konger kjempet
when kings fought

Viking Age runes were specifically Scandinavian. They developed from the runic script created in the centuries following the birth of Christ and used by many Germanic tribes. The earliest known runic inscriptions are from Scandinavia and date from around AD 200. There were twenty-four characters at that stage, formed mainly of vertical and diagonal lines, particularly suitable

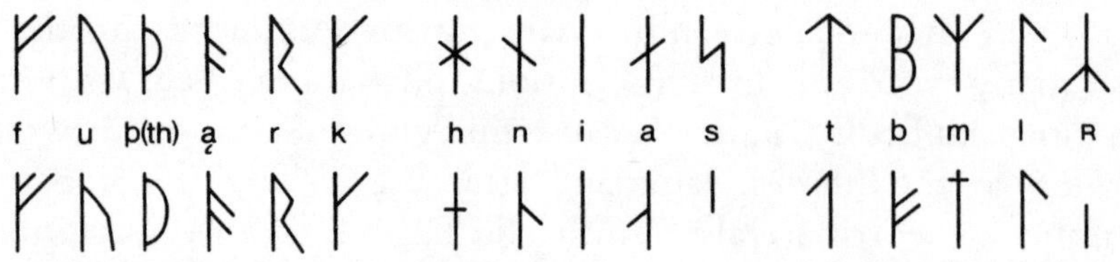
f u þ(th) ą r k h n i a s t b m l R

The sixteen Viking Age runes. Above are the so-called 'normal' or 'Danish' runes, below are the 'short-twig', or 'Swedo-Norwegian' runes.

for carving on wood. Horizontal lines, which might be confused with the grain of the wood, were avoided.

Around AD 800 the number of runes was reduced to sixteen, and the shape of some characters was simplified, making them quicker to carve. They became more difficult to read, however, for most of the characters had multiple meanings, as a simple character had to denote several sounds. For example, the u-rune can be read as u, o, y, ø and w; the k-rune can be read as k, g, nk and ng. Simultaneously, however, a system of symbols developed to divide individual words or sentences. Today many runic inscriptions are difficult, if not impossible, to understand.

This younger runic alphabet, like the older, was called the *fuþark*, after the first six characters (the character *þ* is now represented by the Latin letters 'th'). There were two main variants of the younger runic alphabet: the so-called 'normal', or 'common' or 'Danish' runes, and the 'short-twig runes', or 'Swedo–Norwegian' runes. In the short-twig rune system some characters have fewer and often shorter twigs on the vertical staves – when carved in wood the twigs may be merely a deep cut made with a knife-point – and a few characters consist of just a part of the stave of the normal rune.

Some think that the two variants are due to different local developments, while others maintain that both types were known and used over large areas; the normal runes were mainly used epigraphically for solemn inscriptions on stones, while the short-twig runes, being quicker to carve and probably preferred by merchants, were used mainly for everyday communications.

The reasons for the development of the new runic alphabet of sixteen characters are not known. It is often argued that such a fundamental change must have been imposed by a central authority, rather than being a 'natural' development. Certainly the change took place during a period when many other fundamental social and economic changes occurred.

Many among the upper classes must have been able to read runes, judging by the number of inscriptions on stones which were intended to be seen and read, but runes also occur on all kinds of wooden or bone objects, wherever they can be scratched or carved – on ships, handles, mounts, brooches, weaving tablets and combs. Often they simply spell the owner's name or are just jottings. Some inscriptions may be magic formulas, but this has often been assumed to be the case simply because the runes could not be understood. One of the strangest magic inscriptions is on a piece of human skull from the eighth-century trading centre in Ribe, Denmark, which bears the name of the chief god Odin. Sometimes an inscription merely indicates the name of the object – someone once amused himself by writing the word *kabr* (comb) on a comb, for example. Various sorts of messages have also been found, such as 'Kiss me' on a piece of bone. More important, however, are messages, 'letters', carved on wooden sticks, such as one found at Hedeby, probably from the ninth century. Much of the inscription is incomprehensible, but it is a communication to a man named Oddulv, who is to undertake something – which unfortunately we do not understand.

Most Viking Age runic inscriptions (other than those on stone) have been found in towns and trading posts, where more people needed to read and write than elsewhere. Such a message is actually mentioned in the ninth century in Rimbert's account of the life of the missionary Ansgar. This relates that when Ansgar left Birka in 831 he took evidence of his activities to Emperor Louis the Pious which King Björn had written 'by his own hand with letters formed according to their custom' – presumably in runes. The great majority of Scandinavian runic inscriptions, however, are from the late Viking Age or the early Middle Ages, when the ability to read and write had spread outside the upper classes.

The order of characters in the *fuþark* was quite different to that of the Latin alphabet, nor were they normally written in horizontal lines. On stones they generally ran in vertical bands or in the later Viking Age followed the curves of a snake or dragon's body or framed a picture or ornament. Runic characters were not intended for parchment, long letters or books, unlike the Latin alphabet used by the Church and the administrative bodies in Europe.

The Latin alphabet accompanied the introduction of Christianity into Scandinavia in the tenth and eleventh centuries, along with the increase in European influence and the growing centralization of power. Significantly the earliest inscriptions from the 990s on Scandinavian coins are in Latin letters and the earliest known charter in Scandinavia – a deed of gift by the Danish king St Cnut to the St Laurentii church in Lund in 1085 – was written in Latin letters with pen and ink on parchment, according to European custom.

Runes remained more practical, however, for brief everyday messages, and continued to be used well into the Middle Ages. A knife and a piece of bone from the last meal, or a twig from the nearest tree, were readily available, unlike pens, inkwells and costly parchment.

Naming customs were also distinctly Scandinavian in the Viking Age. Most personal names differed from those in use elsewhere in Europe, which enables Scandinavian place-names in the Viking colonies to be distinguished from others, as one element is often a personal name.

Our knowledge of personal names used in Scandinavia is mainly derived from runic inscriptions; foreign written sources which mention Vikings usually give names in Latinized forms. Other important sources are place-names in the Viking colonies. Because of the nature of these sources, considerably more male than female names are known. Below are some names in their modernized forms.

Names such as Thorsten, Ulf and Grim were common throughout Scandinavia, while others were more local. Among typical West-Norse names are Ejulf and Oddketil, while typical East-Norse names include Manne, Toke and Asved, which is how we know that the Scandinavian immigrants in Normandy were mainly Danish – the Danish name, Ake, for example, is the prefix of the place-name Acqueville.

Naming customs have obvious roots in the preceding age, but

some new names made strong headway in the Viking Age, among them those based on the name of the pagan god Thor (Toke, Thorsten, Thorkild and many more), which remained popular even after the advent of Christianity. Animal names were common, either on their own – Orm (snake), Ulf (wolf) and Bjørn (bear) – or as part of compound names such as Gorm, Gunulf, Ulfbjørn, Styrbjørn. Certain names were much used in particular families: Harald, Svein and Cnut in the Danish royal family in the late Viking Age and early Middle Ages; Harald and Olaf in the Norwegian royal family.

Some people had a by-name, which might indicate a family relationship (son of, daughter of); the place from which they came (Ketil the Norwegian, for example, who lived in Denmark); a possession (Asgot with the Red Shield), or an attribute (Asgot Clapa, which probably means clumsy). In later ages many colour-ful by-names were invented to describe people from the 'olden days'. The great personalities of the Viking Age – Sigrid the Ambitious, Harald Finehair, Ivar the Boneless, Ragnar Hairy Breeches, Harald Bluetooth – were probably not known as such while they were alive. In contemporary sources they are called by their first names, if mentioned at all.

Many of the first names of the Viking Age are still in use in Scandinavia, such as the male names Ivar, Ragnar, Toke, Bjørn, Kolbjørn, Aslak, Rolf, Kjeld, Svend, Knud, Harald, Olav, Håkon and Erik. Among the female names are Sigrid, Thora, Ingrid, Ragnhild, Gunhild, Gudrun, Tove and Åse. Christianity intro-duced a large number of Biblical and saints' names, and other international connections also brought new names. Magnus, which may have derived from the Latin name of the mighty Emperor Charlemagne – Carolus Magnus – or so the Icelandic historian Snorri Sturluson thought, is first known to have been associated with Vikings in tenth-century Ireland, but it quickly became popular in Scandinavia. The first Norwegian king named Magnus was Magnus the Good, who reigned from 1035 to 1047, and later it was also a Swedish king's name.

SOCIETY

No contemporary sources give us precise and detailed knowledge about Viking Age society. Evidence occurs only in brief glimpses and the picture has to be pieced together bit by bit from rune stones and other written sources, and from archaeological finds. Using material from a later age, such as legal texts, is fraught with difficulties, as explained on p. 13); they often claim to be ancient, as age gave authority.

It is clear that great social and economic differences existed in Viking society. The dead might be buried in splendidly furnished graves in large mounds, or at the other extreme, carelessly discarded. We read about kings and chieftains, about free, self-confident farmers, about slaves, and various social stations in between. We know least about these middle groups and the mobility and interrelationships of the groups. There were many poor people who were not slaves and we know of many terms for those whose status was somewhere between the ordinary free farmer and the supreme warrior upper class: *hauldr*, *þegn*, *landsmaðr* and others. The meaning of such words has been much debated; often it is not clear whether a term signifies a specific occupation within a centrally administered military hierarchy (this may be the meaning of the word *þegn* in Denmark), or whether it refers to a rank within the local community, or is a more generalized term for a social class.

SLAVES

There were certainly many slaves in Viking Age Scandinavia, but as they were poor and had no political and economic influence, very few traces of them remain.

Certain crimes were punishable by slavery and the children of two slaves had the status of their parents. The purpose of many Viking expeditions was no doubt to capture slaves; the warriors might keep them, sell them or possibly exchange them for a ransom from rich relatives or from the Christian Church, which was opposed on principle to Christians being the slaves of pagans. The ransoming of Christian captives as an act of piety is frequently mentioned in the accounts of the conversion of Scandinavia.

The Vikings' superb ships made it easy to abduct slaves from foreign lands. The Annals of Xanten, a monastery on the Rhine, record that in the year 837

Immense whirlwinds frequently erupted and a comet [Halley's comet] has been seen with a great train of light in the east about three cubits long to the human eye, and the pagans laid waste the Walcheren [an island at the mouth of the river Schelde in southern Holland] and abducted many captive women as well as an immense amount of various goods.

Trade with slaves is mentioned in Scandinavia as well as in Eastern and Western Europe and it seems highly likely that people were one of the Vikings' most important trading commodities. Around the year 1075 the cleric Adam of Bremen wrote that

These pirates, called Vikings by the people of Zealand [the Danish island of Sjælland], by our people Ascomanni, pay tribute to the Danish king for leave to plunder the barbarians who live around this sea in great numbers. Hence it also happens that the license granted them with respect to enemies is frequently misused against their own people. So true is this that they have no faith in one another, and as soon as one of them catches another, he mercilessly sells him into slavery either to one of his fellows or to a barbarian.

Slaves were subject to their masters, but their exploitation appears to have been regulated by certain rules. They worked in houses and in the fields, and it is likely that they provided some of the labour on the many large building projects of the Viking

Age. Ibn Fadhlan's description of Vikings on the Volga mentions that slave women they had brought with them did all kinds of work as well as providing unlimited sexual gratification on trading voyages of this kind. At home on the farm, however, female slaves of high rank, and also particularly beautiful or accomplished girls, could live in comfortable circumstances and enjoy much respect. The same was probably the case for men with special skills, such as craftsmen, and for faithful old house slaves.

Sometimes slaves accompanied their master in death, as mentioned on p. 31. Several double burials are known, where the grave contains furnishings for one person, and the other has suffered a violent death, including one on the Isle of Man from the Viking period. A woman could be buried with a male slave, a man with a female slave, or either with a slave of the same sex. Ibn Fadhlan described such a burial on the Volga, with its dramatic rituals (p. 157). For slaves who were not buried with their masters there would scarcely be more than a hole in the ground.

Slaves were sometimes freed by their owner, allowed to work to buy their own freedom, or it could be bought for them. In some places full free status could only be obtained after several generations, if they remained in the local community. Most freed slaves were probably members of the landless class who often became farm workers or servants, and there are likely to have been a number of freed slaves among emigrants and craftsmen. A rune stone from Hørning in Jutland – the only one to tell of slavery – was raised by a freed man who did well in life: 'Toke the smith [i.e. craftsman] set up the stone in memory of Thorgisl, Gudmund's son, who gave him gold [or proclaimed him a member of the family] and freedom.'

The social position of craftsmen in general is uncertain but we know that accomplished blacksmiths and ship-builders as well as rune carvers and scalds were greatly respected and lived well by their skills.

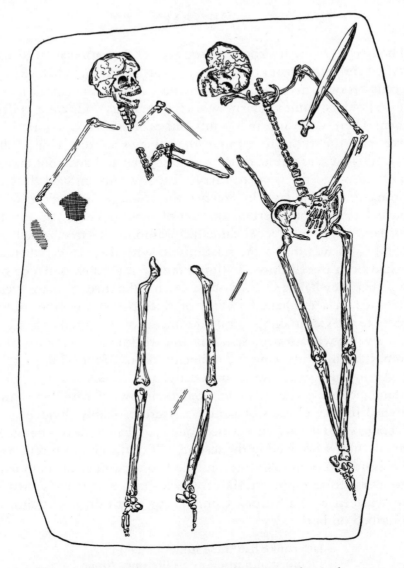

Double grave from Stengade, Langeland, Denmark, tenth century. A
master (left) is buried with a slave. The latter seems to have had his
feet tied together, and his head lay in an unnatural position. He had
presumably been decapitated. A large spear lay obliquely across them
both. Remains of cloth were found on the master's lower right arm.
Langeland Museum, Rudkøbing.

THE FREE

The free were the backbone of society. The group was large and varied and, apart from the aristocracy proper, it included owner-occupiers of farms and large landowners as well as tenant farmers, lease-holders, hunters, farm workers, servants and some crafts-men. There were also merchants and professional warriors. The free had the right to express their views at the Thing (the assembly) where public issues were discussed and decisions taken. They also had the right to carry weapons, and enjoyed the full protection of the law. In practice the concept of freedom may have depended on a certain amount of wealth. There also appear to have been some legal differences among the free, based on family and wealth, on the relationship with their land (whether it had been passed down within a family for generations) or on whether they held a Crown office. Such differences in status were reflected in a graduated system of fines payable by the guilty party to the victim or his family if someone was injured or killed – one's value was assessed. Standing and wealth were naturally also important in influencing the public decisions of the Thing.

Agriculture was the basic occupation almost everywhere. Many people owned and worked their own farms, but some owned immense tracts of land that were probably divided into average-sized farms and leased out. Jarlabanke was one such landowner, who lived in the second half of the eleventh century. To assure his own undying fame he had a number of memorial stones raised in Uppland, six of which survive. A stone which is now placed by Vallentuna Church, just north of Stockholm, is inscribed on both sides:

> Jarlabanke had these stones raised in
> memory of himself in his lifetime. Alone
> he owned the whole of Täby. God help
> his soul.

> Jarlabanke had these stones raised in
> memory of himself in his lifetime, and
> made this Thing place [where the
> assembly met], and alone owned the
> whole of this hundred [an
> administrative district].

Land conferred status and self-confidence and rune stones else-where also tell of large land holdings, which was an essential part of the power base of royalty and the aristocracy. The term *bryti* (leaseholder, steward) is known from rune stones and place-names, and archaeological research confirms that farms varied greatly in size and prosperity. It also demonstrates that entire villages might be totally restructured, as was the case with Vor-basse in Jutland (p. 98). In the past, it was assumed that Viking Age farming communities were democratic and static. Neither was the case.

In the world beyond the local community wealth and pros-perity could be achieved in many ways: by piracy, by expeditions to far-off countries, by entering the service of a great chieftain or king, by trade or by emigrating and acquiring land abroad. Large assets changed ownership during the Viking Age and were channelled into Scandinavia, from both the East and the West. The assets were acquired by a great many people, and in the communities at home where gold, silver and heroic deeds com-manded great respect, newly acquired wealth and honour would have brought enhanced status.

The most vivid picture of the international nature of Viking society comes from Uppland, in central Sweden, because in the eleventh century the custom of raising rune stones flourished so strongly there. These stones bear tales of journeys to nearly all corners of the known world (though mostly eastwards), and of the prosperity which was acquired or sought in far-off lands. These rune stones were raised by self-satisfied, rich farmers, whom the Swedish historian Erik Lönnroth has dubbed *nouveau-riche* upstarts. They needed to show off their wealth and fame, unlike the aristocracy, who often buried their dead in family burial grounds in ships with rich furnishings (as at Vendel, Valsgärde and Tuna). Most of these nouveau-riche farmers were also Christians, like the king, but in contrast to the aristocracy, and the king may well have made use of this ambitious stratum of society to strengthen his power in the area. In return, the par-venus may have been given administrative posts and special favours.

In the past it was assumed that the ties of kinship governed how Viking communities operated and that the family or lineage formed a large and coherent unit on the basis of descent in the male line. This was not in fact the case. Runic inscriptions and other evidence demonstrate that a person's kin was made up of the families of both father and mother, and it was usually the relationships between married couples, brothers and sisters, and parents and children – the immediate family – that decided opportunities in life. It was to them that the individual owed obligations. Only in royal families are more distant relatives frequently mentioned, although the duty to contribute to the *wergeld* (a fine or compensation made to the injured party for a killing committed by a member of the family) went a long way into the branches of the family.

Other ties were also important in both the civilian and the military worlds. Members of a *félag*, or fellowship, owed each other mutual obligations. The *félag* might consist of the joint owners of a ship, it could be a trade association, or a band of warriors (a warrior was often called *dreng*) under a lord to whom they owed allegiance. A rune stone from Århus in Jutland tells of one Asser Saxe, who appears to have been a member of a military fellowship as a *dreng*, and a civilian fellowship as part-owner of a ship. Like many other rune stones, this one was raised by his comrades rather than his family:

Toste [?] and Hove jointly with Frøbjørn erected this stone in memory of Asser Saxe, their partner, a very noble 'dreng'. He died as the greatest 'un-dastard' among men; he owned a ship together with Arne.

Naturally there were other important fellowships which transcended family ties. In villages and towns, where many people lived cheek by jowl, certain common rules were necessary. And there were fellowships connected with defence obligations, religion, the legal system, and the Things, or assemblies, where all major social decisions had to be accepted by free men to gain formal validity.

WOMEN, SEXUAL ROLES AND CHILDREN

There is much evidence that women held their own in Viking society, even though men had the upper hand. Many exercised independent authority and were respected as members of their own social class, and their status may have improved during the Viking Age, since men were often away on long military expeditions or trading voyages, leaving the women in charge of everything at home. Many rune stones all over Scandinavia were raised by women or in memory of women, but they and other sources tell us that the world of women was normally very different to that of men. They were praised not for having undertaken long journeys and warlike deeds, but for good house-keeping and other traditionally feminine qualities and skills that are so important in farming communities. Odindisa from Väst-manland in Sweden was given this obituary by her husband: 'There will not come to Hassmyra a better mistress who holds sway over the farm.' And Gunnvor had this written about her young daughter Astrid on a fine stone in Dynna, in southern Norway: 'She was the handiest [most skilful] girl in Hadeland.'

Given the importance of the family unit, consisting of spouse and siblings, in Viking society, it is not surprising that the largest and most splendid runic monuments mention women. Stones at Jelling in Denmark were raised by King Gorm in memory of his queen Thyre, and by their son Harald in memory of his parents. The Bække monument was raised by two sons in memory of their mother Vibrog, and the Glavendrup and Tryggevælde monuments (all in Denmark) were raised by Ragnhild in memory of her two husbands.

Royal descent on the mother's side was sufficient to establish a legitimate claim to the throne. Svein Estridsson (1047–74), for example, fought for the Danish crown on the basis of his legal right, derived from his mother Estrid, who was the daughter of Svein Forkbeard and sister of Cnut the Great, whose son Har-thacnut died without issue in 1042. According to the eleventh-century Uppland rune stones, women could also inherit land from children who died without descendants, and in some places women may have inherited a share of their parents' wealth, although the shares of sisters and brothers were not equal, notably because daughters had to be provided with dowries on marriage.

Viking graves give a similar picture of women's position. Within the same social sphere women's graves were just as splendid as men's graves – in fact the woman's grave at Oseberg in Vestfold, southern Norway, is the most magnificently furnished of all Viking Age graves. In pagan times women were buried with accoutrements that reflected the female role in society. Instead of the tools, weapons and hunting dogs that accompanied men, women took household utensils, implements for needlework, spinning and weaving, jewellery and lapdogs with them on their journey to the next life. The sexual roles were so deeply rooted among the warrior aristocracy that the two sexes had different realms for the dead in pagan times (cf. p. 149).

Outside the family and the farm women had far fewer opportunities than men. They were not involved in *félag*, as far as we know, and no female merchants or craftsmen are known, although one female scald and one female rune carver, Gunborga, from Hälsingland in northern Sweden, are mentioned. Medieval Irish historians describing the exploits of the Vikings in Ireland included some exciting episodes about wild female warriors, but these were probably dramatizations. Contemporary sources tell us that the women belonging to the great army that invaded England around 890 included wives, and attempts were made before battles to take them and their children to safety. They were there because the army had roamed Western Europe for many years and now the Vikings sought land to settle on. If any female warriors did exist, there cannot have been many. With Scandinavia's conversion to Christianity, church congregations replaced the old fellowships, and these seem to have attracted many women. In their capacity as landowners, some women lent their names to new settlements, both in Scandinavia and abroad, although most place-names of the period are based on a man's name.

Marriage was an alliance between equals and between their families. It is likely that the woman normally brought a dowry and that the man contributed a certain sum, and that both were the personal property of the woman in the marriage. According to two astonished Arab emissaries who visited Viking communities, one in Hedeby around 970, and the other possibly in Ireland in the mid-ninth century, women had very free conditions within marriage, 'the right to divorce among them belongs to the women; the wife divorces when she wants,' one wrote. Adultery by both sexes was punished harshly. Around 1075 Adam of Bremen relates that in Denmark men were punished by death for adultery, while women were sold, and that there was also capital punishment for the rape of virgins. He also rages against the Scandinavian men's excesses with regard to women. Of the Swedes he writes, 'a man according to his means has two or three or more wives at one time, rich men and princes an unlimited number. And they also consider the sons born of such unions legitimate.' These cannot have been actual marriages, but relationships with mistresses or slave women. All in all, the appetite of Scandinavian men for women, or perhaps the openness with which they satisfied it, made a deep impression in both the East and the West.

Children were regarded in a particular way. In the pagan period unwanted children could be exposed to the elements and left to their fate, but Christians reacted strongly against this practice, and it was eventually banned, except in the case of deformed children. Only a few children's graves from the pagan period have been found and certainly in Denmark no children appear to have been buried in adult cemeteries until Christian times. There are no rune stones raised in memory of children, nor is anything known of beliefs about the afterlife with regard to children.

Childhood and youth were brief in Viking times. As in every age all over the world children had stories, songs, rhymes and a few toys modelled on the adult world – miniature ships, weapons and tools – but from an early age they were given daily tasks to do. Cnut, later Cnut the Great, was only a teenager in 1013 when he accompanied his father, King Svein, on the expedition that began the conquest of England. After his father's death in 1014 he became the leader of the army, probably in fact as well as in name, and two years later he was ruler of all England.

RULES OF CONDUCT

The whole of society was bound by conventions and moral codes which today can be discerned through poetry and runic inscriptions. Those who broke the codes lost their honour – their good name – and forfeited their place in society. Loyalty was expected towards the family and those with whom one was in fellowship (*félag*), between a lord and his men, between friends, and between the master and mistress of a household and their servants. There were conventions about hospitality and the giving of gifts; oaths had to be kept (though not necessarily all peace treaties made on expeditions abroad); injustice and violations had to be avenged, and so on. Personal honour was enhanced by praiseworthy qualities: physical courage, skills, magnanimity, generosity (with food too), eloquence, cleverness, moderation in some matters, self-control, fellowship, the ability to execute unusual deeds, and, in Christian times, good deeds for society such as bridge-building and church-building.

The significance of honour is interpreted in the eddaic poem *Hávamál*, 'The Speech of the High One', which goes back to the Viking Age: honour, reputation, is the only thing which endures for ever.

> Cattle die,
> kindred die,
> every man is mortal:
> but the good name
> never dies
> of one who has done well.

> Cattle die,
> kindred die,
> every man is mortal:
> but I know one thing
> that never dies,
> The glory of the great dead.

Hávamál also gives many down-to-earth and practical rules of conduct that are quite different to the attitudes expressed in the warlike poetry composed in honour of princes. Many people had a fatalistic outlook, a conviction that life's vicissitudes were predetermined by fate, which must have been useful in such a violent age, when the world was very uncertain.

The man who stands
at a strange threshold
should be cautious
before he cross it,
glance this way and that:
who knows beforehand
what foes may sit
awaiting him in the hall?

Better gear
than good sense
a traveller cannot carry,
a more tedious burden
than too much drink
a traveller cannot carry.

The tactful guest
will take his leave
early, not linger long:
he starts to stink
who outstays his welcome
in a hall that is not his own.

It is best for man
to be middle-wise,
not over cunning and clever:
no man is able
to know his future,
so let him sleep in peace.

Not all sick men
are utterly wretched:
some are blessed with sons,
some with friends,
some with riches,
some with worthy works.

The halt can manage a horse,
the handless a flock,
the deaf be a doughty fighter,
to be blind is better
than to burn on a pyre:
there is nothing the dead can do.

KINGS AND KINGDOMS

Before the Viking Age there were several kingdoms in Scandinavia, but it is not clear how big the territories were, what powers the kings or chieftains had, nor how they exercised their authority. The same applies to a certain extent to the Viking Age, and we know very little about the unification of the three countries as they exist today, but the main historical developments will be outlined on pp. 73–7. Nearly all of modern Denmark, as well as the districts of Skåne and Halland, which are now part of Sweden, was probably subject to the Danish king before the year 800. Norway, or rather most of the regions near the sea and the deep fjords, was first united under one king at the end of the ninth century. It is uncertain when one king first ruled over the whole of Sweden. Important parts of the country had the same king at the beginning of the eleventh century and again later, but the main parts of Sweden were not finally united before the twelfth century.

Power was far from centralized in the Viking kingdoms. The individual regions retained their own customs and laws and a high degree of independence. The old aristocracy also had great power in the regions, even though this diminished as royal administration became more effective. Nor was there a consistent development, for the power of a king always depended on his interaction with the chieftains and on international politics. Both in the Viking Age and later, a kingdom might be divided for a time; several kings lost the support of the chieftains and were exiled or killed. A kingdom, or part of one, could also fall under foreign sovereignty.

A need for peace and prosperity amongst the leading groups in society must originally have led to the unification of large areas under one king, and explains the people's willingness to accept him as a sovereign and contribute to his maintenance and the execution of his duties. From journeys in Europe, Byzantium and the Arab countries, the Scandinavians knew of the advantages that accompanied more developed administrations. In Scandinavia the need arose for larger and firmer political units around the beginning of the Viking Age. The need grew apace throughout the period, as the economy and the structure of society became ever more complicated. The production of goods increased and trade and crafts expanded rapidly. Great wealth was amassed by more people than before, trading stations grew up, towns were established, goods were distributed over a wider area, and relations within Scandinavia and with countries abroad grew closer. The wealth and valuables which had to be carried over long distances were an open invitation to robbery, and pirates could travel quickly in the new sailing ships of the age. But so could armed guards, so a king with a big enough army was able to keep the peace and provide protection over a large area – in return for fees. This power became the prerequisite for a flourishing community.

A power structure with a leader who could quickly assemble a large force also became increasingly necessary to avert threats from aggressive neighbours and from large, organized bands of warriors. Furthermore, it was desirable that connections with both gods and foreign kingdoms should be in the hands of a single powerful person. The gods were in charge of peace and prosperity in all areas of life, and as international relations increased it also became important to be able to make beneficial agreements between two kingdoms. Finally, to maintain a kingdom of a certain size, an administrative organization was necessary. The king needed a court and representatives throughout the country. This presented new opportunities for members of the aristocracy and for the ambitious.

ACCESSION TO THE THRONE AND PERSONAL POWER

In Scandinavia it was the rule that the king should be descended from a king on his father's or mother's side. A king's legitimacy was often strengthened by making gods and great heroes of the past into distant ancestors. Usually, a deceased king was succeeded by his son, but there was no fixed order of succession. A king had to be chosen and several members of the family might aspire to the throne, each supported by his own party. Generally, agreement was reached, but sometimes the problem was solved by dividing the kingdom or by joint kingship. In other cases, the claimants had to resort to battle.

The Frankish Annals give a dramatic and quite detailed insight into matters relating to the accession of a new king in Denmark at the beginning of the ninth century. After the killing of King Godfred in AD 810, his sons went into exile and his nephew Hemming became king. After Hemming's death two years later, two parties fought for the throne. One was led by Sigfred (another of Godfred's nephews), the other by Anulo (nephew of an earlier king, Harald). Both died, but Anulo's party was victorious, so it was agreed that Anulo's two brothers should be kings. The following year, in 813, they were overcome by the sons of King Godfred, who took the throne, and this branch of the family retained power for many years.

Royal power could also be shared, for example by a father and a son as well as by brothers, but never by a woman. Sources also tell us that the title of king was not always connected with a particular geographical area: there were many army leaders on expeditions in Europe who bore the title of king without having any established power base in their own country and despite the fact that there was a strong ruling king at home.

Occasionally, a new dynasty came to power. This probably happened in Denmark at the end of the ninth century, and again just before the middle of the tenth century, when Gorm the Old suddenly emerged. A claim of legitimacy may have been made, but power was no doubt seized with weapon in hand and much silver, as when Olaf Tryggvason, who was of royal blood, became king of Norway shortly before 1000. His power was based on vast amounts of silver acquired during the raids in England. The might of chieftains and kings was founded on personal fame and wealth in land, animals and easily converted assets; it was maintained by the ability to gather the right men around them, by leadership, the achievement of results, and rewarding good service well.

The hunt for glory and silver, the prerequisites for gaining power, is therefore a dominant theme in the history of the Viking Age. Viking kings were surrounded by glittering splendour, and the scalds, who composed their poems in honour of princes, praised victorious battles, swords and ships, great booty and distant expeditions, courage and loyalty, as well as rich rewards for the prince's men. The weapons found in pagan graves of the upper classes reflect these military ideals, and dead heroes went to Valhalla, ruled by the warrior god Odin, where the time was spent fighting and feasting in noble company with like-minded men. In life, the chieftains as well as the king surrounded themselves with a *lið*, a band of warriors who constituted a *félag*, and were bound to their lord by mutual loyalty. They were his bodyguards, they accompanied him on expeditions and other journeys, and aided him in word and deed.

Some of the most splendid monuments of the Viking Age are the result of new dynasties wanting to make their mark on newly acquired territories. King Gorm's son Harald Bluetooth erected the largest royal memorial known from the Scandinavian Viking Age at Jelling. It comprises two rune stones, two huge mounds, a royal grave and a church, and celebrates his parents as well as the great deeds of Harald himself (p. 162 and Plate 12). The inscription on the larger rune stone has a clear political and religious message:

King Harald commanded this monument to be made in memory of Gorm, his father, and in memory of Thorvi [Thyre], his mother – that Harald who won the whole of Denmark for himself, and Norway and made the Danes Christian.

Similarly, some of the large burial mounds in Vestfold, southern Norway, mark the power of the Ynglinga family. Harald Finehair, who unified large parts of Norway, was one of them. Some of the mounds – Oseberg, Gokstad and one of those on the impressive complex at Borre (Plate 11) – were examined in the nineteenth century, and they contained large ships as well as an abundance of grand furnishings of the ninth and tenth centuries, worthy of kings and queens.

The Ynglinga dynasty probably came originally from Sweden. One of its scalds, Þjóðólf, traced it back in his great poem *Ynglingatal* through thirty generations to Yngvi, the legendary ancestor of the illustrious kings of Uppsala, but he also connected the family with Borre. We cannot tell which members of the family are buried in the mounds that have been excavated, and others probably lie in some of Vestfold's other large grave mounds.

There are also large mounds in Old Uppsala, the heart of the Swedish kingdom of the Svear. The two mounds that have been excavated date from the fifth and sixth centuries, but unfortunately nothing is known about the relationship between those buried here and the Swedish Viking Age kings, nor about their connection with Uppsala. We do know, however, that *c.* 1075 there was a central cult place with a pagan temple here.

ROYAL POWER

We have a surprising amount of information about the Scandinavian kings' areas of responsibility, power bases and administrative systems, although it is very uneven and much of it concerns the later period. Traditionally, royal power was considered weak: a king was a military leader and the leader of the prevailing religious cult; the economic basis for the office was strictly limited, royal administration was probably non-existent and all important decisions were made by the Thing. This interpretation was based on the general perception of Scandinavia as a primitive, barbaric region.

The native and foreign written sources (not least the Frankish and German ones) and the archaeological and numismatic evidence, studied together and in the light of what we now know about contemporary Europe, alter the general picture in several respects. It is true that the function of a king was primarily that of a military and perhaps a religious leader, but he also exercised a monopoly of power: he gave protection within the kingdom.

In addition, he was the official head of state in relations with other countries. In principle, important decisions – apart from levying armies in response to foreign aggression – were made by free men at the Thing, but their real influence varied from place to place at different periods, depending on the understanding between king and aristocracy.

Rimbert's account of Ansgar's mission to the north in the ninth century makes no mention of a decision by the Thing prior to King Horik of Denmark granting Ansgar permission to build churches in his country. At Birka in Sweden the situation was slightly different, though perhaps not in essence. When Ansgar journeyed there to spread the Gospel, he approached King Olaf, who thought it necessary to cast lots to ascertain the opinion of the gods, and to obtain the opinion of the people at the Thing, 'for it is the custom of that country that every public concern depends more on the people's uniform will than on the power of the king'. This sentence has often been taken as clear evidence of the very limited power of the Scandinavian kings in the Viking Age, but the rest of the account modifies this impression. The reason why King Olaf scrupulously observed the formalities on this occasion was that there had been a pagan backlash following recent attempts at a Christian mission. Olaf himself favoured Christianity. He first gathered his chieftains and debated with them about Ansgar's mission, then they went into a field and threw lots which revealed that the gods indicated they should accept Christianity. On the day the Thing assembled the king had the matter proclaimed by a herald. First it aroused opposition, but after a man pointed out the value of the Christian God as a protector on the hazardous journeys to Dorestad, the large Frisian trading town, the Thing decided to follow the king's lead. So, as in Denmark, the opinion of the king was decisive for the outcome of the case.

The account of Ansgar's mission and other contemporary sources mention a circle of aristocrats around the king who advised him, influenced decisions, and appeared on his behalf at official functions as representatives of the realm. This happened at the great peace treaty between the Frankish emperor Charlemagne and Denmark's King Hemming in 811. Peace oaths were made between twelve nobles from the two kingdoms. These must have been lords who periodically or permanently stayed at court. The many diplomatic missions to foreign rulers were also undertaken by men close to the king. In addition, he had representatives throughout the country to act on his behalf, protect his interests, and secure his income. There is also evidence of special coastal guards in times of unrest, as in Western Europe, and in 817 a man named Glum is mentioned as being responsible for the security of Denmark's southern border. Royal representatives in towns and markets helped maintain peace and collected income for the king.

In written sources, royal officials have a number of different titles, the precise meaning of which is sometimes unclear. They were often local lords who resided on their own property but were given a new title and new tasks. Others lived on the king's large, scattered properties; in the late Viking Age the place-name Huseby was connected with a number of such royal centres with administrative functions. Huseby-names are still found in many parts of Scandinavia, but they are most common in central Sweden.

Some of the mightiest royal officials who were given responsibility for a district had the title of earl, but this title was also borne by some independent rulers and by royal representatives in charge of smaller areas. Originally it probably just meant a prominent man. The title was presumably in use throughout Scandinavia, but we know most about the earls in Norway and the Orkneys. The mightiest Norwegian earls had their seat in Lade, near Trondheim, certainly from the end of the ninth century, and they held power from Trøndelag northwards. For more than a century the title was passed from father to son and several Lade earls became the most powerful men in the realm. The Orkney earls' power and title was also inherited, and they were largely independent, although they recognized the supremacy of the Norwegian king.

We do not know of any permanent royal residences, but we know that there was a network of royal estates, many of them visited by kings on their journeys around the country. The royal estates in Borre must have had a special significance in the ninth to tenth centuries, and that at Jelling became important in the middle of the tenth century. Kings often took up residence in trading centres such as Hedeby, Birka and Trondheim, and were furthermore connected with religious centres such as Lejre and Roskilde in Denmark, probably Uppsala in Sweden and Trondheim in Norway. We do not know exactly what a royal estate looked like, although the grand hall (measuring 48m × 11m) excavated in Lejre may well have been royal, while the large farm in late Viking Age Vorbasse illustrates the layout of a magnate's farm. The Danish circular fortresses from around 980, although royal, were mainly military structures.

The rights and economic basis of Viking kings, including the degree to which they could impose public obligations on their subjects, must have varied considerably. Strong kings no doubt had many such opportunities, and royal power, as opposed to the personal power of individual kings, increased during the Viking Age. The people had a basic duty to defend their country. They had to take up arms under the king's command and by the late Viking Age a levy system existed in Norway and Denmark to raise men, ships and equipment, probably on the basis of land ownership. The erection of ramparts and other defences must normally have been a public obligation, for how else was the Danevirke rampart stretching for 7 km built in the 730s? Some of the other great structures, such as the Jelling monuments of the mid-tenth century, may also have been built with conscripted labour.

The economic basis of the crown was land ownership and the returns this yielded; if the king also owned much land privately, the returns were all the greater. In addition there was income from towns and trade, presumably from customs duties levied on the passage of goods, and sometimes from independent trading and from minting coins. Granting licences for piracy was a source of income in Denmark around 1070. In addition large sums were paid to the king by outlaws to recover their 'peace'. Levy-fines, imposed on those who did not fulfil their duties when a levy was called, were another lucrative source of funds. Both are documented in the late Viking Age. The king was entitled to a certain amount of free transport, and there was probably a further obligation to house him and his men when they travelled around the kingdom. After internal unrest and revolts, the king's landholdings and income could be increased dramatically by seizing the property of his adversaries.

Decoration on rune stone from Ledberg in Östergötland, Sweden, with a warship, warriors and dogs. The stone was raised by Bise and Gunna in memory of Bise's father Torgöt.

There was also considerable potential for earnings abroad, from tributes and tolls exacted at intervals from subjugated areas or countries, or from individuals who asked for a king's or a chieftain's protection and 'peace'. Furthermore, a king could obtain vast wealth through straightforward plunder and through tributes paid by defeated or terrified enemies in return for his withdrawal.

Income and honour were indispensable to the Viking kings, and they often fought at the head of their armies. Many therefore died young. According to the saga, Norway's King Magnus Barefoot, who was killed in 1103 during an expedition to Ireland at the age of about thirty, said 'Kings are made for honour, not for long life.'

POLITICAL DEVELOPMENTS

A brief chronological survey of the political conditions and developments in each of the three Scandinavian countries is given below.

Because Denmark bordered Christian countries with a well–established literary tradition, there is much information about Danish kings, but nothing is recorded of when or how the country was unified; presumably it was already unified by 800, when foreign sources began to take an interest in it. The later Danish histories throw no light on its unification either. The main steps in the unification of Norway can be deduced from scaldic poems in honour of kings and earls and from kings' sagas. It was a lengthy and complicated process, leaving many dead. There is hardly any written information about the history of Sweden during the Viking age and also very little about Swedish kings.

DENMARK

Denmark is named after its people, the Danes, but the meaning of the suffix -mark is disputed. A few pieces of written information and large-scale building works, such as the first phase of the ramparts known as the Danevirke, erected in 737, and the Kanhave canal on the island of Samsø in 726, indicate that there was an organized central power of considerable strength, certainly in Jutland, in the eighth century. An area almost the same size as in the Middle Ages was presumably unified under one king before AD 800, but in the ninth and early tenth century we hear most about southern Jutland, since the many border disputes were of interest to Frankish and German writers. A number of kings are mentioned, including Godfred, who posed a threat to Charlemagne in about 800, and two joint kings, Harald and Reginfred, who also ruled over Vestfold in southern Norway in 813. Around 850 the kings Horik the Older and Horik the Younger permitted Ansgar to build two churches. There are also several references to the Danes' interest in the Slav regions and political alliances with Slav tribes.

From the mid-tenth century we know of a continuous succession of kings, beginning with Gorm the Old. His son Harald

Bluetooth's message on the large rune stone at Jelling makes it quite clear that the kingdom was unified. Harald's long reign saw border fights with Germany, the subjugation of Norway, the introduction of Christianity and the undertaking of many large building projects. Harald was presumably successful in extending royal authority, but he was ousted by his son Svein Forkbeard around 987 and died. For a time King Svein also held sway in Norway and he conquered England in 1013, but died in 1014. In Denmark he was succeeded by his son Harald, who died in 1018; his brother Cnut the Great, who had already become sole ruler of England in 1016, became king. For a time he also ruled over Norway and part of Sweden and in a letter to the English people in 1027 he called himself 'Cnut, king of all England, and of Denmark, and of the Norwegians, and of part of the Swedes'. He died in 1035 and was succeeded in Denmark by his son Harthacnut, who became king of England in 1040, dying without issue in 1042. His successor in Denmark was the Norwegian king Magnus the Good, who died in 1047. During this period the Slav Wends often attacked Denmark and Magnus' uncle Harald Harðráði (Hard-ruler) may have ruled part of Denmark for a time, but Cnut the Great's nephew Svein Estridsson (1047–74) was successful in gaining power over the whole realm. He was succeeded by five sons in turn, one of whom, Cnut, was killed during a revolt in 1086 and soon after became Denmark's first royal saint.

NORWAY

Norway, which means the north way, after the sailing route along the country's long west coast, was first unified in the 880s or a little later by Harald Finehair, the king of Vestfold, at the battle of Hafrsfjord (close to Stavanger). This unification included only southern Norway and the coastal districts and the fjords, not the far north. Harald probably died around 930; his son Erik Bloodaxe had been joint ruler, but he was ousted soon after his father's death because of the severity of his rule. Erik then led Viking expeditions in the west and during two periods was king of York, but he was expelled and killed in 954 when northern England came under the English crown. In Norway the throne passed to his brother Hákon Aðalsteinsfostri (foster-son of Athelstan: he had been brought up by the English king Athelstan). Hákon was a Christian, but he let the Norwegians keep their old religion and pursued a cautious policy, partly by maintaining a good relationship with Trøndelag's mighty Earl Sigurd, whose seat was in Lade, near Trondheim. Around 960 Hákon was killed in battle fighting an alliance of Erik Bloodaxe's sons and Danes.

In the following decade Norway came under strong Danish influence through Erik's son Harald Gráfell (Grey-cloak). His power seems to have been greatest in southern Norway, however, and control of Trøndelag and the lucrative trade in goods from the north eluded him for most of his reign. In the 960s he killed Earl Sigurd, who was succeeded by his son Earl Hákon; c. 970 the king was killed in battle against an allied army of Danes and Hákon's Trøndelag men.

During the following years Earl Hákon was the most powerful man in Norway, but in the beginning he submitted to the Danish overlordship of Harald Bluetooth; around 995 he was killed by a slave. At this time Olaf Tryggvason, a grandson of Harald Finehair, returned to Norway from lucrative Viking expeditions in England and elsewhere and became king. Trøndelag was his base and within a few years he held power along the Norwegian coast from the south to Hálogaland in the north. He was a Christian and started systematic missionary activity. On his way to the south coast of the Baltic in c. 1000 he was killed in the battle of Svöld (the location is not known), leaving the alliance of Hákon's son Earl Erik, the Danish king Svein Forkbeard and the Swedish king Olof Skötkonung victorious.

Svein Forkbeard then ruled Norway with Earl Hákon's two sons Erik and Svein as loyal earls; Olof Skötkonung probably took Ranrike on the east coast of the Oslo fjord. The unity of the realm was again lost and who ruled what and how is unclear. In 1014 Earl Erik took part in the conquest of England and in 1017 he became Cnut the Great's earl in Northumbria.

In 1015 Olaf Haraldsson, a distant descendant of Harald Finehair, returned to Norway and became king, having been on Viking expeditions for many years. The process of unifying the kingdom and the conversion to Christianity began again. He also took the inland regions under his dominion and strengthened

Norway's hold on Orkney and Shetland. But in the 1020s the relationship with the wealthy north Norwegian chieftains deteriorated and Cnut the Great laid claim to the country. He came to Norway in 1028 with a fleet; Olaf was also threatened by an army of Trøndelag men led by Earl Hákon, son of Erik, and fled across Sweden to take refuge with Prince Yaroslav of Kiev. Hákon now became Cnut's earl in Norway, but shortly afterwards he drowned in 'the English sea'. In 1030 Olaf returned, but in the summer, possibly on 29 July, he was killed in battle against a Norwegian army at Stiklestad (*Stiklastaðir*), near Trondheim. Shortly after this he was worshipped as a saint.

About the same time Cnut the Great's illegitimate son Svein and his English mother Alfiva (or Ælfgifu) assumed power in the country on behalf of Cnut. They became unpopular, however, and the Norwegians united around St Olaf's young son Magnus, who had been in Russia since 1028 and was brought home around 1035. Svein Alfivason fled to Denmark and died shortly afterwards. Royal power over Norway was again strengthened under Magnus and after the death of Harthacnut in 1042 he also became king of Denmark. In the mid-1040s his father's half-brother, Harald Harðráði, who returned from Russia and Byzantium with great wealth, claimed a share of the Norwegian throne. He became sole ruler of the kingdom after Magnus died without issue in 1047, but he had to surrender Denmark. Harald Harðráði was killed by King Harold Godwinsson at the battle of Stamford Bridge, when he attempted to conquer England in 1066.

SWEDEN

Sweden is named after the Svear people from central Sweden, the core of the realm. Throughout the ninth century several kings are mentioned in Birka, among them Björn and Olaf, who received Ansgar and permitted his mission, but the extent of their power is unclear, and very little is known about the political history of the country in the Viking Age. We do know that Blekinge in the south and the coastal area north of here, as well as the islands of Öland and Gotland, belonged to the realm of the Svear by 890, from Wulfstan describing a sailing voyage on the Baltic to King Alfred. Olof Skötkonung (*c.* 995–1020) is the first king known to have ruled over Sweden, that is as king of both the Svear and the Götar (Skåne and Halland belonged to Denmark), but there may have been others before him, and it certainly did not amount to the whole country being united. Olof was Christian, although the majority of the population, especially among the Svear, still observed the old religion. After a revolt he seems to have retained power only in Västergötland. He was succeeded by his son Anund Jakob, who was also Christian. In 1027 we know that Cnut the Great called himself king of 'part of the Swedes', and around 1030 he had coins struck in Sigtuna, just north of Birka. Anund Jakob died c. 1050 and was succeeded by his half-brother Emund Slemme, who was followed by Stenkil.

Two wild animals with swords and shields weave their long tongues into a mask. Decoration on rune stone from Lund in Skåne, Sweden, c. AD 1000.

TRAVEL, TRANSPORT AND SHIPS

Effective means of transport and established routes were essential for social and economic growth in Scandinavia and for expansion overseas. This applied chiefly to ships and sailing routes, but also to land transport.

Many people travelled a lot, and many travelled far – to local and national Things and religious festivals, to family celebrations and markets. Trade, war and diplomatic missions took them abroad. Many Vikings emigrated and some even undertook voyages of exploration. Travellers' tales and descriptions made good entertainment, and journeys to far-away countries were so prestigious that they were mentioned in scaldic poems and on rune stones. The splendid Viking ships were immortalized in poetry, on stone memorials, coins and jewellery, and became favourite motifs for graffiti. The rune stones of the late Viking Age also celebrate the building of bridges and causeways.

Adam of Bremen, writing around 1075, gives us an indication of typical routes on land and at sea: if you sail from Skåne in southern Sweden to Sigtuna, you get there on the fifth day, while a journey overland, through the land of the Götar, Skara and Södertälje, takes a month. If you wish to go to Trondheim, you can sail from north Jutland to southern Norway in one day; from there you sail along the west coast of Norway, and on the fifth day reach Trondheim. From Skåne there is also a route overland to Trondheim: 'this route, however, is slower in the mountainous country and travellers avoid it because it is dangerous'. It must have followed the large valleys which cut deep into Norway from the region around the Oslo fjord.

To travel up through Jutland, from Schleswig in the south to Ålborg by the Limfjord in the north, would take five to seven days. Adam of Bremen also records that according to King Svein Estridsson, you can easily traverse Norway in a month, whereas the difficult journey through Sweden takes at least two. This is presumably because of the large forests, lakes and marshy areas as well as mountainous terrain; in Norway many land routes passed through large tracts of unforested mountain plateaux.

TRAVEL ON LAND

In Viking times people walked, rode horses or drove wagons, while in the winter sledges, skis and skates were much used. Busy routes over even ground consisted of broad bands of wheel tracks that kept to dry land where possible. The main road through Jutland, for example, which came to be known as the Army Road and the Ox Road, ran along the ridge and the watershed. In the lake-lands of central Sweden, one could follow the gravel ridges over long distances, and the same was (and still is) the case in Vestfold in southern Norway. In many places, however, the roads were interrupted by lakes or rivers which had to be crossed by boat, ford or bridge.

Ever since the Stone Age people had built causeways and fords, but bridges were not built in Scandinavia until the Viking Age. The earliest that have been discovered are in Denmark, all built within a short period at the end of the tenth century. The Danes may have learnt how to build them from the Slavs, as south of the Baltic large-scale bridge-building had been undertaken for a long time.

The largest and possibly the earliest bridge in Denmark is that over the Vejle river valley in Ravning Enge near Jelling, dated by dendrochronology to 979 ± one year. It was built of oak and was 700 m long, about 5.5 m wide and supported by more than 1,500 large oak timbers. The bridge can only have been in use for a few years, for it was never repaired, and wooden bridges require repair after ten or fifteen years. It was probably built by order of King Harald Bluetooth, who also had large fortresses built in various parts of his realm at this time. The bridge made it much easier to cross the wide Vejle river valley and the Army Road presumably made use of it while it was in good repair. The king may have charged tolls for passing over it, but prestige was certainly an important reason for building it. The bridge was on a royal scale and it must have made the approach to Jelling an impressive experience for the traveller from the south, as well as facilitating troop transport to the vulnerable border regions.

In many other parts of Scandinavia at about this time much effort was expended on improving land transport, presumably because of an increasing demand for trade and other forms of communication, including Christian church-going. Remains of several bridges and causeways from the late Viking Age have been found and a number of rune stones – always raised by Christians, it seems – mention road clearance or the building of bridges and causeways (the word *brú* can mean a causeway and probably a ford as well as a bridge). The most famous is Jarlabanke's *brú* in Täby in central Sweden, dating from the end of the eleventh century. A causeway about 150 m long and 6.5 m wide was built over a marshy hollow and edged with raised stones; two rune stones were placed on each bank, with almost identical inscriptions:

Jarlabanke's causeway in Täby, Uppland, Sweden. Drawing by Peringskiold, seventeenth century when it was still in good condition.

Jarlabanke had these stones raised in
memory of himself in his lifetime. And he
made this bridge for his soul. And alone he
owned the whole of Täby. God
help his soul.

Good bridges and causeways were a convenience for those
walking and riding but were essential for vehicular traffic. There
is much evidence that wagons and carts were in common use in
Scandinavia on suitable terrain: wheel ruts, wheels, broken axles,
bodies of wagons (used as coffins in women's graves), items
of carriage harness, pictures of vehicles on stones and textiles,
references to them in written sources and even an entire four-
wheeled wagon found in the Oseberg woman's grave.

This ninth-century wagon consists of an undercarriage with
spoked wheels and double shaft, and a round-bottomed body.
The end panels are decorated with fine carvings, and it lies loose
on the cradles. Unfortunately, the undercarriage gives us no clear
idea of normal construction methods, for its design prevents the
wheels from turning properly. Nor is there any wear on the
wooden wheels. These and other details strongly suggest that the
undercarriage was made specifically for the burial and hence no
attention was paid to whether or not it worked. The same applies
to some other things in the grave.

Horses and oxen were used as draught animals. Carriages for
transporting people rather than goods were primarily used by
women. The horses that drew them often wore a breast harness,
for more effective traction. This harness may have been introduced in the Viking Age, like so much else.

In mountainous regions and over difficult terrain everyone had
to walk or ride, and goods had to be carried on people's backs or
on pack animals. On fairly even and firm ground special sledges
were used for heavy loads, such as large stones, while turf and
other building materials were moved over short distances in
barrows carried by two people. These consisted of boards tied
together and lashed to two carrying poles.

It was mostly men who travelled, both on land and sea. If they
did not have much luggage and could afford a horse they rode
when the terrain allowed. The horses were somewhat smaller

then than today, but the tack was much the same: bits, saddles, stirrups and spurs were all used. Those of the rich were splendid and showy, sometimes inlaid with copper and silver, which gleamed against the dark iron. Indeed, remains of riding equipment made of solid gold have been found at Værne Kloster on the east side of the Oslo fjord, including a spur decorated with an animal ornament in magnificent filigree. Some walkers also had stylish accessories: a couple of handsomely carved walking sticks have been discovered.

The most lively travel account from the Viking Age is of a long journey, partly on foot, undertaken around 1020 by the scald Sigvat and other emissaries from the Norwegian king Olaf Haraldsson (the Holy) to Earl Ragnvald, probably in Väster- götland in Sweden. On his return Sigvat composed the poem *Austrfararvísur*, which tells of sore feet and lack of sleep, how they got soaking wet crossing a lake in a leaky boat, and had problems finding shelter for the night; of pagans who held a sacrificial feast, and how they rode fast to get women to come out of their houses.

WINTER TRANSPORT

In many parts of the Scandinavian peninsula – for example, in mountainous districts and in central Sweden's large lake district, which at that time had even more water than today – transport was easiest and fastest when ice and snow covered land and water throughout the long winter. The frozen lakes were passable and uneven ground was covered over. Then sledges, skis, snowshoes and skates were the everyday means of transport; sledges and skates (and probably skis) were also used in southern Scandinavia.

Our knowledge of sledges and skis comes from archaeological finds and from pictures such as the large stone in Böksta, in Uppland, depicting a skier on an elk hunt with bow and dogs. Skiing is also mentioned in scaldic poetry. The most splendid sledges are from the woman's grave at Oseberg, which contained three handsomely carved luxury sledges for personal transport and also a small goods sledge, very like those used by children today. The large sledges must have been drawn by horses; to secure a foothold in slippery conditions horses were shod with crampons. Skates, known as 'ice-legs', have been found in great numbers. They were cheap and easy to make: usually a horse's foot bone (metapodial) was smoothed flat on the underside and sometimes bored with a hole so that it could be tied on with a strap. A spiked staff made it easy to push oneself along at great speed on smooth ice. Experiments in modern times have fully confirmed the effectiveness of these Viking designs – and have caused much amusement.

SHIPS AND SAILING

Ships have become the symbol of the Viking Age, and with good reason. A reliable description of the main type used in Scandinavia, and some insight into its specialization, can be given on the basis of the many ships and fragments discovered. This main type has also been found in England and in the Slav regions south of the Baltic, with local modifications. It was probably introduced in both places as the result of Scandinavian influence. The ships which William the Conqueror, a Viking descendant, had built for his invasion of England in 1066 were of the same type.

The finds also tell us that within Scandinavia ships varied according to local natural conditions, and there is evidence that they developed technically during the Viking Age. Sails seem to have been introduced during the centuries preceding the Viking Age, although sailing ships had then been used in Western Europe for many hundreds of years. In Scandinavia sailing ships rapidly attained a level of sophistication that was outstanding for their time. Without sails, the far-flung exploits of the Vikings would have been impossible.

The best-preserved and the most famous Viking ships are the magnificent Norwegian burial ships from Oseberg and Gokstad in Vestfold, excavated in 1904 and 1880 respectively (Plate 2). The Oseberg ship is the older, probably from the early ninth century, while the Gokstad ship is from the end of the ninth century or the beginning of the tenth. Elsewhere kings, chieftains and high-ranking women were also buried with ships. Other finds include five ships of different types from around AD 1000–

1075, which were scuttled at Skuldelev in Denmark in order to obstruct the passage through Roskilde fjord. When the wrecks were excavated in 1962 they were in varying states of preservation. In addition there are a number of wrecks sunk at anchoring places and in harbours.

All these Scandinavian ships and many small boats have a clinker-built hull (of overlapping strakes) joined with iron rivets and caulked with animal hair. The hull has a keel and tapering prow and stern, and evenly curving lines between keel and gunwale, between the keel and the prow and stern, and between prow and stern. The hull is reinforced inside with a number of symmetrical frames placed across the width of the hull, their lower portion resting on the keel. A crossbeam (*bite*) was laid across the ends of the frames, attached by knees to the strakes at each end to reinforce the structure. Some pictures show ships with a triangular or pointed infilling beneath the prow or beneath both prow and stern, but no examples of this design have been found. They may be the Frisian ships called cogs, which differed in construction and design from the Scandinavian ship type or have been influenced by the cog.

Scandinavian ship-builders attempted to combine lightness with strength and flexibility by using excellent craftsmanship and carefully selected timber. Timber whose grain followed the shape of the finished pieces as closely as possible was used. The frames were thus hewn from naturally curved timbers and the strakes were split radially from logs and then shaped. They were not sawn. In this way optimal use was made of the natural strength and flexibility of the wood, and the joints between the hull and the frame were made flexible by the use of ties or trenails.

The ships were steered with a large and equally flexible steering oar, placed near the stern on the right hand side, to this day called starboard (*stýra*: to steer). They were propelled by a square sail, which could be reefed, reducing the sail area in strong wind. Some ships also had oars. Anchors were used, and some iron anchors have been found which closely resemble those used today.

Written sources have many different words for ships and ship types, but it is often difficult to apply them to surviving Viking Age ships. The words in the much later sagas fit contemporary vessels, and many of the words in scaldic poetry are synonyms employed for artistic reasons rather than precise designations. However, the extensive poetic vocabulary demonstrates how fascinated people were by the elegant ships. The poems are about warships (called *skeið*, *snekkja*, *knörr* amongst other things) and the ideal was a long, slender, supple vessel, which could also be rowed at speed.

In terms of construction, the surviving Scandinavian ships can be divided into two main groups: war- and travel-ships, and cargo ships. The two types certainly existed from the tenth century and perhaps even earlier. In addition smaller ships with other functions have been discovered: ferries and fishing boats, a few clinker-built rowing boats, dug-outs, and one flat-bottomed barge from *c.* 1100.

WAR- AND TRAVEL-SHIPS

These were low and narrow relative to their length. Those that have been found are built of oak. A deck ran the entire length of the ship. Oar-ports were evenly distributed along the whole length, with two to each 'room', the space between the frames, so the number of oar-ports is an indication of the number of the crew. On some ships the oar-ports could be closed with flaps when not in use. The mast could be easily lowered and raised thanks to the design of the mast fish (which supported the mast at deck level) and of the mast step in the keelson (which was fitted on top of the keel, fastened to the frames by knees). It was useful to be able to lower the mast in many circumstances, including military cover manoeuvres and surprise attacks. The combination of a sailing and rowing vessel also gave unique manoeuvrability; the ships could pass under low bridges, were not in danger of being becalmed and could manage many difficult conditions of wind and current. The shield-batten on the outer side of the uppermost strake, which allowed shields to be placed close together along the sides, is a characteristic feature of these ships.

Some ships of this design were probably travel-ships and 'royal' ships rather than warships proper. This is true of the Oseberg and Gokstad ships, for example, which are very different to each other but are somewhat wider relative to their length and thus more spacious than the warships and indeed of particularly handsome craftsmanship. The Oseberg ship's construction is also comparatively weak and its prow and stern are decorated with elaborate carvings. These two ships were presumably used only by the high-ranking people buried in them and by their families, for ceremonial purposes and other journeys. They were not ordinary Viking ships.

Of the five wrecks found at Skuldelev in Denmark, numbers 2 and 5 are more representative. They were slender, fast vessels, built for the efficient transport of many men. This was the kind of ship used for Viking raids in Scandinavia, the Baltic and Western Europe in the late Viking Age. The remains of a very narrow ship also from the late Viking Age, almost 20 m long, found in Hedeby harbour, display a perfection of craftsmanship similar to that of the Norwegian 'royal ships'. It must have been a chieftain's war- and travel-ship, like those ships buried with chieftains or kings in Ladby on the island of Fyn, and at Hedeby in the first half of the tenth century, of which only impressions in the earth and the iron rivets survive.

The Oseberg ship is 21.4 m long and 5.10 m broad. The height from the bottom of the keel to the gunwale is 1.58 m amidships and there were twelve strakes on each side. The high prow and stern have elegant spiral terminals, and the leading edge and the uppermost strakes of the prow are embellished with complicated animal ornament. The upper strake has fifteen oar-ports on each side. The shield-batten was very thin. The ship contained thirty oars and a great deal of other equipment when it was discovered.

The Gokstad ship is 23.3 m long and 5.25 m broad amidships. The height from the bottom of the keel to the gunwale is 1.95 m amidships and there were sixteen strakes on each side. The third strake from the top has sixteen oar-ports on each side. The ship was found with thirty-two shields tied to each side on the shield-batten, half of each overlapping the next. They were painted alternately yellow and black. The ship contained thirty-two oars and other equipment which included the remains of three rowing boats; the largest was just under 10 m long. The number of shields indicate a crew of about seventy, which allowed rowing in shifts.

Skuldelev 5 was 17.4 m long and about 2.6 m broad. There were seven strakes on each side and twelve oar-ports in the upper strake on each side; the upper strakes had been re-used from

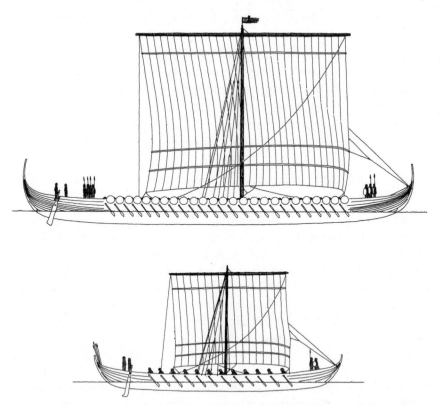

Reconstruction of two warships from Skuldelev, Denmark (numbers 2 and 5). They were 29 m and 17.4 m long, respectively. The Viking Ship Museum, Roskilde.

another ship. A shield-batten ran along the outside. Skuldelev 2 is badly preserved, but the length has been estimated at 28–29 m and the breadth at around 4 m. There were more than seven strakes to each side, but the upper strakes are missing. The number of oar-ports must have been between twenty and twenty-five on each side, which means it would have had a crew of at least forty or fifty men. Dendrochronology says that is was built in Ireland.

Much of the outer adornment of all these ships has now been lost. Some spiral iron bands from the Ladby ship and from a Viking ship burial on the Île de Groix off Brittany must be neck-curls from the prow's dragon-head, all that remains of such ornaments. However, their original splendour and glory can be imagined from gilded bronze prow-vanes (later used as weathervanes on churches), from the Oseberg ship's carvings and the Gokstad ship's rows of painted shields, as well as from pictures and literary descriptions, which also give an impression of the formations and movements of war fleets.

This magnificent passage describes King Svein Forkbeard's fleet which sailed from Denmark in 1013 to conquer England. The author was a learned monk from the monastery of St Omer in Flanders who around 1040 wrote the *Encomium Emmae Reginae*. With poetic licence he combined expressions from classical Roman literature, including Virgil's *Æneid*, with impressions of Scandinavian ships and fleets.

When at length they were all gathered, they went on board the towered ships, having picked out by observation each man his own leader on the brazen prows. On one side lions moulded in gold were to be seen on the ships, on the other birds on the tops of the masts indicated by their movements the winds as they blew, or dragons of various kinds poured fire from their nostrils. Here there were glittering men of solid gold or silver nearly comparable to live ones, there bulls with necks raised high and legs outstretched were fashioned leaping and roaring like live ones. One might see dolphins moulded in electrum, and centaurs in the same metal, recalling the ancient fable. In addition I might describe to you many examples of the same celature [embossing], if the names of the monsters which were there fashioned were known to me. But why should I now dwell upon the sides of the ships, which were not only painted with ornate colours but were covered with gold and silver figures? The royal vessel excelled the others in beauty as much as the king preceded the soldiers in the honour of his proper dignity, concerning which it is better that I be silent than that I speak inadequately. Placing their confidence in such a fleet, when the signal was suddenly given, they set out gladly, and, as they had been ordered, placed themselves round about the royal vessel with level prows, some in front [i.e. on the starboard side] and some behind [on the port side]. The blue water, smitten by many oars, might be seen foaming far and wide, and the sunlight, cast back in the gleam of metal, spread a double radiance in the air. What more?

Scandinavian poetry has similarly evocative descriptions of ships and fleets. The scald Arnór, for example, in a poem about King Magnus the Good (who died in 1047) says that when the king lets the ships run across the sea, it is just as if the Heaven-Lord's crowd of angels were floating together across the waves.

CARGO SHIPS

Cargo ships were completely different – high and wide in relation to their length, with half-decks fore and aft to allow for a hold amidships. The mast was fixed in the mast step and could not be easily lowered and raised. Cargo ships were sailing ships. The oar-ports, situated above the half decks, were few and oars would only have been used in narrow channels and in certain manoeuvres. Among the Scandinavian cargo ships from the Viking Age are the Klåstad ship found near the trading centre of Kaupang in Vestfold, Norway, and the Äskekärr ship found near the mouth of the river Göta in Sweden. They were 16–20 m in length. The best-preserved and most thoroughly examined cargo ships are numbers 1 and 3 of the five Skuldelev ships, dating from around AD 1000. Another very large ship found in Hedeby harbour is thought to be slightly later. So far only partially examined, its length is estimated at 22–25 m.

The most important factor for cargo ships is, of course, how much they can carry, both in weight and volume. This has been calculated for several ships on the assumption that a ship must have a freeboard of two-fifths of its height amidships to be properly loaded for seagoing. Precise figures are available for the two Skuldelev ships because full-size, accurate replicas, Saga Siglar and Roar Ege, have been built, so the draught of the ships in sail-ready and loaded state, as well as the number of crew needed, has been tested. The test reveals that the loading capacity is often surprisingly big – so big that the ships must have been built to carry everyday supplies as well as luxury goods. This clearly influences our ideas of what was traded in the Viking Age. Furthermore, it means that each member of the crew would have had a considerable share of the cargo if they had a right to equal shares, as was the case with many ships. The loading capacities of the Klåstad, Äskekärr and Hedeby cargo ships are tentatively estimated at 13 tons, 18–20 tons and 38 tons respectively.

Skuldelev 1 is made of pine, which implies that it was built in western Norway. It was 16.3 m long and 4.5 m broad amidships. The height from the bottom of the keel to the gunwale was about 2 m amidships and there were twelve strakes on each side. The ship was very solidly built, with numerous reinforcements on the

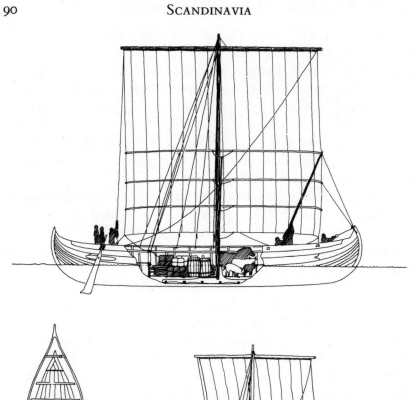

Reconstruction of two cargo ships from Skuldelev, Denmark (numbers 1 and 3). They were 16.3 m and 13.8 m long, respectively. The Viking Ship Museum, Roskilde.

inside. There were a few oar-ports above the half-decks fore and aft. The sail area is estimated at about 100 m². The draught was around 125 cm and the loading capacity 24 tons, or 40 m³. Fully loaded, this ship could thus carry an average of 0.6 tons per cubic metre. It could be sailed efficiently by six men, who would have had equal shares in the cargo of 4 tons, or almost 6.5 m³.

Skuldelev 3 is the best-preserved of all the Skuldelev ships, since three-quarters of the length survives – the whole of the front of the ship and the hold amidships. It was built of oak, presumably in the Roskilde area, where it was found. It was small but capacious: 13.8 m long and 3.4 m broad. The height from the bottom of the keel to the gunwale was about 1.6 m amidships and there were eight strakes on each side. The prow is 3.7 m long, up to 0.55 m wide and hewn from a single piece of timber. On each side the curved lines of the strakes converge elegantly on the tip of the prow. Above the half-decks fore and aft there were a few oar-holes. The sail area was about 45 m². The draught was 84 cm and the loading capacity 4.6 tons, or 12 m³. When fully loaded the ship could thus carry an average of 0.38 tons per cubic metre. It was manned by five men, whose share of the cargo would have been about 920 kilos, or 2.4 m³.

These cargo ships were obviously not suitable for river traffic, which needed oars as well as sails. On certain routes, such as along the river Göta to central Sweden and along the Polish and Russian rivers, the craft had to be small and light enough for land portage, whereas the replica of Skuldelev 3, Roar Ege, has a hull that weighs about 2 tons. Fragments found in Lake Tingstäde Träsk on Gotland may be of a boat used for river voyages. It was about 8 m long and 2 m broad. A replica, Krampmacken, has been built based on the remains of this boat and of Slav boats found on the south coast of the Baltic, and on the many sailing ships represented on Gotland picture stones. It has been sailed up the Eastern European rivers, the Vistula first, and drawn overland, with a crew of ten men and a cargo of iron, as far as Istanbul. It is likely, however, that the Vikings often used specialized local river boats on their long journeys in Eastern Europe.

The ship which the chieftain Ohthere from Hálogaland in northern Norway used for his long sea voyages may well have resembled the very sturdy Skuldelev 1, and ships of this type may

have sailed the routes to Iceland and Greenland. The replica Saga
Siglar performed well on rough journeys in the North Atlantic,
while Roar Ege proved that Skuldelev 3 would have been an
excellent ship for Kattegat and the Baltic.

Trials such as these have also shown that under good wind
conditions the boats can maintain an average speed of 6–8 knots,
so long distances could be covered quite quickly. Saga Siglar is
even said to have maintained 10 knots over a period of six hours
in a strong wind in the North Sea. Roar Ege's maximum speed
is nearly 9 knots with a side wind. However, wind conditions
were not always favourable, so Viking Age cargo ships had to be
able to tack. They appear to have been able to sail about 60° into
the wind, with a speed of $1\frac{1}{2}$–2 knots up-wind while tacking.

The Vikings normally sailed along the coast, made landfall and
halted at night. Ohthere did this on his journey from Hálogaland
to *Sciringesheal* in southern Norway, which took about a month.
But there are also accounts of sailing for several days without a
break, as when a merchant called Wulfstan sailed across the Baltic
from Hedeby to Truso in the Gulf of Gdansk. This took him
seven days and nights and he must have navigated partly by
means of depth measurements with a plumb line.

On the open sea, sailing from Norway to Iceland, or from
Denmark direct to England, this method of navigation would be
of no use, of course. We know very little about Viking navigation,
but much of it must have been based on precise sense of time
and speed, on knowledge of sea-birds, wave-formations and the
position of the sun and fixed stars – as it is done today in some
parts of the Pacific Ocean. The height of the sun may have helped
the Vikings follow a degree of latitude. In addition it was normally
unnecessary to sail without landfall for any length of time. The
voyage from the mouth of the Limfjord, on the west coast of
Denmark, to Tynemouth, on the east coast of England, for
example, only took thirty-six hours under optimum conditions.
Between Norway and Iceland there was landfall on the Shetlands
and the Faroes. Various authorities have credited the Vikings with
ingenious navigational instruments, on very slender evidence, but
in fact they were not really necessary for their journeys.

There are many good natural harbours along the Scandinavian
coasts and many ships had such a shallow draught that they could

sail up on to the beach and easily be pushed afloat again. This is especially true of the slender and well-manned warships. Large cargo ships such as Skuldelev 1 must have been loaded and unloaded by means of small boats when there were no harbour facilities, but there were jetties at the largest towns and trading stations of the age, such as Hedeby, Birka and Kaupang.

A large number of special buildings, *naust*, where ships were stored for the winter, have been found in Norway, while traces of repair yards have been found in Hedeby and at the trading centre of Paviken on Gotland, and a shipyard from the late Viking Age has been excavated on the Danish island of Falster. Here extensive recycling of parts from broken-up ships took place; such recycling can be seen on the warship Skuldelev 5.

Many canals may have been built in the Viking Age where a narrow stretch of land impeded shipping, but so far the partly timber-lined Kanhave canal, about 1 km long and 11 m wide, on the island of Samsø in the middle of Denmark, is a unique find. It allowed ships with a draught of up to 1.25 m to pass directly from the deeply indented Stavnsfjord to the sea west of the island. The canal has been dated by dendrochronology to the year 726 and its purpose was presumably military: to command central Danish waters, which could be surveyed from a high point on an island in the Stavnsfjord.

LIVELIHOOD AND SETTLEMENT

At the end of the Viking Age, around 1075, the cleric Adam of Bremen described many aspects of Scandinavia in his history of the Archbishops of Hamburg. This is a summary of his account of the occupations and settlement conditions in the various countries:

The soil in Jutland is sterile; except for places close to a river [perhaps the Eider], nearly everything looks like a desert. It is a salt land and a vast wilderness ... Hardly a cultivated spot is to be found anywhere, scarcely a place fit for human habitation. But wherever there is an arm of the sea it has very large cities ... From this port [Schleswig] ships usually proceed to Slavia [on the south coast of the Baltic], to Sweden or to Samland [in the south-eastern corner of the Baltic], even to Greece [that is, the Byzantine Empire]. [From Ribe] one sails for Frisia ... for England or for our Saxony ... [From Århus] one sails to Fyn or Zealand [Sjælland], to Scania [Skåne], or even to Norway.
[On Fyn] is the great city of Odense. Small islands encircle it, all abounding in crops ... [Sjælland's] largest city is Roeskilde, the seat of Danish royalty ... [Sjælland] is very celebrated as much for the bravery of its men as for the abundance of its crops ... There is very much gold in Zealand, [Sjælland], accumulated by the plundering of pirates ... as soon as one of them catches another, he mercilessly sells him into slavery either to one of his fellows or to a barbarian ... Scania is the province of Denmark fairest to look upon ... well provided with men, opulent of crops, rich in merchandise ... [Bornholm] is the most celebrated port of Denmark and a safe anchorage for the ships that are usually dispatched to the barbarians [non-Christians] and to Greece.
[Sweden is] shut in by exceedingly high mountains ... The Swedish country is extremely fertile; the land is rich in fruits and honey besides excelling all others in cattle raising, exceedingly happy in streams and woods, the whole region full of merchandise from foreign parts ... they regard as nothing every means of vainglory; that is, gold, silver,

stately chargers, beaver and marten pelts, which make us lose our minds admiring them ... Skara is the great city of the Goths [Götar] in Västergötland; [near the Baltic is the great city of the Svear people, Sigtuna, and also Södertälje is mentioned. The town of Birka is mentioned several times even though it had been abandoned at the time when Adam wrote.] On the east ... there is an immense wasteland, the deepest snows [...] where hordes of human monsters prevent access to what lies beyond.

[Norway] is the farthest country of the world ... On account of the roughness of its mountains and the immoderate cold, Norway is the most unproductive of all countries, suited only for herds. They browse their cattle far off in the solitudes [this must refer to summer pastures]. In this way do the people make a living from their livestock by using the milk of the flocks or herds for food and the wool for clothing. Consequently, there are produced very valiant fighters ... not softened by any overindulgence in fruits ... the Danes ... are just as poor ... Poverty has forced them thus to go all over the world and from piratical raids they bring home in great abundance the riches of the lands. In this way they bear up under the unfruitfulness of their own country. Since accepting Christianity, however ... they have already learnt ... to be content with their poverty ...

The metropolitan city of the Norwegians is Trondhjem ... [where many] flock together [because of] the miraculous cures [of] Olaf, king and martyr.

[Far north] along the ocean [live heathens] ... superior in the magic arts ... I have heard that women grow beards [there] and that the men live in the woods ... They use pelts of wild beasts for clothing ... can hardly be understood by the people nearest to them. [Another people live in] that mountain region [with] perpetual snows ... In those same mountains there are such large numbers of big game that the greatest part of the country subsists only on the beasts of the forest. Aurochs, buffaloes and elk are taken there as in Sweden ... Only in Norway, however, are there black fox and hares, white martens and bears of the same colour.

It is abundantly clear that Adam regards the whole of Norway, and the northern regions of the Scandinavian peninsula in general, as very remote and harsh, and finds the people and their means of livelihood so exotic as to be hardly credible. Nor does he think the Jutland peninsula much better; he really only portrays eastern Denmark and Sweden in a positive light. Adam writes that his information came largely from the Danish king Svein Estridsson, who had served the king of Sweden for twelve years. Adam apparently never visited Norway and Sweden himself, and may not have travelled much in Denmark. His knowledge is limited, he generalizes and simplifies, and he moralizes in favour of Christianity. All the same, the account is interesting as a contemporary opinion, which probably also reflects Svein Estridsson's views.

However, conditions in Scandinavia were far more varied during the three centuries of the Viking Age than Adam's picture implies, and in some respects it is completely misleading. Let us see how it compares with Scandinavian sources. The economy of the three countries was of course dependent on local conditions. In most places agriculture was the backbone of the economy, but the life of a Danish farmer was very different from that of a farmer in northern Scandinavia, where crops were much less important and people's livelihood (mainly sheep and cattle) was often heavily supplemented by fishing and hunting reindeer, elk, birds and animals for their pelts. Seals, walruses and whales were also hunted, and natural resources such as iron deposits, or certain types of stone suitable for making cooking-pots, whetstones and querns, were another source of wealth.

Experience of many different types of farming allowed the Vikings to colonize areas as varied as verdant Normandy and the mountainous Faroes in the middle of the Atlantic. Before and during this expansion, the inhabited regions within Scandinavia were being extended. From archaeological finds and the distribution of the place-names in common use in this period, such as names with the suffixes -by, -torp, -toft, -tved, -setr, we know that new land was claimed between existing settlements; forests and stony wastes were cleared, or new settlements were established in higher and less fertile areas or in places where new resources could be exploited.

The first Scandinavian settlements in the northern coastal districts of the Scandinavian peninsula date from a much earlier period, however. We know most about those in Norway, where the Gulf Stream makes life easier. In the Viking Age there were farm settlements far north of the Arctic Circle: rune stones and farms have been found up to around Tromsø (70° N), and other scattered finds even further north may indicate temporary stops on journeys north of the permanent settlements.

Lapp tribes also lived north of the Arctic Circle, but mostly in the interior of the country. Their economy was mainly based on hunting and fishing (not till much later did they begin to keep large herds of reindeer). There is much evidence of communication with the Vikings, in spite of undoubted language difficulties, and some Lapps may have lived quite far south. The cultural patterns on the Åland islands at the mouth of the Gulf of Bothnia were chiefly Scandinavian, rather than Finnish, in the Viking Age, as indeed they were before and after.

DENMARK

Since the 1970s our understanding of the development of settlement in Denmark has been completely altered by a large number of excavations. This new evidence about the distribution, appearance and structure of farms and villages has given us important insights into the Viking Age economy.

There were some single farms, but it is now clear that villages predominated in most of the country. Despite Adam of Bremen's testimony, there were numerous villages in Jutland, as has long been demonstrated by place-name research. The best-known Danish village is in central Jutland, at Vorbasse, where the extensive excavations (200,000 m² by 1985) clearly reveal its lay-out and appearance.

The excavations, close to the present village of Vorbasse, have uncovered traces of its many predecessors dating back to around 100 BC. These were structured in different ways in different periods, and the site of the settlement moved within a small area every century or two. This seems to have been typical in most parts of the country, but we do not know whether it was the result of a decision made by the villagers or by a large landowner. Nor are the underlying reasons known, but some have suggested that they may have been partly agricultural: a plot that had become infertile could be built on, while a built-up area might have become well-manured and fertile from discarded waste and thus suitable for cultivation. As the houses were built of timbers dug into the earth, their lifespan would have been short in the Danish climate (reconstructions have shown that extensive repair is necessary after only twenty or thirty years), so why not take a big decision from time to time and move the village to an exhausted field?

We also do not know for certain why the village finally moved nearly half a kilometre around the end of the Viking Age and then remained on that site, but the sites of most Danish villages today go back to the eleventh or twelfth centuries at the earliest, and are often better situated for the cultivation of crops than

Plan of Vorbasse village in Jutland. All the buildings and fences are marked. The village was moved to this site in the first half of the eighth century and its basic lay-out was retained until the late Viking Age. There were seven farms on fenced-in plots, each with a gateway giving on to a communal street. Four farms lay to the north of the street and three to the south. There were several buildings on each plot, but not all were in use at the same time. The extent of the excavation is marked with a dotted line. Main buildings and sunken-featured buildings are shown with horizontal hatching, other buildings with vertical hatching. Fences are indicated by a line. Wells, some of which have been dated by dendrochronology, are marked with a W. An attempt has been made to distinguish buildings and fences from the village's earliest phase and these are marked with dots.

earlier ones, whose location was more suited to animal husbandry. Hence the reason for moving the settlement to another type of soil in Vorbasse and elsewhere may have been an increased emphasis on crops and a new form of field cultivation, perhaps including the introduction of the plough and manuring. By the twelfth and thirteenth centuries society and conditions of land ownership had become increasingly regulated and many taxes and obligations to the Church and the king based on land had been introduced. As early as 1085 a charter mentions a land valuation (Latin *mansus*), the military levy system, which was probably based on land ownership, and various dues to the king. From the early twelfth century the Danes paid tithes and the country was divided into parishes; most acquired a stone church in the course of this century. A village move in the High Middle Ages would therefore have been troublesome.

In the first half of the eighth century, when the site of Vorbasse was moved some hundreds of metres to the south, it was divided into seven farms, four to the north and three to the south of a street some 8–10 m wide. Six of the farms were of almost equal size, while the seventh was somewhat larger. The farms were all similar in layout: large, square, fenced plots, with a wide gateway to the public street. There was a large main building, more or less in the middle of the yard, with living quarters at one end and a byre at the other. Smaller buildings often lay close to the inside of the fence. In addition there was a hay-loft, and some small 'sunken-featured' buildings (which were half-dug into the earth), often near the gateway. Some of the farms also had a well and one had a smithy. Because of the fire hazard, this lay at the western edge of the settlement, as was customary.

Only those parts of buildings and fences that were sunk into the ground have left traces: dark marks of timber in the light coloured soil and, in the case of the sunken-featured buildings, dark traces of the pit. We know most about their ground plan, therefore, and less about how the buildings looked above ground. This site was inhabited for around three centuries, and buildings and fences were repaired and renewed many times. Sometimes the site of a building was changed, or a fence was slightly realigned. All these traces add up to a somewhat confusing picture, but the fences are unusually well-preserved, which makes it possible to distinguish what was in contemporary use in the village and how it looked at a given time. Vorbasse is unique in this respect, and because it is the only complete Viking Age village to have been excavated; but during its lifetime it was probably quite ordinary.

The main building of a farm had curved side walls and a curved roof ridge. It was about 30 m in length with stalls for twenty or thirty animals, probably cattle, in the byre (the number can be deduced from the traces of stall partitions). The roof was supported by solid timbers and probably covered with straw or reeds. The walls were made of timbers with planks in between, or wattle and daub.

The hay-loft in each yard was always built around four posts set in a square. The other buildings were presumably dwellings for servants and slaves, workshops, stores for food and winter fodder, and perhaps byres for animals which did not require stalls. They were usually built in the same way as the main building.

Sunken-featured buildings were common in many parts of northern Europe (though obviously not in wet regions, or on rocky ground) from about A D 400 to after the end of the Viking Age. They were often rectangular, quite small and half-buried – the soil that was dug out formed the walls above ground, which were often lined on the inside with planks. The roof rested on two posts, one in the centre of each end of the pit. Sunken-featured buildings were popular because they were easy to build and were well insulated by the earth and by the low roof, which meant they were cool in summer and easy to heat in winter. In Vorbasse nearly all sunken-featured buildings were rectangular, about 2.5–3 m wide and 3–4 m long, and were apparently used for weaving, an important occupation in all households. Elsewhere sunken-featured buildings have been found of a slightly different size and shape, and were used for other purposes, such as workshops, dwellings or storage.

The economy of the Vorbasse village must have revolved around animal husbandry. The area given over to byres was very large and the village was sited close to good pastures and hayfields. A certain amount of grain was grown too, as traces of cultivated fields have been found. The farms were doubtless self-sufficient in terms of basic requirements, but they produced a surplus and bought goods from outside, even from far away – finds include sherds of soapstone pots and whetstones from the Scandinavian peninsula, fragments of Rhenish pottery (Pingsdorf ware) and of many Rhenish querns. Similar finds have been made in many other villages, which shows that imported goods reached far beyond towns and trading centres. House timber, too, seems to have not been local, apparently because no suitable trees grew in the district.

Some time in the eleventh century Vorbasse changed again. The site extended westwards, where three farms were built, one twice the size of the other two. The total number of farms in the village appears not to have changed, but those on the previously inhabited area were larger than before, and the public street was no longer there.

The picture of this phase of the village is unclear, for few traces of fences survive, but on most farms the main dwelling and byre were now separate buildings and there were no sunken-featured huts. The interior was also grander, since the roof was no longer supported inside; sloping posts placed at regular intervals outside, following the curved long walls, supported the top of the walls against the pressure of the roof. This design of house, divided into two gable rooms and a central hall three times their size, was the same as the houses in the large royal circular fortresses of about AD 980 (see p. 136).

The large farm to the west was enlarged at some point. It had many buildings, craftsmen working in bronze, silver and iron, and the byre could house perhaps 100 head of cattle at once. This was clearly the property of a very wealthy farmer and even though a large number of hands would have worked on it, a considerable surplus must have been produced for sale.

This farm and others like it give firm evidence of some of the products Denmark traded with other countries, mainly agricultural goods, usually in animal form (these and grain were Denmark's most important exports until very recently). We know that butter was among the gifts presented by the Danish Archbishop Asser to Bishop Otto of Bamberg in 1120. This is the earliest mention of farm produce being sent abroad, and it coincides with the latest phase of the large farm, or dates from shortly after the village moved to its present site.

It is not known whether a surplus of grain was produced in other parts of Denmark in the Viking Age, but we know that some of the farm land was normally sown. The most important crops were barley, rye and oats, as well as peas, beans and cabbage. Wheat was grown, and probably flax too. The soil would have been worked with wooden shovels and spades, wooden hoes or digging sticks with iron blades, or with an ard or plough and a harrow. The ard scratched up the soil, but unlike the plough did not turn it. It is not known when the plough was introduced in Denmark. The oldest traces of ploughing date from the eleventh century, but only a few hundred kilometres to the south it was in use shortly after AD 1. As no ard nor plough from the Viking Age has survived in Scandinavia, their precise appearance is unknown.

Many harvesting implements have been found, however – sickles, short scythes and leaf knives. At Lindholm Høje in north Jutland part of a field 30 m wide by more than 40 m long has survived. It was preserved by a thick layer of sand deposited after a storm some time in the eleventh century. When this was excavated the field emerged exactly as it was before the storm, with the footprints of animals and people from its last ploughing, and crossed by wheel tracks. The field consisted of many long, parallel beds, which were slightly curved and separated by narrow furrows. The beds were 50–100 cm wide, less than 10 cm high and appear to have been ploughed. It has not been possible to determine what was grown there, but it was probably crops which have to be weeded – people could walk along the furrows between the beds, which also provided drainage after heavy rain.

Cattle, horses, pigs, sheep were common farm animals in Denmark, and goats were seen. Hens, geese and ducks were also kept. Measurements of bones reveal that the animals were considerably smaller than those of today. Cows' milk was made into many kinds of dairy produce and cattle were reared as draught animals, for meat and hides, from which straps, sheaths and shoes were made. Calfskin could be worked into parchment, which was in great demand in Western European centres of learning. Horses were used for riding or for pulling carts; their flesh was eaten (at least in pagan times) and their hides were used too. Sheep provided milk, wool for textiles, meat, warm fleece and leather for shoes, among other things. Goats were eaten and milked. Their skins were used for shoes and perhaps exported, as goatskin could also be used for parchment. Poultry provided eggs and meat, while their feathers were used for eiderdowns and pillows. Certain animal bones were made into skates, handles, spindle whorls, flutes or needles; horns were often used as drinking-horns. There were also cats, rats and several breeds of dog.

Hunting was not an important source of food or wealth in Denmark, but it was a favourite sport. Fishing was important in coastal and lakeland areas and there seems to have been some trade in fish products, but it was not a major part of people's livelihood there. Their diet was supplemented by mussels and oysters, and lots of wild fruit, berries and nuts. No evidence of gardens survives anywhere in Scandinavia, but we know that in Hedeby there were plum trees and some peach trees.

Bee-keeping was no doubt important in many places in Scandinavia. Honey was the only known sweetener, was used as a preservative and was an important ingredient in alcoholic drinks, while beeswax was necessary for certain metal-casting processes and it was also the best material for candles. We have no evidence of bee-keeping in the Viking Age but it is mentioned in slightly later written sources. Hops were gathered for ale brewing.

SWEDEN AND NORWAY

In the flat and fertile parts of Västergötland, and possibly in the most fertile open valleys of southern Norway, the settlements were presumably like those of Denmark – mainly villages, with some single farms – but this is difficult to establish in the absence of large excavations. In the fertile Mälar district, in Uppland, it is thought that settlements were mostly single farmsteads until the end of the Viking Age, when villages sprang up. This is based on the study of cemeteries, which seem to have survived almost complete, since they were normally sited on stony, uncultivated areas. The distance from one cemetery to the next, the estimated number of graves in each, and the estimated number of individual farms within this district all seem to support this view. Cattle and some crops were no doubt the mainstay of the local economy, as Adam of Bremen relates.

In other parts of the Scandinavian peninsula conditions were such that only single farms or a couple of farms at most could be supported. One of the farms that has been excavated lies in Ytre Moa in western Norway, near the head of the 200-km-long Sognefjord. The farm dates from the ninth or tenth century and consisted of a number of fairly small, rectangular buildings with internal wooden walls, protected from cold and rain by stone walls on the outside. Each building probably had a different function: dwelling, byre, store, barn, cook house (for baking, ale brewing, washing, preparing large quantities of food for feasts, or for slaughtering).

In western Norway people often earned their living from a combination of animal husbandry (cattle, pigs, sheep, goats), fishing, some cultivation of grain, and perhaps some hunting in the mountains, depending on the locality. On the coast the mild climate meant that cattle and sheep could stay outside all the year round and find their own food. If food supplies such as heather were plentiful, considerable numbers of animals could be supported. In other places on the coast and on the islands, fishing was the main source of food, supplemented by a few animals and a little grain. Settlements along the fjords would also exploit the mountain pastures during the summer and build up supplies of winter fodder from there.

Graves and other archaeological finds indicate that there were also permanent settlements in the mountainous regions of southern Norway, where people lived by hunting, trapping, fishing and trading goods, mostly hides and furs, with the farming population and with merchants. In many places there are also traces of large-scale iron extraction, the basis for an extensive iron trade. Around Lake Møs (Møsvatn) in Telemark, southern Norway, iron production, using bog-iron ore, increased dramatically during the Viking Age (Plate 7). In Sweden iron was extracted in Dalarna and in southern Norrland, and also in Småland, which had great resources of bog-iron. There is no evidence so far of iron extraction in Viking Age Denmark; much of this important product was probably acquired in the north.

Soapstone was quarried in several parts of Norway and in what

1   Scandinavia

2 The Oseberg ship, Norway

3 Utensils from the Oseberg ship

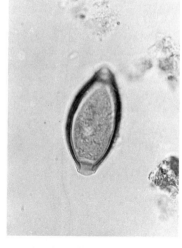

4 Viking head, Sigtuna, Sweden

5 Intestinal parasite, York

6 The Hon hoard, Norway

7　Iron extraction area at Mösstrand, Norway

8　Weapons from Norway

9   Birka, Sweden

10   Glasses from Birka graves

11   Burial mounds at Borre, Norway

12   Jelling rune stones, Denmark

13　Reconstruction of a Fyrkat house, Denmark

14　Trelleborg fortress, Denmark

15 Picture stone from Hammars in Lärbro, Gotland, Sweden

Notes on the Plates

1 Satellite photograph of Scandinavia and the Baltic region.
2 The Oseberg mound in Vestfold, southern Norway, during excavation in 1904. The mound covered a ship in which a high-ranking woman, perhaps a queen, was buried with a wealth of fine grave goods. First half of the ninth century.
3 Household utensils from the Oseberg grave: buckets, barrels, troughs, bowls, scoop, axe, ladle, and a knife. The bucket (centre back) is of Irish or Scottish origin. University Museum of National Antiquities, Oslo.
4 Viking warrior: the carved tip of an elk-horn mount found at Sigtuna, Uppland, Sweden. The length of the head (including beard and helmet) is 4 cm. National Antiquities Museum, Stockholm.
5 Egg of a human intestinal parasite (a whip-worm) from a Viking Age cesspit in York, England. Length 0.055 mm.
6 Viking hoard from Hon in Buskerud, southern Norway, probably hidden in the 860s. It consists of 2.5 kilos of gold objects, with some silver and beads. The large trefoil mount with plant ornament in filigree is one of the finest examples of the art of the Frankish gold-smiths, while the coins are of Roman, Byzantine, Arabic, Anglo-Saxon and Frankish origins. University Museum of National Antiquities, Oslo.
7 Mösstrand in Telemark, Norway, one of the places where iron was extracted from bog-iron in the Viking Age.
8 Norwegian weapons – offensive and defensive: swords, spear-heads and axe-heads, with the helmet from the chieftain's grave in Gjermundbu and one of the shields from the Gokstad ship. University Museum of National Antiquities, Oslo.
9 Aerial photograph of Birka on the island of Björkö, Sweden, seen from the north. The island still has birch trees, which gave it its name.
10 Drinking glasses from graves in Birka. They were all manufactured in Western Europe, except the straight-sided one with cut decoration, which is Oriental. National Antiquities Museum, Stockholm.
11 Snow-clad burial mounds at Borre, Vestfold, Norway, which scaldic poetry links with the Norwegian kings.

12   The two rune stones at Jelling, Jutland, Denmark. On the right is King Gorm's memorial stone to his wife Thyre. On the left is King Harald's memorial stone to his parents and to his own deeds: most of the long inscription is on one face of the three-sided stone; the face with a picture of Christ is shown in Plate 18, while the large strutting animal entwined with a snake on the third is seen here. Pictures and ornament are in low relief and the background has been blackened with soot to make them stand out more clearly.

13   A full-scale reconstruction of a house, from Fyrkat, one of the Danish geometric fortresses, completed in 1985. The building is 28.5 m long and 7.5 m wide at the centre, while the gables are 5 m long, since the long walls are evenly curved. It is divided into three: a large central hall, which is three times the length of the gable room at each end. There are four entrances: a door in each gable and one in each of the long walls. The latter opens into the hall just by the two partition walls and are both protected by an outside porch. The gable rooms also gave access to the hall. Some houses had a hearth in the centre of the hall and low platforms, c. 1.5 m wide, along their outer walls. The main roof and that of the porches were supported externally by sloping posts.

      The house was built of oak timbers, split radially and finished with an axe. The upper ends of the wall timbers were secured by a horizontal plank, the wall-plate, while the lower ends were sunk into the ground. The house was held together crossways by truss beams at the top of the two partition walls and presumably by another two above the hall. The roof was presumably raftered, supported by the walls and the external sloping posts, and also by side purlins. The bow-shaped walls of the house may have been a stylistic feature, but they also meant more floor-space around the central hearth and made the house more stable in strong winds. The roof ridge and roof surface were also curved.

14   Aerial photograph of the geometric royal fortress of Trelleborg on Sjælland, Denmark, seen from the east. Internal diameter 134 m. The fortress is situated on a promontory between the rivers Tude and Vårby. In the foreground is the full-scale reconstruction of a Trelleborg house, built in 1942.

15   Picture stone from Hammars in Lärbro, Gotland, Sweden, eighth century. Height above ground 3 m. At the base is a warship in full sail with shields at the gunwale, perhaps depicting the journey to the realm of the dead. Above it are scenes with people, horses and birds, including scenes of fighting, and in the third strip from the top a sacrificial scene. The man hanging from a tree on the far left may be a human sacrifice or it may be Odin hanging on the World Tree, Yggdrasil. By hanging there he obtained wisdom and the knowledge of runes.

is now south-west Sweden. Soapstone is so soft that it can be cut with a knife and was an excellent material for cooking-pots. They were hewn directly from the stone face, shaped on the spot and sold at home and abroad. Slate whetstones from the mountains gained even wider distribution; vast numbers have been found made of a characteristic light-coloured slate which appears to have come from the Eidsborg district of Telemark in Norway. Quern-stones, rock crystal for beads, the antlers of reindeer and elk, which were made into combs, berries, meat, fur and skins – all these mountain resources supplemented the economy of many farms, while for some people, notably the Lapps, they were the main source of income.

OHTHERE FROM HÁLOGALAND

The Norwegian chieftain Ohthere's account of his sources of income provides a unique insight into the trading patterns that were established in the Viking Age. Around the year 890 he visited the court of King Alfred the Great in England, who included Ohthere's story in his extended translation of the Spaniard Orosius' classic history of the world, at that time over 400 years old. The English, naturally enough, found his living conditions alien.

Ohthere related that he lived in Hálogaland, farthest north of all Norwegians; only the Lapps lived further north. Even though he was one of the most important men in his country he only had twenty cows, twenty sheep and twenty pigs; only a little land was ploughed; this was done with horses. His wealth consisted of 'wild animals' and Ohthere had 600 tame reindeer, among them six decoy-reindeer, which were highly valued by the Lapps, as they were used to catch wild reindeer. But most of his wealth came from the tributes paid by the Lapps in the form of animal skins, feathers, whale bones (or walrus tusks) and ship-ropes. The Lapps paid according to their rank: the highest ranking gave fifteen marten skins, five reindeer skins, one bear skin, ten measures of feathers, a jacket of bear or otter skin, as well as two ropes, each 60 ells long, one made of seal skin and one of whale-hide. Fish is not mentioned – perhaps this was too ordinary a commodity to both Ohthere and the English – but we are told that whale-hunting in his country was good. With five others, he had in two days slain sixty whales, of a kind which grew to 48–50 ells.

Once he had sailed northwards to find out how far the land stretched and who lived there, and thence eastwards and south into the White Sea. Another important reason for his journey, however, was the walruses, 'because they have very fine ivory in their tusks . . . and their hide is very good for ship-ropes'.

He also told of a journey south along the coast of Norway to the trading centre of *Sciringesheal* (this is most likely Kaupang in Vestfold). If one halted at night, this journey could be done in under a month with good winds. From *Sciringesheal* he took five days to sail to Hedeby. Kaupang was an international trading centre and Hedeby was Scandinavia's largest trading post. The purpose of the journey was no doubt to sell products from northern Scandinavia, which were considered luxury goods and would fetch a good price, and buy luxury goods which were difficult to obtain in his home area. Ohthere may have carried back with him fine textiles and ceramic tableware, precious metals and glass, jewellery, base metals, delicious foods and wine.

Such voyages with a cargo of furs, skins, feathers, ropes and walrus tusks were no doubt undertaken at regular intervals by Ohthere and other chieftains, for walrus tusk was the ivory of that age and was used by craftsmen to produce beautiful art objects. Ohthere took King Alfred some tusks as a gift. Fine skins and furs were luxury goods in southern Scandinavia and Western Europe as well as being the best protection against the bitter winters. The demand for furs and walrus ivory was so great that a century after Ohthere's journey it became an important economic basis for the new Scandinavian settlements in Greenland.

Ohthere probably lived near Tromsø, perhaps on the island of Bjarkøy. This is where the most northerly 'court-site' is found – this is a group of houses laid out with their gable ends facing a semicircular or oval open space, situated close to chieftains' residences. The court-site on Bjarkøy may have existed in Ohthere's day, and later on a chieftain certainly lived on the island.

Ohthere was not the only chieftain in Norway north of the Arctic Circle who lived off tributes from others. In Borg on Vestvågøy, an island in Lofoten, remains of an early Viking Age chieftain's farm have been found. An 80-m-long building situated on a windswept hill had a magnificent view across the land and safe and easy access from the sea. The owners of the house had gold and silver, glass cups and fine jugs made in Western Europe. A short distance from the farm was a 'court-site' and a large *naust* (boathouse). The Norwegian kings' sagas tell of several mighty chieftains in this district. During the reign of St Olaf, at the beginning of the eleventh century, the Bjarkøy chieftain was chieftan Þórir Hundr. Like Ohthere, he went on a journey to the White Sea, but this was no explorer's voyage: first he traded, then he raided.

Successful exploitation of so many different resources, local as well as imported, lies behind the prosperity of Scandinavia in the Viking Age and the enormous wealth which survives in graves and hoards. Adam of Bremen gave a very one-sided explanation when he wrote that Norwegians became Vikings because of poverty.

Naturally, however, the economic opportunities must not be allowed to eclipse the fact that many people lived on the bread line, where even the slightest reduction in the norm had disastrous consequences. Many lived in isolated places and had to exploit a number of different resources to the maximum. Even to those who had more at their disposal, the harvest, farm animals, fishing or hunting from time to time failed so badly that shortage and starvation followed. For many people everyday life was a tough struggle for survival.

EXCHANGE, SILVER AND MERCHANDISE

Among the many innovations in Scandinavia during the Viking Age was the establishment of systems which meant that luxury goods and, for the first time, everyday wares, both bulky and small, reached villages and farms. This started as early as the eighth century. The plundering of foreign land and tributes paid by subjugated people were partly responsible for the spread of wealth and goods. Trade and industry also grew apace, and though barter was widely used, money payments for goods became increasingly common. Scandinavia was full of foreign goods and many people owned beautiful and useful things made by others.

Efficient means of transport and a governing power which could guarantee a reasonable degree of safety and a suitable framework for trade were prerequisites for this expansion. It was fuelled by surplus production, increasing occupational specialization, the establishment of new trading posts and a new type of settlement – towns – where trade and industry were more important than agriculture. A standard unit of value within a large area was also necessary. In the world of the Vikings this came to be silver according to weight and in some areas silver coins were eventually struck.

EXCHANGE OF GOODS

It is often impossible to determine how specific goods and means of payment were acquired, and how foreign goods reached the North. Furthermore, the modern concepts of imports and exports, as well as internal trade, are anachronistic in relation to the loosely associated kingdoms of the Viking Age, and trade was only one form of exchange.

As well as trade, the giving of gifts played a part in Viking society, as elsewhere. Kings and chieftains rewarded exploits with gifts, scalds were given gold rings for splendid poems, and gifts were presented at the beginning of visits and negotiations. It is related that Halfdan, brother of the Danish King Sigfred, handed a sword with a golden hilt to King Louis the German when he visited him on a diplomatic mission in 873. The missionary Ansgar carried fine gifts from the Emperor Louis when he set off in 830 to visit King Björn in Birka, but on his way the gifts were stolen by pirates, together with forty books intended for use in church services. Archaeological finds include luxury goods that were presumably gifts from one noble to another; a peacock whose remains lay in the Gokstad burial mound is one possible example. No doubt many everyday objects also changed hands in the same way, and marriage dowries were another way in which goods were redistributed.

Tributes and taxes, plunder and trade, were of much greater economic significance, however. The merchant Ohthere told King Alfred that the tribute from the Lapps was an important part of his income. Like most of the dues paid throughout the Middle Ages, for example to large landowners, payment was in kind. This was probably also true of some of the tributes paid by subjugated peoples, such as that paid to the Danish king by the Slav Abodrites, and by Norwegians in periods of Danish supremacy. Part of the Norwegian tribute may have been in the form of furs, iron, walrus ivory, soapstone and whetstones. A large portion of kings' and chieftains' income from tributes and taxes was distributed among their men or stored in the treasury, but some was no doubt sold.

Much of the loot from Viking expeditions at home and abroad was also sold or bartered, or, in the case of precious metals and coins, used to buy goods. This explains the agreement between a Viking army and the king of the Franks in 873, which permitted the Vikings to live on an island in the Loire river and trade there for a short period. The gifts and books of which Ansgar was robbed in the Baltic must have fetched a good profit, and the masses of silver which a certain Ulv from Yttergärde, in Uppland, won in England around the year 1000 (p. 254) must have led to great commercial activity in his home district.

SILVER AND COINS

The vast amounts of silver and gold acquired by the Vikings on expeditions in Eastern and Western Europe must have stimulated the economy enormously, as the supply of goods expanded to match their buying power, both in Scandinavia and wherever Vikings set foot – from Dublin in the west to the Volga in the east. Written sources relate that in the ninth century the Frankish rulers and their men defrayed at least 44,000 lbs of precious metal to the Vikings. To that must be added payments which are not mentioned in the sources, and all the goods and precious metal that were simply stolen. Through official channels in England the Vikings received more than 150,000 lbs of silver in tribute (Danegeld) in the years between 991 and 1014 – the equivalent of at least 36 million contemporary coins.

The written sources give no figures for Eastern Europe, but more than 1,000 hoards have been discovered from the Scandinavian Viking Age which tell their own tale of silver from the East and the West. A hoard is normally defined as two or more objects made of precious metal deliberately hidden in the ground; silver and gold were rarely placed in graves, perhaps to avoid grave robbing. Hoards contain coins, jewellery, ingots, mounts and so on, as well as unidentifiable fragments. In Scandinavia the hoards range from a couple of objects to 8–9 kilos of silver. The largest known Viking hoard, from Cuerdale in England, contained about 40 kilos of silver (Plate 26).

A few Viking hoards consist solely of gold, but most of them contain silver, with perhaps one or two gold objects. In the Slemmedal hoard, found near Tønsberg in Norway, the silver totalled 2.116 kilos and consisted of eight neck-rings, seven arm-rings, three large bosses from a penannular brooch, four gilt Frankish sword-belt mounts (two of them with runic inscriptions on the reverse), another mount and five coins, four Islamic and one Anglo-Saxon. The gold amounted to 291 grams: four arm-rings, one finger-ring, one medallion, one cross pendant and two small pieces of gold. The coins reveal that the hoard must have been buried after 918.

Coins are our key to establishing the origin of much of the Scandinavian silver, as most of them have inscriptions, which reveal where and when they were minted. The origin of some pieces of foreign jewellery and mounts can also be identified by the form and ornamentation – the Frankish sword-belt mounts in the Slemmedal hoard is an example – but most precious metal from abroad was melted down and made into new jewellery and decorative objects to suit local tastes. However, in many places a number of foreign coins survived for use as small change for payments made according to weight – they weighed between about 0.5 and 3 grams, the heaviest being the Aramic or 'Cufic' dirhems (named after the cufic script on the coins which originated in the city of Cufah in Iraq).

More than 200,000 coins from the Viking Age have been found in Scandinavia. The vast majority come from Sweden and of these two thirds come from Gotland. Only a few Frankish and Anglo-Saxon coins from the ninth century have been found, despite the large payments mentioned in written sources, but there are quite a lot of Russian rings. Coins until c. 970 are predominantly Aramic; more than 85,000 have been found in Scandinavia. Many were minted in the eastern parts of the Caliphate, in what is now Samarkand and Tashkent. It is worth remembering that the vast numbers that fell into the hands of the Vikings represent only a small percentage of the silver of the Orient. After 970 the Scandinavians had to turn to Western Europe for silver, as the Eastern supply routes began to dry up rapidly. The exploitation of German silver mines in the Harz Mountains increased and about 70,000 German coins of those that ended up in Scandinavia have been found. In addition there are more than 40,000 Anglo-Saxon coins from the second half of the tenth and the eleventh centuries, more than have been found in England itself. A fair number of these no doubt came from the large payments of Danegeld.

The contents and composition of the hoards in terms of jewellery, coins, hack silver and so on in the various regions also cast light on other aspects of the Viking economy. Small folding balances and sets of weights, which fitted into a small box, were used to weigh silver as payment for a particular item; if the weight was a little short, a piece of an arm- or neck-ring would be cut off and added. These pieces of jewellery were often of a standard weight and thus of fixed value, so they became a sort of 'ring-money'. Coins of fixed weights could, of course, be used for payment without being weighed. The silver content of an object was often tested before a transaction by nicking or pecking it.

The cutting up of jewellery was particularly common in southern Scandinavia (Denmark and Skåne) at the end of the tenth and the beginning of the eleventh centuries. The small pieces found in the hoards often weigh the same as Arabic or European coins and so would have been used in small transactions and for direct payment without weighing as were coins, clipped into halves and quarters. In northern Norway there is no evidence of hack-silver, presumably because barter was still the most common form of trade there.

It has long been thought that the many large hoards on Gotland represent the surplus generated by extensive trading and that much of the silver was profit from trade in Russia. We know that Vikings did trade there, but the hoards may in fact be the result of plunder and extortion rather than trade. Active traders tend not to bury their silver at home but to let it circulate, and cut up Arabic coins are not common in the Gotlandic hoards, although tiny pieces have been found at the trading centre of Paviken, which indicates that there was some market trading on the island.

The date when a hoard was buried can usually be determined fairly precisely if it contains coins. The reason for its concealment may have been unrest in the district, leaving home, or, as on Gotland, that it was customary to keep valuables buried on the farm. If it remained in the ground, the owner, with his knowledge of the hiding place, must have come to a sad end at home or abroad. Hence the size and number of hoards found in various districts do not reflect the relative wealth or economic development of the region.

Denmark was the first part of Scandinavia to produce coins. As early as the eighth century coins were used as currency at the trading centre of Ribe, for many have been found there. These are known as sceattas and may be Frisian, though some authorities

Scandinavian silver coins minted before A D 1000. a and b were probably struck in Hedeby *c.* 800, a was inspired by the coins of the Frankish Emperor Charlemagne struck in Dorestad in Frisia, but on the Scandinavian coins the letters have become ornamental, the pictures on b are entirely Scandinavian. c was struck during the reign of Harald Bluetooth in the second half of the tenth century, and the cross indicates that he and his country were Christian. d, e and f were all struck shortly before 1000, by King Svein Forkbeard in Denmark, King Olaf Tryggvason in Norway and King Olof Skötkonung in Sweden (respectively). They were modelled on the English coins minted during the reign of King Æthelred, who at that time paid vast numbers of silver coins to the Vikings in an attempt to gain peace. These three Scandinavian coinages are the earliest to carry the name and title of the king and also the names of the moneyers, who were English. The diameter of a is 20 mm.

have suggested they were Danish. Coins were certainly minted in Hedeby early in the ninth century – imitations of the coins of Charlemagne, minted in the Frisian town of Dorestad, and other types based on Carolingian models. The production of coins was limited, however, and ceased in the second half of the century. It was resumed around the year 900, but large quantities were not minted until 975, during the reign of Harald Bluetooth, when the number of mints increased and Byzantine models began to be used. The master of the mint was presumably always the king, as in the rest of Europe, but the oldest coins did not bear a legend.

Just before the year 1000, at the time of the English expeditions and the large payments of Danegeld, coins, albeit of limited number and short duration, were issued in all three Scandinavian countries, modelled on Anglo-Saxon coinage. The name of the king now appears in the legends: Svein (Forkbeard) in Denmark,

Olaf (Tryggvason) in Norway and Olof (Skötkonung) in
Sweden. Olof's successor Anund Jakob also minted coins for a
time and around 1030 the name of Cnut the Great appears on
coins minted in Sigtuna. After this coins were not produced in
Sweden for more than a century. In Norway minting started
again in the reign of St Olaf (1015–30). Under Harald Harðráði
(1047–66) coins first indicated the mint and a coin economy was
established. Hoards with a mixture of jewellery and coins ceased
to be buried.

In Denmark coinage probably continued during the reign of
Svein Forkbeard and Harald Sveinsson. Under Cnut the Great
(1018–35) and his successors it was carried on with great energy.
The coins were still based on English ones, often struck by English
moneyers and from many named mints. Soon the Danes became
so used to handling coins that jewellery, ingots and hack-silver
cease to appear in the hoards. After an extensive reform of coinage
around 1070 foreign coins largely disappeared, and, as had long
been the case in England and in many parts of Western Europe,
only native coins became legal tender. After a very long process
of development there was now a national coin economy to the
advantage of trade and royal profit.

GOODS

Written sources give some indication of the goods which were
traded in Scandinavia, notably slaves and furs. Archaeological
and scientific research has provided more information, but it is
impossible to draw up a comprehensive list of the range of goods
in the period, for often the home-made cannot be distinguished
from the professionally manufactured, nor can the place of production always be identified. Also, many types of goods have
almost or entirely perished, such as food and textiles, both of
which must have played an important role in the economy.

Some foreign goods are easily distinguished – those made of
raw materials not found locally, such as silk or certain types of
stone and metal. The animal bones found in a settlement indicate
whether meat acquired elsewhere was eaten. Sometimes the origin
of artefacts like jewellery can be determined. The fashion and

cut, and the technique used, and any remains of the production processes, can help us decide whether everyday articles, such as shoes or combs, were home-made or the work of specialized craftsmen.

The professional manufacture of market goods, including many articles of everyday use, increased greatly in the tenth century as a result of steadily growing trade, although the prosperity of different regions varied. Lots of people owned something made by professional craftsmen, and a number of items from abroad or for which the raw materials were imported. People were mostly self-sufficient, but there was a demand for more, and the means to acquire it. The relationship between home-made goods and those produced by craftsmen was not much different from that which existed in the countryside right up to the time of industrialization.

There are a lot of exotic single finds, which must have been souvenirs, loot or gifts received from foreigners, but the following gives an impression of the types of goods which changed hands regularly in Scandinavia in the Viking Age.

The goods obtained from outside Scandinavia were mostly luxury items. All metals apart from iron were probably imported, although copper mining may have begun in Falun in Dalarna, Sweden, during the period. Many good sword blades and coats of mail came from the Frankish empire, though there were several interdicts against selling such things to the Vikings. Good quality salt came from this area too, and the Rhineland produced high-quality textiles, walnut shells for dyeing local textiles, querns of Mayen lava, fine drinking vessels of glass and pottery, other glassware and wine. Silk and other fine textiles, furs, spices, glassware and other handsome drinking vessels, beads of semi-precious stones, such as cornelian and rock crystal, came from the Orient, Russia and Eastern Europe. Slaves were seized wherever there was an opportunity and their economic significance must have been considerable, both as commodities and as a labour force.

Scandinavian products sold or bartered abroad included slaves, skins and furs, walrus tusks, iron, whetstones, soapstone cooking-pots. In addition, within Scandinavia there was an exchange of the same sorts of objects as well as feathers and down, ropes made from the skin of sea mammals, textiles, foodstuffs and probably timber. Then there were craft products, including leather footwear, combs made from the antlers of red deer, reindeer or elk, forged iron articles for everyday use, bronze jewellery and glass beads. All these goods are discussed in more detail in other chapters.

Scandinavian goods may not appear as exotic and exciting as the luxury objects imported from East and West, but this trade was of central economic and social significance. It tied Scandinavia together and created a basis for imports, just as local trade led to the emergence of many markets, trading centres and towns.

TRADE AND TOWNS

Scandinavia's many resources and the extent of local trade have only recently been recognized. Previously the wealth of Scandinavia was almost inexplicable. Many thought that the Vikings were middlemen who procured luxury goods from the distant Orient, bringing them along the Russian rivers to the Baltic and on to Western Europe, and that Western European goods travelled in the opposite direction. (The more direct trade routes via the Mediterranean region were thought to have been closed by the advance of the Arabs.) This theory has now been drastically revised. Although the Scandinavians did take some Western European luxury goods to Russia, and others, including furs, back to Western Europe, this hardly amounted to a large-scale transit trade, for there were still direct trade routes between East and West, for example across Europe from Mainz to Kiev, and the luxury goods from the rest of Europe and the Orient which reached Scandinavia seem to have been for personal use.

In Scandinavia, as we have seen, there was a large market with strong purchasing power – and silver and goods could be acquired in other ways than by purchase. Trade flourished and the market grew with the Vikings' expansion in the North Atlantic, Western Europe, the British Isles and the Baltic-Russian areas, and with the establishment of colonies and trading stations there.

Many foreign merchants travelled to Scandinavia, among them Frisians, Saxons, Slavs and Eastern Europeans, as we know from the burial customs in the large cemeteries at Hedeby and Birka. English merchants presumably went there too; a Spanish-Arab merchant, At-Tartūshi, who visited Hedeby in the middle of the tenth century, commented, however, that the town lay 'at the very end of the world ocean'.

The many valuable goods and the amount of silver in circulation in Scandinavia attracted pirates and robbers. A guarantee of peace and order was necessary in markets and towns, otherwise merchants stayed away. The guarantor was normally the king or a local chieftain, who in return received dues and perhaps first refusal on goods. The interest the kings had in trade is also seen in their involvement in coinage. They had officials in the important towns and trading centres – Hedeby, Ribe and Birka – owned land there as early as the ninth century and often stayed there. They also appear to have been active in founding towns.

On long journeys several merchants would often band together for safety and there are many examples from Europe of two kings entering into an agreement which safeguarded their subjects on journeys in the country of the other party. The clearest of the agreements which concern Scandinavia is recorded in the Annals of Fulda under the year 873. Here we learn that the Danish King Sigfred's emissaries came to Worms to enter into an agreement with King Louis the German 'to secure the peace in the lands between them and the Saxons, and so that the traders of both realms, when they went over there and over here and brought wares with them, should buy and sell in peace, all of which the king for his part promised to keep'. We also know that the chieftain Ohthere stopped his journey north in the White Sea, when he came to the country of the Beormas; he dared go no further 'for unfriþe'. The term unfriþe meant that there was no security agreement guaranteeing his safe passage among the Beormas or covering trade with them.

Most trade and long journeys abroad took place during the summer, when communications were best. In several places permanent trading stations where merchants could overwinter were established. But in central Sweden's large lake district, where ice and snow improved communications, large markets were held in February. Otherwise winter trade was largely limited to local trade in essential goods.

There must have been merchants in large trading centres such as Birka and Hedeby for whom trade was their sole occupation, but many Scandinavian traders had agriculture, hunting or fishing as their main occupation and only went on trading expeditions from time to time as part of a félag, or fellowship. Others, like

Ohthere, were chieftains or large landowners who came by so
many valuable goods that they could venture out in their own
ship with their own cargo. Many craftsmen probably sold directly
from their workshops or took their wares to market themselves.
Itinerant craftsmen, who travelled from farm to farm or went to
market with their wares or tools, no doubt also existed.

Towns as well as markets and trading posts were a focus
for trade and they mushroomed in the Viking Age. Some are
mentioned in written sources and more and more are discovered
through archaeology. They were normally established in protected natural harbours on the coast or were connected with the
sea by fjords; as trade expanded some inland towns developed at
the end of the period. So far no evidence of Viking Age trading
posts has been found in the sparsely populated northern regions
of Norway and Sweden; outposts probably existed, although
there were no towns as such (nor were there any in the Middle
Ages). The most northerly town was Trondheim in rich Trøndelag.

Towns are often defined as fairly large, quite densely populated,
permanent settlements with some centralized functions, such as
markets, serving the surrounding area. A town might also be a
religious centre, a Thing-place, an administrative centre, or a
mint. The inhabitants made their living from trade and crafts
rather than agriculture, fishing or hunting. Here goods were
produced and distributed for use in the town and outside, and
rare commodities, raw materials and specialist skills were to be
found. The most important towns were links in trading networks
which connected local and non-local trade.

The surrounding countryside supplied foodstuffs and fuel –
meat, grain and wood – while raw materials such as iron and
other metals, antlers, hides or leather, everyday goods which
could not be produced locally and luxury products were obtained
farther afield. Goods might be bartered for necessities such as
knives, dress-fittings, combs, footwear, glass beads, or paid for
with silver or coins. Towns were complex economic and social
structures and are among the innovations of the Viking Age in
Scandinavia.

HEDEBY

Hedeby was Scandinavia's most southerly town. It lay on the eastern side of the Jutland peninsula, a little south of the later town of Schleswig. The old border with the Frisians, Saxons and Slavs was near by, and it was closely linked with the border rampart Danevirke. It was well-placed to become a crossroads for international trade: only a few kilometres separated the town, at the end of the long, narrow Schlei fjord, from the small rivers which flowed into the Eider river and the North Sea, while Jutland's north–south traffic route, later known as the Army Road or Ox Road, ran close by.

The earliest settlement, which lies just south of the later semi-circular wall, dates from the eighth century. Most of the excavated buildings are small, sunken-featured buildings and there are various traces of industrial activity. The first written reference to Hedeby is in the Frankish Annals of AD 804, which record that the Danish King Godfred went there (to 'Sliesthorp') with the army. Four years later the annals relate that Godfred had destroyed Reric, a Slav trading station which had given him a large income from taxes, moved the merchants from there to Sliesthorp and had decided to fortify his southern border with a wall.

Throughout the rest of the Viking Age Hedeby is mentioned in several foreign written sources and on rune stones and in scaldic poetry; the name varies from Sliesthorp, Sliaswich, Slesvic, æt Hæthum, to Haitha by. We know that the town had many centralized functions and was closely linked with the king and had foreign connections in all directions. It was rich and was besieged and conquered several times. The missionary Ansgar obtained the permission of King Horik to build a church here c. 850 – the first in Denmark.

We know far more about Hedeby than about any other Scandinavian Viking Age town, because since the Viking Age the water level at Hedeby has risen by some 120 cm, creating excellent conditions for the preservation of wood and other organic materials. Major excavations have been undertaken in the central settlement inside the Semicircular Wall (only 5 per cent of the total area of 24 hectares, however), in the harbour (only 0.5 per cent) and in the cemeteries.

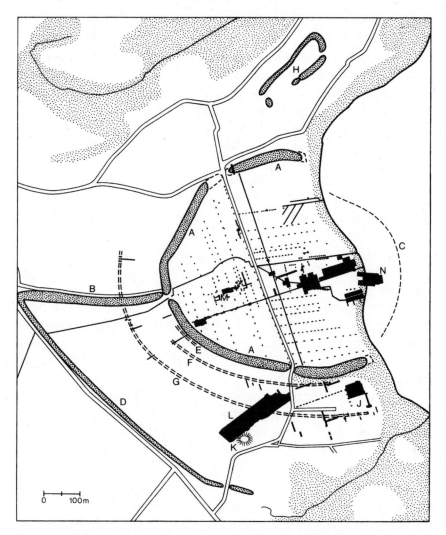

Plan of Hedeby and its surroundings. Low-lying parts are indicated
with dots. The excavation areas inside and south of the
semicircular wall are marked in black. A Semicircular Wall. B
Connecting Wall to Danevirke's Main Wall. C harbour fortification.
D Fore Wall. E, F, G ditches. H Hochburg, which was probably
used as a refuge before the construction of the Semicircular Wall. J
excavated part of the early settlement south of the Semicircular
Wall. K mound with the rich boat-chamber grave. L, M
cemeteries. N harbour excavation 1979–80, with the wreck
of the magnificent warship.

The town was laid out around a stream which ran through the centre from west to east and was very soon channelled. Wood-paved streets ran almost at right angles to the stream or parallel with it and were bordered by small, fenced plots, each with the comparatively small, rectangular house typical of towns in southern Scandinavia. On some plots there was also a small outhouse and often a well. A house that is slightly larger than average, 12 m long and 5 m wide, was particularly well preserved and a full-scale reconstruction has now been built (p. 42).

Several thousand pieces of timber have been dated by dendro-chronology: the oldest to 811 and the most recent to 1020. When King Godfred moved the Reric merchants to Hedeby and built the border wall in 808 the old settlement was presumably rebuilt to make it into an international trading centre. As mentioned on p. 113, the earliest Scandinavian coins were also minted here at that time.

In the harbour, which was protected by semicircular arrange-ments of piles, remains of jetties have been found as well was many small objects thrown or lost in the water. There were also remains of ships, among them a large trading vessel and an exceptionally elegant warship.

The large semicircular wall, which today dominates Hedeby, is 1300 m long and in some places a full 10–11 m high. It was built around the middle of the tenth century, but the enclosed area was never built on in its entirety. It is linked to the Danevirke by the connecting wall that is probably slightly later. It was reinforced several times, and the Fore Wall and a system of ditches to the south were added to make Hedeby a strong fortress. Until these fortifications were built, the inhabitants had probably sought refuge at Hochburg, a hill fort just outside the town to the north.

More than 340,000 objects have been found, as well as bones and botanical finds, which throw light on many aspects of Viking society. There are artefacts from all over the world, although there were clearly stronger connections with the Baltic area than with Western Europe. Leather footwear and glass beads were manufactured here; combs, needles, flutes, gaming pieces and other objects were made of antler and bone; jewellery was cast and hammered; walrus ivory, amber and jet were worked into decorative objects; wooden objects were turned, iron was forged

and ships repaired. There is evidence of increased industrial specialization in the tenth century, and neither the cultivation of
crops nor animal husbandry seem to have played an important
part in its economy.

No traces of royal residences or noble establishments have been
excavated, but Hedeby's cemeteries show that there were great
class differences. Most graves are simple, as befitted the inhabitants
of the small town-houses, but there are some richly furnished
chamber graves from the tenth century and one princely grave,
known as the 'boat-chamber grave'. Here swords, riding equipment, drinking vessels and much else were placed beside the dead
man and his two companions in a grave-chamber under a war-
or travel-ship about 20 m long and covered by a mound.

According to written sources, Hedeby was destroyed several
times in the middle of the eleventh century and the archaeological
finds show that the settlement ceased then. With the decline of
Hedeby, Schleswig grew in strength. There seems to have been
a certain overlap in the eleventh century and it is possible that the
king's residence and his officials' base always lay in Schleswig,
rather than in Hedeby. Schleswig lies at the westerly end of the
Schlei fjord, while Hedeby is situated a little further inland on a
southerly arm; presumably the development of ships with greater
draught was one of the reasons' why Schleswig became more
attractive than Hedeby.

BIRKA

Birka was Sweden's largest town. It lay on the small island of
Björkö in Lake Mälar (Mälaren), 30 km west of Stockholm. In
the Viking Age the land level was 5 m below that of today, so
ships were able to reach the Baltic via the outlet at Södertälje. To
the north there was easy access to Uppsala, the old centre of the
Svear kingdom.

From as early as about AD 400 there was a trade and manu-
facturing centre called Helgö, 12 km east of Birka, which was
probably linked to a chieftain's residence. Many richly furnished
graves in the area from different ages show how wealthy the
region was; in the cemeteries at Vendel and Valsgärde members
of noble families were buried in ships and boats over several

generations with sumptuous grave goods. The economy of these settlements, like Birka's, was presumably based on the trade in iron, furs and skins from the North.

Birka must have been in existence by the beginning of the ninth century and was a flourishing centre when it is first mentioned in written sources in connection with Ansgar's mission around 830. In Rimbert's book about Ansgar's life, written *c.* 875, there are quite extensive descriptions of the town, for several missionaries visited it and lived there for varying periods. Ansgar himself returned in 852 and Sweden's first church was built here. Many functions were centralized here, as in Hedeby. We hear of a king, royal officials, a Thing, worship of gods and international trade, including links with the important Frisian town of Dorestad. Large winter markets were held here, and enormous amounts of fine, warm furs must have been traded.

Some of the settlement was excavated in the 1880s, but only the main results have been published. The houses and the finds, including many imported objects and many traces of industry, are to a large extent comparable with those of Hedeby. Minor excavations in this century concentrated on fortifications and jetties, but new large-scale excavations started in 1990.

The town lay on the north-western side of the island and was fortified in the tenth century on the landward side by a semi-circular rampart, like Hedeby (Plate 9). To the north it extended towards the shore; to the south it was probably linked to a small rocky plateau fortified by a wall: a fortress (Borg). If so, the semicircular rampart enclosed an area of about 7 hectares. There are openings at regular intervals in the remains of the wall; they presumably contained wooden towers. Near the middle of the settlement, known as Black Earth, after the distinctive colour of the soil, is a small bay, accessible to ships of shallow draught. Here jetties have been found, and remains of piles in the water indicate that there was a protected harbour.

At the northern end of the settlement is another bay known as Kugghamn, traditionally thought to have been a harbour for ships with greater draught. If the name is as old as Birka itself, it implies that Kugghamn was used by ships of the Frisian type known as cogs. East of here are two more harbour-like bays with the names Korshamn and Salviken.

Large cemeteries surround the town and attempts have been made to calculate Birka's population on the basis of the number of graves. The conclusions vary between 500 and 1,000 inhabitants, but the population was certainly large. The graves also reveal marked social stratification.

About 1,100 graves were excavated in 1871–95 and this material has been examined and published. The most richly furnished graves, containing Oriental textiles, complete garments of Oriental cut, British vessels, Frisian jugs, Lappish jewellery, among other things, point to a vast consumption of luxury goods, chiefly from the East (Plate 10; illustration p. 155). These graves give a fascinating insight into Birka's cosmopolitan upper class, and the diversity of commodities that could be bought. Hordes of visitors came to this great market, many different languages must have resounded here and many different gods were worshipped.

But around the year 975 the town was abandoned. There are no certain traces of activity after this time. Sigtuna, a little to the north of Birka on the way to Uppsala, presumably succeeded it, there may have been a period of overlap. Sigtuna was certainly closely connected with the king and coins were minted here around AD 1000. The cause of Birka's fall is not known; it may have been that the land level rose, thus blocking access to the sea at Södertälje, or that the area's economy changed as opportunities for obtaining Arab silver in the East declined.

KAUPANG

Kaupang in Vestfold, in southern Norway, on the western side of the mouth of Oslo fjord, lay near the present town of Larvik. The land level has risen here too since the Viking Age, so connections with the sea were much better than they are today. Vestfold was one of Norway's richest and most fertile areas. Harald Finehair of the Ynglinga dynasty came from here and some of the most important Viking Age monuments are to be found in the region: the cemetery for chieftains and kings in Borre, the Gokstad grave, the Oseberg grave. We know that the district was fought over, for the Frankish Annals record that Danish kings were in power here at the beginning of the ninth century.

Kaupang probably dates back to the eighth century, but had played out its role around the year 900. It never became a town with a permanent population and was never fortified. It was an international trading post, presumably with large seasonal markets – the name itself means market-place. It covered an estimated area of 40,000 m², of which about 1,400 have been excavated. Here and in nearby cemeteries many imported goods have been found, which demonstrate contacts primarily with Western Europe and Denmark. There is pottery and glass from the Rhineland, bronze mounts from the British Isles and pottery from Denmark. Traces of industry and a jetty have been discovered and five of the six houses that have been excavated seem to have been workshops rather than dwellings.

A number of graves contained agricultural tools, so some of the people buried here were undoubtedly farmers who lived nearby and engaged in trade from time to time. Others would have been full-time merchants. Kaupang's economy must have been based on supplying whetstones, iron, hides, antlers and soapstone cooking-pots, and very likely also northern Scandinavian luxury goods. Its location means it was probably *Sciringesheal*, the trading station where Ohthere from Hálogaland called in on his long journey to Hedeby around 890.

Kaupang's successor is not known, but around the year 1000 the town of Skien grew up not far away, trading in iron, whetstones and hunting products from Telemark, which were easily transported by water to Skien and on from there.

OTHER TRADING STATIONS AND TOWNS

Norway had no international trading centres that we know of other than Kaupang and no towns in the ninth and tenth centuries. Several places seem to have had the required factors for an important trading centre, for example around Trondheim and Oslo. It is conceivable that organized markets, which simply have not been found, were the beginnings of these towns, and large excavations have confirmed the sagas in that Trondheim was founded by King Olaf Tryggvason just before 1000, while the beginnings of Oslo are slightly later. Trondheim became an important royal seat and the centre for the cult of St Olaf, the royal saint, immediately after his death in 1030. Coins were minted here around 1050, and probably also in Hamar in southern Norway.

Urban development was stronger in Denmark and Sweden and continued into the Middle Ages. Towns that started at the end of the tenth century or the first half of the eleventh include Schleswig and Sigtuna; Viborg, Odense, Roskilde and Lund in Denmark; and Skara, Lödöse, Södertälje and Visby in Sweden. It is often not clear what sort of settlement there was at the beginning, but in many places Christian worship provided a focus. Apart from the last three, all the sites mentioned had a bishop before 1060, and coins were minted in all but the last four (and in yet another couple of Danish towns) before that.

Only two Scandinavian towns can be demonstrated to have older roots: Ribe and Århus in Denmark. In Ribe on Jutland's west coast not far from Frisia, plots with substantial traces of eighth-century workshops have been excavated; we know that glass beads, combs and bronze objects were made and amber-polishing was another specialized craft. The production was clearly aimed at a Scandinavian market, but there were also many imported goods from the Rhineland. A large, well-organized seasonal trading station was established here in the early eighth century, probably by the king. Cattle trading may have been the basis of the economy, as thick layers of cattle manure were found. During the following centuries Ribe developed into a town. Ansgar visited Ribe in 860 and built a church, the town had a bishop in 948, it was fortified in the tenth century and coins were minted from the beginning of the eleventh century. Archaeology has also revealed that the twelfth-century town lay on the other side of the river.

Århus, in the middle of Jutland's east coast, was founded around 950; a strong semicircular rampart surrounding it is nearly contemporary with those at Hedeby and Birka. In the fortified area of 4–5 hectares some traces of crafts have been found, but the only buildings excavated so far are sunken-featured huts in one part of the area. Århus may have been chiefly a fort to begin with, developing into a town with permanent inhabitants a little later. In 948, 965 and 988 there was a bishop in Århus; coins were minted here before 1050 and from *c.* 1060 a bishopric was firmly established.

Most of the international and local trading centres and markets from the Viking Age remain undiscovered. They were not stable settlements and were frequently discontinued or moved. Topographical conditions explain why the site of Ribe was almost stable. Many eleventh-century towns, not just Schleswig and Sigtuna, must have sprung up near to an earlier trading post. For example, Paviken, a trading post at Västergarn on Gotland, which flourished in the tenth century, may have been the precursor of Visby, which became the only town in Gotland in the Middle Ages and perhaps the most important one in Scandinavia.

A new era of urban development began in many parts of Scandinavia in the eleventh century. The Church and the growth of a central power were stabilizing factors, but their impact varied considerably from place to place. Trading stations continued to rise and to decline; Köpingsvik on Öland, for example, flourished in the eleventh and twelfth centuries, but did not become a town.

FORTIFICATIONS, WEAPONS AND WARFARE

Fortifications are built in times of unrest and major defences presuppose a society organized on a local, regional or national level. Apart from the mention of King Godfred's Danevirke in AD 808, there is no documentary evidence about how the fortifications in Viking Age Scandinavia came to be built. Labour and materials were presumably procured chiefly through public defence obligations, and kings, as military leaders, must have been responsible for most of the great defensive works. Many Scandinavian defences were complicated pieces of engineering, and some were no doubt inspired by foreign structures.

RAMPARTS, FORTRESSES AND SEA-BARRIERS

In the mid-tenth century Viking raids in Western Europe became less profitable, partly because many new fortifications had been erected there. The thriving open trading centres in Scandinavia were very vulnerable in comparison, so at the two largest, Hedeby and Birka, a defensive rampart was built. Ribe too was fortified, while Århus probably began as a fortress. The Västergarn rampart on Gotland is probably also from the tenth century. At Hedeby border problems were no doubt responsible for the complicated defensive system that linked the town with the Danevirke (see p. 121).

The ramparts of Hedeby, Birka, Århus and Västergarn were semicircular and faced inland (very little is known so far about the Ribe defences); the harbour at Hedeby, and possibly at Birka, was also protected by rows of stakes in the water. Århus may have had a similar sea defence, but any traces have been obliterated by the modern harbour. The ramparts were built with local building materials; the infill was usually earth from an exterior ditch, and maybe stones, faced with turf or wood, presumably with a wooden palisade on top. They may also have had wooden towers. Traces of timber-lined gateways have been found in Hedeby.

Fortification of other Scandinavian trading centres is not known, for it is uncertain whether the wall at Löddeköpinge in Skåne is from the Viking Age.

Before the ramparts were built at Hedeby and Birka the fortified natural hill just outside both towns – Hochburg at Hedeby and Borg at Birka – would have been a refuge for people and their animals and possessions when an attack was in the offing. This is an ancient type of fortification. The period when Hochburg was used has not been established, but archaeological finds demonstrate that Borg was in use in the Viking Age, and Rimbert's *Life of Ansgar* confirms that Birka's inhabitants sought refuge there during an attack in the ninth century when the town itself was conquered. It has also been suggested that a town garrison may have been stationed at Borg.

In exposed areas the rural population also needed protection in times of unrest, so there must have been many fortified refuges in areas where the terrain did not offer good natural hiding places. Written sources relate that when danger threatened, look-outs would be positioned on the shore and fires would be lit on the hilltops to alert the population. Many early Scandinavian fortresses have completely disappeared and only a few of those that survive have been thoroughly examined, but in the Viking Age it must have been quite common to use and to extend an earlier, delapidated structure when a fortress was needed after a period of peace. Similarly, the Vikings often took advantage of existing structures on expeditions abroad when they needed to defend themselves.

The largest Scandinavian refuge fortress known to have been in use in the Viking Age is Torsburg, just inland on the east coast of Gotland. It covers an area of 112.5 hectares, on a rocky plateau, and is fortified by stone walls for a stretch of about 2 km, where there is no natural protection. There was no permanent settlement there. Scientific dating methods show that it was constructed in the late Roman period and that it was repaired and strengthened before and during the Viking Age. Its precise function is not known but it could have contained the whole of Gotland's estimated population with their animals and fodder. By forced march it was possible to reach this place in a day from most parts of the island. A look-out post on the island's projecting eastern tip could keep watch on enemies approaching by sea. Given the water supply inside the fortress, a siege of about two weeks could be withstood, and a military garrison positioned here could make tactical sorties against an enemy.

Another large fortress on Gotland is Bulverket in the middle of Tingstäde Träsk, the island's largest lake. This is a square timber construction dating from the late Viking Age, about 170 m in size, with an open central area. A number of the objects found and some features of its construction indicate that it may have been built by immigrants from the eastern side of the Baltic, rather than by Gotlanders. In any case this structure is unique in Scandinavia.

The fortress of Eketorp on the long, narrow, flat island of Öland in the Baltic, a little to the south of Gotland, was in use in the late Viking Age. Excavations have shown that, like Torsburg, it dates back to the late Roman period, to AD 300–400. After being enlarged and strengthened around AD 400 it was inhabited continuously for three centuries. It was then presumably in use from time to time for short periods, but gradually fell into disrepair, until around 1000 it was again inhabited. The ruins of the old ring-wall were extended, and given protection by an outer wall. As in the original construction, the building material was local limestone laid without mortar. The walls were roughly circular and the inner wall enclosed an area about 80 m across. Densely packed, long buildings for people and animals radiated out from an open space in the middle. This third and last phase of Eketorp functioned until some way into the thirteenth century and is thought to have been a military garrison. It was certainly not a refuge fortress. The reason for this distinctive fortress must have been the military situation in the Baltic – the Slavs were engaging in piracy and expansion, and the peoples on the eastern shores of the Baltic were launching attacks. Also, after the death of Harthacnut in 1042 Denmark was often politically unstable.

There may have been other fortresses of a similar character on Öland, for there were very few natural refuges on the island and finds show that the somewhat larger fortress of Gråborg, which was enlarged in the Middle Ages, was already in use in the Viking Age.

In many parts of Scandinavia there was a risk of attack and raids from the sea, so defences were often built to protect an area against sudden landings. The rows of piles around the harbours at Hedeby and Birka have already been mentioned. In fjords and bays the sailing channel towards a settlement or a larger area would be blocked by stakes, stones or scuttled ships (such as the five Skuldelev ships: cf. p. 88), so that only people with local knowledge could find their way through a narrow opening.

Such defences were employed before, during and after the Viking Age, and were common outside Scandinavia too (barriers were often used to block the passage of Vikings up European rivers). In southern Scandinavia many of these barriers date from the eleventh century, when there was a great deal of unrest. These constructions were often very large and demanded great resources, both in terms of material and of labour, and they were not always without danger for the local population, as Adam of Bremen noted in connection with Birka:

At that place a bight of the sea which is called the Baltic or Barbarian Sea by extending northward forms a desirable, but to the unwary and those unacquainted with places of this kind, a very dangerous port for the barbarous tribes that lie spread about this sea. For the people of Björkö, very often assailed by the inroads of pirates, who are numerous there, have set about deceiving by cunning artifices the enemies whom they could not resist by force of arms. They have blocked that bight of the restless sea for a hundred or more *stadia* [about 200 m] by masses of hidden rocks, making its passage as perilous for themselves as for the pirates.

THE DANEVIRKE

The Danevirke protected Denmark's southern border and is one of the largest ancient defences in Northern Europe. The complex consists of long ramparts of different periods; parts have often been repaired or extended, to meet the defence needs of later ages. Most of it is Viking Age and early medieval, having been built in AD 737 and extended, changed and maintained until the early thirteenth century. The wall was again extended in 1864 prior to a Prussian invasion and most recently during the Second World War, when the German army made a tank trap there.

The various ramparts cover some 30 km altogether. They form an effective barrier from the Hedeby area at the end of the Schlei fjord in the east to the rivers Rheide and Treene in the west, preventing access to Denmark. Ordinary traffic further west was barred by the rivers and wide, swampy valleys. Jutland's main north–south route, the Army or Ox Road, ran through a gateway in the Danevirke near Hedeby; the area between the wall and the border river, the Eider, about 20 km away, was forested and uninhabited. To the south lived the Saxons, to the west the Frisians and to the east Slav tribes. Conflicts between the Danes and their neighbours were the main reason for building the Danevirke.

Excavations have yielded much evidence about the appearance of the ramparts, and the year of construction of sections of wall has been determined precisely by dendrochronology. The political background can be illuminated by documentary evidence. Three successive lines of ramparts were built at different times (illustration p. 134).

The earliest rampart was built around 737 – this was the year the trees for it were felled, and the timber was not seasoned. The wall was about 7 km long, 10 m wide and 2 m high and was made of earth faced with timber. It consisted of a stretch just north of Hedeby known as the North Wall (which has only one building phase) and the earliest of the Main Wall's many phases. Special foundations were built where the wall crossed marshy ground and over a wet area it took the form of an embankment, which allowed access along the defensive line, on special foundations. On firm ground a ditch ran in front of the wall. Another section, the East Wall, may have been built at the same time.

No written sources record the political and military reasons for the construction of this earliest Danevirke, but it is known that around this time the Danes had a powerful king named Ongendus, who vigorously refused to be converted to Christianity by the

missionary sent by the Frankish Empire, Willibrord (died 739).
A border wall of this magnitude presupposes a central power, so
Ongendus may have built it in an attempt to keep the Saxons or
the Slavs at bay. But it is also conceivable that the wall was built
as the result of the political tension which led to the campaign
against the Saxons in the year 738 by Charles Martel, the mighty
ruler of the Franks.

With the Emperor Charlemagne's conquest of Saxony in the
770s and 780s, Franks and Danes became political neighbours and
at the beginning of the ninth century fierce confrontations arose
on the border. At the same time Danes were raiding the coastal
areas of the Frankish realm and extorting tribute. The Frankish

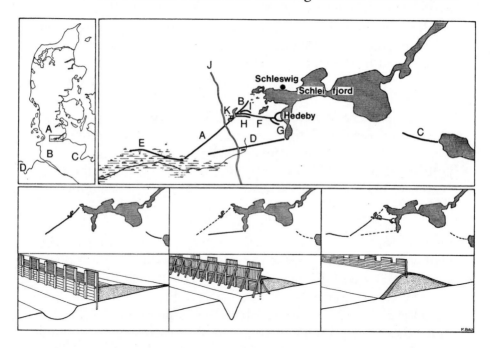

The Danevirke border wall. Top left: A Danes, B Saxons, C Slavs, D
Frisians. Top right: the lay-out of the walls, A Main Wall, B North
Wall, C East Wall, D Kovirke, E Crooked Wall, F Connecting Wall,
G Semicircular Wall and Fore Wall around Hedeby, H Double Wall,
I Curved Wall, K Thyreborg, J Army or Ox Road. The overall length
of the Danevirke is *c.* 30 km and some walls were built in many phases.
Below: the three stages of the ramparts with diagrams showing the
construction of walls and ditches.

Annals tell of the various alliances of Slavic people with Franks and Danes and describe the Danes' proud King Godfred, whose large maritime army landed at Hedeby. In 808 he decided to build a border wall from the Baltic to the North Sea which was to have only one gateway. Immediately after this Charlemagne had a fortress built north of the Elbe and the Slav Abodrites built a fortress in Alt-Lübeck, while the border conflicts continued under varying alliances for some years.

King Godfred's wall was thus part of a complicated piece of power politics, but it is not yet known which section of the Danevirke corresponds to it. No section has so far been dated to his time, and in fact the building activity referred to may have been a repair of the 737 wall. Another possibility is the straight wall Kovirke, south of Hedeby, which was 6.5 km long, built of earth faced with timber and with a ditch in front. It was apparently never repaired and its age is unknown.

The third line of the Danevirke covered 14 km in an immense zig-zag. It included the earliest part of the Main Wall built in 737, and, via the Connecting Wall, incorporated Hedeby's Semicircular Wall and its Fore Wall. To the west the Crooked Wall formed a considerable extension of the earlier defensive lines. This line of the Danevirke was 12–13 m wide and about 3 m high, built of earth with a steep front of turf and was probably crowned by a timber palisade.

The construction of the Connecting Wall is dated by dendro-chronology to AD 968, and the whole of this rampart line was probably built at this time by King Harald Bluetooth. The problems with the German Empire in the 960s are recorded in documentary sources and provide the reason for this magnificent border fortification. In 974 open warfare broke out and although Harald Bluetooth, as overlord of Norway, received military assistance from Earl Hákon of Trøndelag, the Danevirke fell to the enemy and German soldiers were stationed in the border region. The wall was reconquered in 983, no doubt with the help of warriors from the king's recently constructed circular fortresses (see p. 137).

Later on the Danevirke was again extended and faced with stone and then with bricks during the reign of King Valdemar the Great (1157–82). Fighting took place here several times – in the eleventh century the Slav peoples were the main threat – and on a few occasions the Danevirke was conquered, but for half a millennium the wall marked Scandinavia's political and cultural southern border and acted as an effective defence of Denmark.

ROYAL FORTRESSES

As far as we know royal fortresses only existed very briefly in Viking Age Scandinavia, and all are Danish. Those that have been discovered are scattered across Denmark: Trelleborg on Sjælland, Fyrkat in north-east Jutland, Aggersborg in north Jutland by the Limfjord. There was probably also such a fortress at Nonnebakken on Fyn, but the traces of it have been almost obliterated by a medieval monastery, a later suburban development and large-scale soil removal at the turn of the century. The fortresses were all built to the same strictly geometrical design c. 980 (Trelleborg and Fyrkat are precisely dated by dendrochronology), which means that they must all have been built by King Harald Bluetooth, although there is no documentary evidence about them (Plate 14).

All the fortresses had a circular rampart built of earth and turf with internal timber structures, faced with wood and with sloping outer surfaces. There were covered gateways, perhaps crowned with towers, at all four points of the compass; they were linked by two timber-paved streets which crossed at the centre of the fortress, and by another around the inside of the rampart. The rampart was surrounded by a v-shaped ditch separated by a narrow berm. In each of the fortress's quadrants there were large, uniform, timber buildings arranged in a quadrangle.

Despite these similarities the fortresses were not identical. The differences in size are the most striking.

	Internal diameter of fortress area (m)	Width of rampart (m)	Width of ditch (m)	Length of houses (m)
Aggersborg	240	11	4	32.0
Trelleborg	136	19	18	29.4
Fyrkat	120	13	7	28.5
Nonnebakken	120	17(?)	7(?)	?

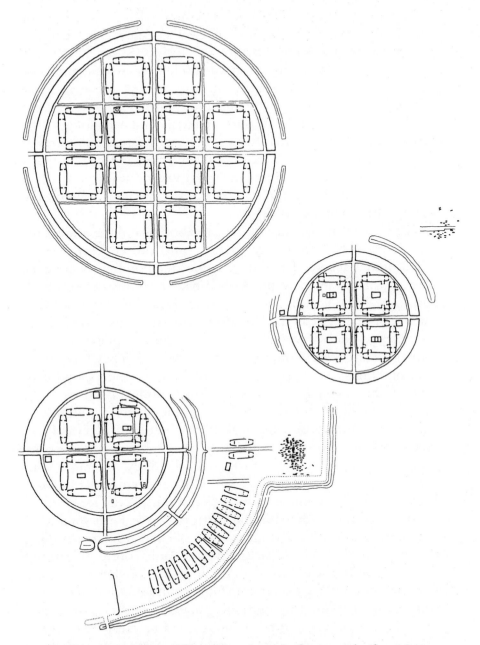

Reconstructed plans of Danish geometric fortresses built *c.* 980:
Aggersborg, Fyrkat and Trelleborg. The basic geometric principle is
the same, but the fortresses vary in size and only Trelleborg had an
outer fortification. Scale 1:4,000.

At both Trelleborg and Fyrkat a cemetery has been found just outside the ring-wall. At Trelleborg and Aggersborg existing villages were demolished before the fortresses were built and excavations at Trelleborg revealed infilled wells containing the bodies of children. The narrow spits of land at Trelleborg and Fyrkat had to be enlarged by enormous infilling, but in spite of the huge investment of labour, materials and technology, the fortresses were abandoned after a few years. There are no traces of repairs, although the timbered houses and timber-faced ramparts would soon have needed them, and Fyrkat's wall soon fell in where it was built on infill. The fortresses disappeared until the 1930s, when excavations began.

The original appearance of the large houses and the models for the fortresses, their precise age and their function have been the subject of much debate. The only traces of the buildings were dark patches where posts and planks had been sunk into the ground, and some large hearths. No wood survives. The appearance of the large buildings had to be deduced from their ground plan and estimates of the individual posts and planks, supplemented by knowledge of the building customs of the age. They were standard buildings, whose general plan and lay-out corresponded to dwelling houses on the large farms of the period, as at Vorbasse (cf. pp. 98–101). In the fortresses, however, they were not all dwelling houses; some were used as workshops where gold, silver and iron were worked, and others would have been stables, barns or stores. Some buildings can also be imagined splendidly decorated with carvings and brightly painted. (A full-size reconstruction of a Fyrkat house was completed in 1985 just outside the fortress.)

Architectural models for the fortresses have been sought all over Europe and in the East. A number of circular fortresses along the coasts of Holland and Belgium have some common features; Souburg, on the island of Walcheren in The Netherlands, has a circular wall with gates at the four points of the compass as well as streets connecting opposite gateways, but there are many differences, such as the type of houses, and its precise date is not known. A recently excavated Viking Age fortress in Trelleborg in Skåne also had a circular rampart but was otherwise different from the classic Danish ones. The Danish fortresses and those in The Netherlands may have been based on the same model, but if so, it was freely adapted, as the building materials and the design of the houses at Trelleborg (in Sjælland) and at Fyrkat and Aggersborg were Scandinavian. The geometric design and the houses set in a square may have been inspired by Carolingian or Ottonian monumental architecture, and the fortresses must have been intended for the exercise of sovereign political and military power. Such centres existed in many parts of Europe outside Scandinavia and in the East. The idea would not have been unknown to the Vikings.

The dating of the fortresses to around 980 and their very short lifespan has overturned a theory that they were built as barracks and training camps for the Vikings who plundered and finally conquered England under Svein Forkbeard and Cnut the Great in 1013. It is clear, too, that the fortresses were not exclusively for warriors. They also housed women, children and craftsmen. Furthermore their location gave them command of the interior rather than of the coast: none of them lay on the sea, but all were near important land routes.

The political and economic problems in Denmark in the years around 980 were caused by an acute shortage of silver, as Arabic silver had ceased to flow into Scandinavia ten years before; the Danes' defeat by the German emperor at the Danevirke in 974; the loss of supremacy over Norway and hence loss of income from tribute. Moreover, throughout his long reign Harald Bluetooth had had an unprecedented number of large structures built, probably chiefly by the imposition of public labour duties, and later sources say that this became the cause of rebellion.

Given this background, it is likely that c. 980 King Harald felt the need to consolidate his power and to regain some of his lost domains and his lost prestige. The fortresses would therefore have been regional centres of royal power designed to keep the population in check and to fulfil administrative functions, as well as housing garrisons which could turn out quickly when foreign princes threatened the country or when the king was on the offensive. They could also collect finances for the king by plunder and extortion outside the realm. Slightly earlier fortresses existed, as already mentioned, at Hedeby and Århus, and the distinctive appearance of the circular fortresses can only be ascribed to concerns for prestige.

The immense Aggersborg was presumably intended for a special role. From here there was easy access to Norway where Harald Bluetooth had vital interests, through a strait from the Limfjord to Skagerak. He could also control and levy tolls on the north–south road traffic through Jutland, there being an important crossing here, and on the through traffic in the Limfjord, which must have been the safest shipping route between Western Europe and the Baltic.

The large bridge across Ravning Enge (cf. p. 79), which was also built around 980, was presumably part of Harald's strategic plan and as early as 983 the lost border area was reconquered. But around 986 rebellion against Harald Bluetooth broke out again. He was exiled and probably died on 1 November 987. It may well be that the royal fortresses, symbols of his unsuccessful policies, were abandoned when his rebellious son Svein Forkbeard assumed power. At any rate, they soon fell into ruins and were totally forgotten.

WEAPONS AND WARFARE

The *lið* (the private fighting units of kings and chieftains), military duties and the public levy system under the command of the king have already been mentioned. In addition there was an obligation on all men capable of bearing arms to defend the country – to spring to the defence of their locality at a given signal. Not much is known about any of these forms of military organization, but the levy system could hardly have been employed for foreign offensives. The Viking armies that fought the campaigns abroad must normally have been organized on a voluntary basis, as a group of *lið*. Other voluntary groups engaged in piracy at home and abroad from time to time.

However, we do know a considerable amount about how the Vikings fought. In many places during the pagan Viking Age it was customary to bury warriors with their weapons, and some have also been found in lakes and bogs, perhaps deposited there as votive gifts. There are also a number a descriptions of military techniques and of battles. The most extensive are foreign: a ninth–century poem written by the priest Abbo about the Vikings'

Royal constructions from tenth-century Denmark: semicircular walls around Århus and Hedeby, a major extension of the Danevirke, the Jelling monuments, the bridge across Ravning Enge, the four geometric fortresses, the first church on the site of the present Roskilde Cathedral. King Harald Bluetooth may have ordered the building of all these.

attack on Paris in 885–6, the various Western European annals, the Anglo-Saxon Chronicle and the Anglo-Saxon heroic poem about the battle of Maldon between Anglo-Saxons and Vikings in 991.

Free men had the right and duty to own weapons. The Vikings fought with swords, axes, spears, javelins, bows and arrows, and stones, defending themselves with shields, helmets and various forms of armour such as chain-mail (Plate 8). In siege warfare special machinery such as catapults and mantlets were sometimes used, or burning ships were sent towards the enemy. Many accounts of Viking campaigns abroad show that they were familiar with field fortifications, and the army at Paris in 885 had a couple of engineers to build large offensive machinery, presumably battering rams.

The finest and most costly weapon was the sword. They were one-hand slashing swords with broad, sturdy blades, about 75–80 cm long, and a hilt wide enough for a broad fist. The total length was normally about 90 cm. Single-edged swords are known from the earliest Viking Age, but the typical sword of the period was double-edged, with a fuller along the centre of the blade to reduce the weight and increase flexibility. Sophisticated craftsmanship produced light, supple but strong blades that might have a pattern-welded central section and specially treated iron for the cutting edges. The quality of the sword and the status of the owner were reflected in how ornate the blade and the hilt were. Simple hilts might be of antler, while richly decorated ones were worked in silver and gold.

Many good sword blades, some with inscriptions, were imported from the Frankish Empire, but the hilts were normally mounted in Scandinavia. Studies of forging techniques and of tools and workshops indicate that quality weapons, perhaps even with pattern-welding, were produced in Scandinavia. Swords were carried in scabbards of wood and leather, lined with wool or fabric, hanging on the left side from a strap across the right shoulder. The scabbards could also be splendidly decorated.

Swords were highly prized. Grand swords were given as princely gifts or were handed down from father to son. They were praised in scaldic poetry and special swords were given names, such as *Brynjubítr* (mail-biter) or *Gullinhjalti* (golden-hilt).

Most people think of axes as the Viking weapon *par excellence*. They were effective and were used by many in battle, but both grave finds and provisions in Norwegian regional laws indicate that by the later Viking Age axes were often a cheaper alternative to the combination of sword and spear preferred by the rich. It is sometimes impossible to distinguish a battle axe from a tool. A few superb, silver-decorated axes are known from rich graves, however, and like fine swords, they must have been status symbols as well as weapons.

Spears were also much used. They had blades up to about 0.5 m long and some had pattern-welded blades or sockets decorated with inlaid silver. Javelins were probably normally undecorated, but the size of many blades, ornamented as well as plain, meant that they have been used both for thrusting and throwing. Of course spears were also used for hunting – a favourite nobleman's sport – as were bows and arrows. One whole bow, 192 cm long and made of yew, has been found at Hedeby. Arrow heads were made of iron and the shafts of wood, with a notch in the end and tied-on feather. The princely grave at Hedeby (the so-called boat-chamber grave), contained a bundle of fine arrows with bronze mounts as well as an exquisite sword.

The most noticeable feature of a Viking army at a distance must have been the large round shields, which were often painted in brilliant colours. Yellow and black shields were found on the Gokstad ship, red shields are mentioned in contemporary literature, and *Ragnarsdrápa* – the earliest surviving scaldic poem – describes a shield painted with pictures from popular stories of gods and heroes. A shield must protect the body from chin to knee and those from the Gokstad ship are in fact just under 1 m in diameter. Shields were made of wood and the edge streng-thened in various ways; in the centre was an iron boss to protect the hand, which held a bar at the back.

Viking battledress must have included protection for the head and body, but very little survives, as dead warriors were rarely buried with their armour. The helmets shown on many pictures of Vikings are conical, sometimes with a nose-guard, and this type of helmet was also common in the early Middle Ages – it can be seen on the Bayeux Tapestry, from the 1070s, worn by Normans and Anglo-Saxons alike. However, the very few remains of helmets are rounded at the top, not pointed, and more akin to the helmets of earlier ages. The only one in a reasonable state of preservation is from a richly furnished grave in Gjermundbu in southern Norway. The round iron shape is strengthened by iron bands and has a spectacle-like guard for the eyes and nose. A neck guard was probably attached at the back.

The best-preserved remains of a mail shirt come from the same grave, but the appearance of mail shirts is still not clear. It was presumably a knee-length shirt with long sleeves, like those known from preceding and later ages. Small fragments of chain-mail have been found in several other places and accounts in Scandinavian poetry give the impression that many warlords owned a mail shirt. Another type of armour consisting of small iron plates tied together has been found in the fortress at Birka, which perhaps reflects Birka's close connections with Russia and the East, where this type was common.

The many descriptions of the Vikings in battle give the impression that, unlike the Franks, they fought on foot. Horses tended to be used for transport to and from battlefields and when scouting for enemy manoeuvres, although sometimes a group of Vikings might engage in a fight on horseback.

The army would often reach the scene of battle by warship, as when King Godfred called up a great force against Charlemagne at Hedeby in 804. Battles were also fought at sea. One of the most famous was the great battle at Svöld, c. 1000, when King Olaf Tryggvason lost his life. Naval battles (and acts of piracy) normally began by the attackers hurling stones and javelins and firing a host of arrows, then the enemy ships would be boarded and the battle engaged with swords, spears and axes.

Before a battle on land the leaders of the two armies often made a rousing speech to their men and sometimes also a speech to discourage the enemy. As a prelude to the battle proper terms of abuse were hurled from both sides, arrow quivers were rattled and the combatants roared wild battle cries to inflame themselves and frighten the enemy. A hailstorm of stones, arrows and javelins was followed by hand-to-hand combat with swords, spears and axes, accompanied by fierce battle cries. Signals were sounded on wind instruments. The king often fought at the head of his army, surrounded by a bodyguard of his best men. The leader's position in the mêlée of battle was marked by the standard; the standard bearer, an especially able man, had to prevent the standard falling. A banner depicting a raven (the symbol of the war god Odin) was captured from Vikings in England in AD 878, and sixteen royal standards were taken from Vikings in 891 at the battle of Dyle (in present-day Belgium) and sent to Bavaria as evidence of the victory.

The Vikings were adept at exploiting the advantages of the terrain. For example pits were dug against the horse-mounted Franks as an army took up its position in a place inaccessible to horses, and field fortifications were often constructed too. Western European sources relate that the Vikings often made use of islands, fortresses, fortified towns and stone churches as secure bases. They rarely undertook long sieges, but when they did, as before Paris in 885–6, they sometimes had siege machines constructed; and their tactics also included digging ditches and building ramparts. Their Western European adversaries were frequently overawed by the mobility and ingenuity of the Viking armies.

According to the German Annals of Fulda, the Vikings would declare peace by raising a shield on high, but on one occasion when the Vikings were besieged in a fortress in Elsloo (by the river Maas, on the present-day border between Holland and Belgium), they tricked the enemy by doing this. Several sources record that a peace treaty was often sworn on weapons, confirmed by mutual oaths and sealed with exchanges of high-ranking hostages and gifts. Other sources relate that the Vikings sometimes swore on a holy ring. When a Viking army abroad was victorious, the conclusion of peace normally involved payment of tribute and supplies to the army.

Many of the Viking Age finds are weapons, and fighting and the ideals of warriors – courage, strength, delight in weapons, the splendour of battle, loyalty to one's fighting comrades, faithfulness to one's lord unto death – are a constant theme in poetry in honour of princes and also on many rune stones.

> I've been with sword and spear
> slippery with bright blood
> where kites wheeled. And how well
> we violent Vikings clashed!
> Red flames ate up men's roofs,
> raging we killed and killed,

and skewered bodies sprawled
sleepy in town gate-ways
(stanza by Egil Skallagrímssoñ, *c.* 925)

'Sakse' raised this stone in memory of Asbjörn his partner, Toke's son.
He fled not
at Uppsala
but struck
while he had weapon.

(Sjörup rune stone, Skåne, *c.* 1000)

But these ideals were not unique to the Vikings. They were fundamental to the age, and were also expressed in Anglo-Saxon heroic poetry, such as the poem about the battle of Maldon, where Brihtnoth and all his men were killed. Of course, in Scandinavia, as well as elsewhere, there were also people who viewed the world with more peaceful eyes.

THE OLD AND THE NEW
RELIGION

Throughout most of the Viking Age the Scandinavians had a non-Christian religion. The Christians called them pagans, *paganos*, a derogatory term applied to all those of a different faith. Apart from the Muslims in Spain and elsewhere in the Mediterranean area, the whole of Western and Southern Europe was Christian. In Northern and Eastern Europe, the Slav, Baltic, Finnish and Lappish peoples, like the Scandinavians, had different religions.

Christianity is a missionary religion. Scandinavia's nearest neighbours to the south were converted around the beginning of the Viking Age – the Frisians during the eighth century, and the Saxons at the end of that century, as the result of their integration into the Frankish realm. In Saxony it took the form of an exceptionally brutal forced conversion by Charlemagne. The mission continued northwards and eastwards when political conditions permitted. Denmark became officially Christian c. AD 960, Norway followed at the beginning of the eleventh century, and Sweden was very gradually converted during the eleventh century.

Conversion in these countries was used to strengthen royal power, as it was in Poland, in the Russian state of Kiev and in Hungary, which officially became Christian in the years 966, 988 and 1000 respectively. Around the year 1000 the Viking colonies in the Atlantic also accepted Christianity. In the following centuries the Scandinavians helped spread the new religion in the Baltic area, in Finland and among the Lapps, often with sword in hand.

Missionary activity was not co-ordinated, however, and Christianity far from united. The Church of Rome and the Orthodox Church were rivals; both the Pope and the Patriarch in Byzantium thought they had the monopoly of true Christianity. Many Swedes came across the Orthodox faith through their close links with Eastern Europe and Byzantium, but in Scandinavia the Roman Catholic Church prevailed. This was not free from rivalries, however, for missions were usually sent by an archbishop whose prestige, influence and income grew with the acquisition of new Christian regions. This could cause strife between archbishoprics, and because church organization in a country was closely linked to royal power, missionary activity and church politics often went hand in hand with national power politics.

But the introduction of Christianity caused a cultural divide everywhere. It brought not only new rituals and a new faith but also a change in the moral code and a gradual erosion of deeprooted cultural patterns.

THE OLD FAITH

Virtually all documentary evidence about the pre-Christian religion in Scandinavia was written by Christians, and the fullest accounts were written several centuries after the conversion. The most important sources are old poems about the gods from the anthology known as *The Elder Edda*, written down in the thirteenth century, and Snorri Sturluson's book about the art of poetry from about 1220 (pp. 13 and 178). This contains a detailed Norse mythology, which is as reliable as it could be, given that it was written some 200 years after the introduction of Christianity; Christian influence can often be discerned in these sources, however. The descriptions of Arab travellers, accounts of Western European Christians, scaldic poems in honour of princes and rune stones yield some fragments of contemporary information. Further knowledge of pagan customs can be gleaned from laws of prohibition in early legal texts and from a detailed study of twelfth- and thirteenth-century historical works. Archaeology has shed light on burial customs, pagan monuments, divine symbols and sacrifice, but has not uncovered any temples. Pictures (Plate 15) can rarely be interpreted precisely, but they give an impression of ceremonies and rituals and also confirm some of the stories about the gods, while place-names can demonstrate the popularity of gods in different parts of Scandinavia.

Our picture of the pre-Christian religion is thus based on information from many periods and places, which was often recorded by people with a completely different religious background. This may well explain why the underlying concepts often seem unclear and somewhat primitive. Religious concepts also changed in the course of the Viking Age, no doubt partly as a result of Christian influence, and there were regional variations. Unlike Christianity, the old religion was tolerant, had many gods and also adopted new ones. For example, the *Life of Ansgar* relates that the people of Birka had started to worship a former king, Erik, and religious influences from Eastern Europe may also have been absorbed here. However, the main features of the religion were common to all Scandinavia.

The gods were each responsible for an important aspect of human existence. They were represented as human beings and to a large extent they behaved like mortals. They lived in firmly structured communities, just as the wealthy farmers of the age did, and they were divided into two families, the Æsir and the Vanir.

The Æsir was the larger family. Its head was Odin, the omniscient god of power, of wisdom, poetry and battle. Unlike the other gods, he was wild and unpredictable and possessed many strange abilities, acquired by mystical and supernatural deeds connected with death. He was one-eyed, having exchanged his other eye for a draught from the well of wisdom. His weapon was the spear and he rode an eight-legged horse named Sleipnir. His ravens Hugin and Munin flew into the world every day and gathered knowledge of all that happened there.

Odin resided in Valhalla, the hall of the slain. His chosen warriors were led here from the battleground by the Valkyries, females who were not strictly goddesses. The warriors passed their time in Valhalla waiting for the last great battle against the powers of evil; they fought and feasted, just like warlords on earth, except that real women were not present in Valhalla. Odin and his warriors lost the battle against evil. He was swallowed up by the wolf Fenrir and Ragnarök, the destruction of the world, followed, but a new world arose.

Odin was primarily worshipped by kings, chieftains and their men. He could meet their needs, if he so wished, and place-names indicate that there was an official cult of Odin in Denmark and in the Götalands in Sweden. He seems to have been less popular in Norway and Iceland. The eight-legged horse with a rider depicted on picture stones on Gotland must be Sleipnir, perhaps being ridden by Odin (p. 23). Around 1075 Adam of Bremen wrote that one of the three idols in the large heathen temple in Uppsala was 'Odin – that is the Furious – who carries on war and imparts to man strength against his enemies'. Odin's many strange qualities and his supreme position explain why his name does not form part of personal names, and why he is not invoked on rune stones, but we know that in the eighth century his name was scratched on a piece of human skull, found in Ribe.

According to Adam of Bremen, Thor was the mightiest of the three gods in the Uppsala temple. 'Thor, they say, presides over the air, he governs the thunder and lightning, the winds and rains, fair weather and crops . . . If plague and famine threaten, a libation is poured to the idol Thor.' Thor was the son of Odin, but had quite a different nature. He was down-to-earth and reliable. He represented physical strength and, according to the west-Norse literary sources, fought evil, symbolized by the giants and the World Serpent. A widespread and popular story, also known from picture stones in Uppland, Gotland, Denmark and north-west England, tells of the fishing trip when he caught the World Serpent; it escaped because the giant Hymir cut the line. Thor drove in a cart drawn by goats and his weapon was the mighty hammer Mjöllnir. He was worshipped all over the Viking world, and the sign of the hammer, fashioned as a pendant, was a widespread divine symbol – the only pre-Christian one to be identified with certainty (Plate 16). With the introduction of Christianity it was supplanted by the cross. Thor is also invoked on a number of rune stones; scalds made poetry in his honour and his name was an element in many personal names and place-names which are still in use.

There were many more members of the Æsir family, among them Odin's good son Baldr and the strange Heimdall, the watch-man of the gods. But the third god in the temple of Uppsala was Frey of the Vanir family. Adam tells that he 'bestows peace and pleasure on mortals. His likeness, too, they fashion with an

Thor's fishing expedition depicted on the Altuna stone in Uppland, Sweden. Thor is sitting in the boat, his hammer at the ready in his right hand, having caught the World Serpent, using an ox head as bait. He thrust so hard against the bottom of the boat that his foot went through it. According to the story, the giant Hymir is with him in the boat (not shown in this picture), and cuts the line so the evil World Serpent escapes.

immense phallus'. When marriages were celebrated, offerings were made to Frey. Frey was a fertility god. He was first and foremost the god of the Svear and, according to the poem *Ynglingatal*, he was the ancestor of the Ynglinga dynasty, who became kings in Uppsala and in Vestfold in Norway. But place-names, personal names and poems indicate that he was also worshipped in the rest of Scandinavia. Some tales relate that ritual feasts were held in the spring in his honour, with processions and fertility rites. Adam of Bremen recounts that the pious bishop Egino smashed a famous statue of Frey in Västergötland, probably in Skara. A small bronze figure of Frey from the late Viking Age has survived, found in Södermanland in Sweden. It is a seated man with an arm-ring, pointed hat, crossed legs and a large, erect penis.

Tiny gold-foil plaques found all over Scandinavia show a man and a woman in a tender embrace, a motif associated with a fertility cult, possibly centred on Frey or Freyja. Freyja was Frey's sister, his female counterpart, the goddess of love and fertility. She too was worshipped by many. She was the leader of the *dísir*, female beings who represented fertility in nature and in mortals. There was probably a public cult of *dísir* among the Svear, but place-names reveal that they were also worshipped elsewhere in Sweden and in Norway, often at private feasts.

Quite separate from the two divine families were the Norns, the goddesses of Fate, to whom both mortals and gods were subject, and the Valkyries. There were also evil giants, the enemies of gods and mortals, who lived in the outer circle of the world and in uninhabited places on earth; the strange, cunning and unreliable Loki, father of the World Serpent, and the wolf Fenrir, who moved among gods as well as giants, played them off against each other and tricked both many times. Dwarves also lived in deserted places. They were clever, cunning and good craftsmen. Elves lived in the ground and *fylgjur* were the guardian spirits of a family or an individual, who represented what we today would see as inherited qualities. The dead of a family had to be well-treated as they went on to an afterlife. The world was full of spirits who had influence on the life and happiness of mortals and with whom people had to be on good terms. They had to behave properly, honour the gods and other supernatural beings and give them their due. No sacrifice was made to the Norns, however, who spun the thread of man's inevitable fate.

Many place-names give evidence of pre-Christian cult places but not much is known about how the gods and other beings were actually worshipped. Adam of Bremen's description of the temple in Uppsala, with its priesthood and the large idols there and elsewhere, dates from *c.* 1075, when Christianity had become solidly rooted in Scandinavia. The temple, priests and statues may all have been influenced by Christian worship, for they are not known from earlier sources.

In the main, the cult seems to have been decentralized and led by local chieftains or wealthy farmers. On certain occasions the farmers from a region would meet to honour the gods at a sacrificial feast, or *blót*. This normally took place in the hall of the chieftain's farm (a hall of this kind was probably called a *hof*). There was also private worship in the home. In the poem *Austrfa-rarvísur* from *c.* 1020 the Christian scald Sigvat relates that it was impossible to find shelter one evening (probably somewhere in Västergötland) because *blót* was being celebrated on all the farms; a woman explained that it was elf *blót*.

The Spanish Arab At-Tartūshi relates after a visit to Hedeby in the second half of the tenth century:

They have a feast, when they all gather in order to honour the god and in order to eat and drink. He who slaughters a sacrificial animal erects a wooden scaffolding by the door of his house and places the animal upon it, be it an ox or a ram or a he-goat or a pig. Then people know that he has honoured his god.

Gods and other supernatural beings could also be worshipped out of doors: in groves, in specially consecrated places called *vé*, on hills and mountains, and by springs. A *hǫrg* may have been a kind of altar – a heap of stones, either in the open air or later in the Viking Age inside a building. The largest of the boat-shaped stone settings, known as ship-settings, found especially in Sweden and Denmark may also have been places of worship. They rarely contain graves but often small pits with charcoal and other burnt material. Being up to 90 m long, they could accommodate many people.

It is doubtful whether kings exercised religious cult functions which differed from those of other leaders, but large, official cult feasts took place in Lejre in Denmark and in Uppsala in Sweden. In both places large monuments are still visible (in Lejre, the remains of a ship-setting some 80 m long and in Uppsala three large mounds), and they both seem to have been associated with royal power.

The Lejre cult is described by the German Thietmar of Merseburg half a century after Christianity was introduced in Denmark, while Adam of Bremen tells of contemporary conditions in Uppsala, though he never visited it. The two accounts are remarkably similar. In both places people met every ninth year and both human beings and animals were sacrificed: in Lejre, ninety-nine people and ninety-nine horses, dogs and cocks; in Uppsala, nine of all kinds of living males, whose corpses were hung in a holy grove near the temple. Adam relates that the whole of Sweden celebrated this religious feast together. Everyone, including the king, sent gifts and Christians could only opt out by buying dispensations. Lejre is called the most important place in the realm (*caput istius regni*). Recently a very large hall has been excavated here – 48 m long and up to 11 m wide, with a floor area of approximately 500 m².

The sacrificial sites themselves, and the Uppsala temple, have not been identified, but in other parts of Uppland and on Gotland the remains of large Viking Age sacrifices containing partly destroyed weapons have been found in bogs and other marshy places. At Gudingsåkrarne on Gotland more than 500 items have been found, predominantly spear and arrow-heads. There are few material traces of cult ceremonies, but the Oseberg tapestry depicts what must be a religious procession: people in wagons, on horseback or on foot, some equipped with spears and shields, and one disguised by an animal mask. People in animal disguise must have played a role in certain ceremonies, as they are also depicted on finds from Sweden, and the textile finds from Hedeby harbour include two very realistic three-dimensional animal masks, one the head of a small animal such as a fox, dog or sheep, the other the head of an ox. The Oseberg tapestry and other finds also show men wearing horned head-dresses, but these have nothing to do with helmets worn by Vikings on military expeditions.

We do not know much about the rituals associated with death

Opposite: rich male grave from Birka, Sweden, tenth century. The man was buried with magnificent possessions, probably in a sitting position, in a timber chamber 2.35 m long. On the east side was a pit with two horses. Other finds were a sword (1), a large knife (2), two large spear-heads (3–4), an axe (5), twenty-five arrow-heads (6), shield bosses and mounts (7–8) from two shields leant against each end of the grave, stirrups (9), a knife (10) and whetstone (11), twenty-eight gaming counters, three dice and three weights (12), a quarter of an Islamic silver coin minted AD 913–33 (13), a ring-pin (14), a silver mount of eastern origin with silk and four silver pendants, all from a hat (15), a bronze bowl (16), a strap-mount with an iron ring (17) and iron buckle (18), a comb (19), two horse bits, some iron mounts and iron rings, four crampons for horses (20–23), an iron hook (24). In addition, some large iron mounts and mounts from a gaming board, which probably lay south of the large knife (2).

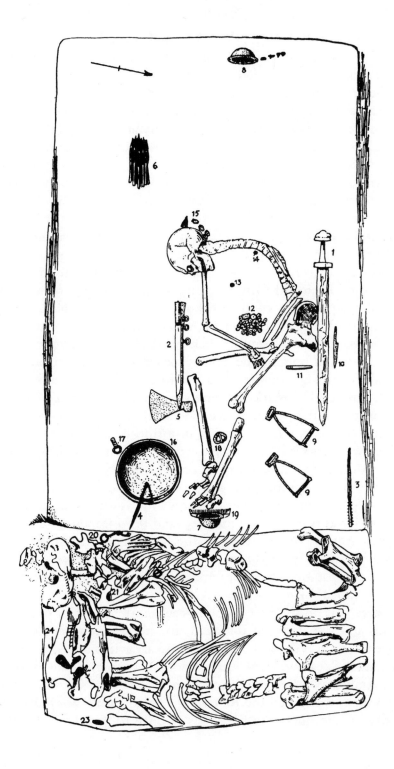

and burial. The old religion contained several concepts of the afterlife and archaeological finds confirm that burial customs were tremendously varied. Written sources tell of several realms of the dead, but these fragments are partly contradictory, so they give a very incomplete picture of pre-Christian concepts.

One realm of the dead was the gloomy and murky Hel, whose grim mistress of the same name was a sister of the World Serpent and the wolf Fenrir. Both men and women came here. Odin's Valhalla was for chosen warriors, but there are also said to have been warriors in Freyja's hall. There are stories too about the dead living on in the grave. One source tells of a dying woman on her way to Freyja, but nearly all the surviving stories are about men.

Burial customs were very different from the Christian ones. Many people were buried with possessions for use in the afterlife. Grave-goods ranged from the single knife of a poor man to the splendid equipment of the Birka aristocracy and the Oseberg queen. In Norway the emphasis was often on tools for work in the fields, the workshop, kitchen or at the loom, but weapons and status symbols of the upper classes are found throughout Scandinavia. The contents of a group of warlords' graves from tenth-century Denmark appear to mirror the ideals of Valhalla. In Norway and Sweden, as we have seen, it was not uncommon for the aristocracy to be buried in a ship or a boat; men were buried with horses all over Scandinavia, while the coffins of upper class women in tenth-century Denmark often contained the body of a wagon, to symbolize a whole wagon. Food and drink were usually placed in the graves. All this indicates that the realm of the dead was reached by a journey, and this idea also emerges in written sources. An element of the burial custom which today seems particularly macabre was the possibility of being buried with a companion, a male or female follower, presumably usually a slave, killed for the burial.

There was no simple equation between the quantity of grave-goods and the status of the dead, for not all rich people were buried with grave-goods. And in some areas it was customary to cremate the dead with their grave-goods and to bury the remains. The Arab envoy Ibn Fadhlan, who attended a Viking funeral on the Volga, was given the following explanation: 'We burn him in fire in a moment, and he goes at once to paradise.' Archaeological finds confirm that the burial rites witnessed by Ibn Fadhlan were similar to those used in Scandinavia. The following is a shortened version of his eye-witness account:

When a chieftain dies, slaves and servants are asked who will die with him. The one who volunteers cannot alter the decision. In this particular case it was a woman who was treated with great courtesy while the burial was being prepared. On the day of the funeral the chieftain's ship was drawn up on land and people walked around it and said words. A bier was placed on it and cloths and cushions laid on it by an old woman called the Angel of Death. She was responsible for the preparations. The dead body which up to now had been laid in a grave was taken up and dressed in splendid garments specially made for the occasion. He was seated among the cushions in the tent on the ship, with alcoholic drink, food, aromatic herbs and all his weapons. Then a dog, two horses, two cows, a cock and a hen were killed and placed in the ship.

The woman who was to die went round to each tent in the camp and had sexual intercourse with its owner. After this she performed various other rituals. She was raised three times above something which looked like a door frame and said: 'I see my master sitting in paradise, and it is beautiful and green and with him are men and slaves [or youths] and he calls me. Lead me to him.' Then she killed a hen and was taken to the ship, took off her jewellery, drank two beakers and sang, and was finally taken into the tent to her dead master by the Angel of Death. Six men followed her into the tent and had sexual intercourse with her, then she was killed. The closest relatives of the deceased now lit the firewood under the ship. Others threw more flaming brands on the fire and within one hour everything was burnt. Then they built a mound on the spot and raised a pole at its centre with the name of the chieftain and his king on it, and went away.

In Scandinavia graves were often placed close to farms so that people could maintain contact with their ancestors. In the villages there was often a communal cemetery in an open area nearby. The graves were marked by a pole, stones, a stone setting of various kinds (such as small ship-settings), or by a mound. Rune stones are not usually associated with graves, as they were memorial stones, raised in places where many people passed by.

The prestige of a large, costly burial obviously reflected on the family, and many aristocratic graves were marked in grand style by large mounds as at Borre, Oseberg and Gokstad in Norway, Skopintull on Adelsö near Birka in Sweden, and Jelling in Denmark. The north mound at Jelling (p. 163), Denmark's largest burial mound, was raised to King Gorm, the first king of a new dynasty and the country's last pagan king. In the 950s he was laid to rest in a large burial chamber with a horse and riding equipment, a silver cup, carved and painted wooden objects, a chest and many other things which have almost totally disappeared.

CONVERSION

When Christianity became the official religion in the Scandinavian countries, some people were already Christians, and most had heard of the new faith. Everywhere the king supported its introduction. Many Vikings on military expeditions, trading voyages or diplomatic missions in Europe and the Byzantine Empire had seen churches and monasteries, listened to bishops and priests, and had understood some of the traditions and precepts of the Christian faith. They had been impressed by the awe-inspiring stone cathedrals, moving ceremonies, glorious singing and great riches (which they sometimes stole). They had witnessed the respect paid by mighty kings and emperors to Almighty God and his son Christ.

Many Vikings were baptized abroad, some of them several times, for baptism was often a condition in a political alliance or in a propitious peace treaty, and the ceremony meant new clothes, a baptismal gift and a baptismal feast. Some Scandinavians received the *prima signatio*, the sign of the cross, as a first step towards conversion. This was often useful in relations with Christians, for example in trade, but did not preclude worship of the old gods. Others had become familiar with Christianity from friends and relatives who had emigrated to Christian countries such as England, Ireland and Normandy, where the immigrants quickly accepted the local faith. For several centuries before the conversion, there had also been Christian traders and diplomatic envoys in Scandinavia, as well as missionaries.

So throughout the Viking Age there were Scandinavians who professed the Christian faith sincerely, and others who had included Christ in the large pantheon of Scandinavian gods, and even made sacrifices to him on certain occasions.

The first missionary we know of is the 'Apostle of the Frisians', Willibrord, who tried in vain to convert the king of the Danes, Ongendus, at the beginning of the eighth century. Ebo, Archbishop of Reims, preached in Denmark in 823 and is said to have baptized many people. His actions were presumably part of the political support given to King Harald Klak by Louis the Pious, Emperor of the Franks. Harald Klak was the first Scandinavian king to be baptized, with his family and attendants, in 826 in Mainz. The event was celebrated at a splendid ceremony in the imperial palace in Ingelheim.

Ansgar, somewhat misleadingly known as the 'Apostle of the North', travelled back to Denmark with Harald Klak and was active there until the king was exiled in 827. A few years later the Svear asked for a missionary and Ansgar travelled to Birka with rich gifts, which were stolen on the way. He worked there for some years with the king's permission. Around 850 he was on an active mission in Denmark, here too with the king's approval. He died as archbishop of the newly established see of Hamburg-Bremen, which became the centre of the Scandinavian mission and then the head of the Scandinavian church until 1103, when an archbishopric was established at Lund in Skåne.

Ansgar's mission concentrated on the great trading centres of Birka, Hedeby and Ribe, where there were already Christians or where Christian traders visited. Many people were baptized and churches were built. Permission for bell-ringing was granted in Ribe and Hedeby, although the pagans did not like it. However, the Life of Ansgar points out that official recognition of Christianity and the possibility of attending church services encouraged international trade, so this was undoubtedly a strong reason for royal support of missionary activity in these places.

Ansgar's activity in Scandinavia aroused a pagan backlash on several occasions, and in the second half of the ninth century the political climate appears not to have favoured missions. In the 930s Archbishop Unni travelled to Birka to continue the Church's work and in 934 the Danish king is said to have been forcibly baptized after his defeat by the German king Henry the Fowler. By 948 there are references to bishops of Schleswig (Hedeby),

Ribe and Århus, who must have been missionary bishops whose task was to travel around and preach the Gospel.

Christianity now spread northwards and eastwards. More and more bishoprics were established as peoples and countries accepted the new faith, though the process was interrupted by pagan reactions in Norway and Sweden. The converted were baptized. Baptism was a dedication to Christianity but sometimes did not take place until the death-bed – several Uppland rune stones were raised in memory of men who died 'in white clothes' (*í hvítavaðum*), the garment worn during baptism and for a week afterwards.

What was the appeal of Christianity, and what were the methods of its missionaries? Christianity was above all a victorious religion. That God and Christ were strong and good helpers could be seen in the power and splendour of churches abroad and in pictures of the triumphant Christ. The impotence of the old religion was revealed when missionaries destroyed sanctuaries and did not suffer retribution. It may also have seemed appealing to have a single god rather than the many who often proved to be of no use. In these violent times the Church preached peace and mercy to others, and good missionaries practised these qualities in their way of life, by redeeming prisoners of war and slaves, for example, and giving alms to the poor. They also preached non-violence and man's equality in the face of God. They stressed that it was a person's own actions that decided whether they did well in life and came into 'light and paradise', as it says on an Uppland rune stone; it was not the thread of the Norns, nor Odin's arbitrary decision. In the one true realm of the dead all would meet again if they had lived as they ought.

For the Viking kings the new faith meant the strengthening of central power, in the short as well as the long term, as the Church was centrally organized and traditionally very dependent on the king. The priesthood took over the cult functions of the local chieftains, which weakened their power. The break in tradition also made it easier for kings to impose new social rules and new methods of government. Furthermore, Christianity encouraged peaceful relations with the rulers and inhabitants of other Christian countries – if Cnut the Great had been a pagan, he would never have been accepted as king of England. Official acceptance of Christianity prevented other countries from using the dissemination of the one true faith as a basis for military expansion and the conversion of a country by its own king might be enforced without undue pressure.

To be successful the missionaries needed to be familiar with local ways and customs and able to preach in the local language. They normally sought permission from the king or local lord and it is mentioned several times that they brought them rich gifts and held great feasts. They were treated as guests and were given a form of guest protection. Christian documents praised missionaries for their sincere preaching of the Gospel, their piety, learning, good sense in daily life, chastity and good deeds. That they lived according to their teaching impressed the pagans. On a purely practical level, they often bought boy slaves in order to bring them up in the Christian way of life, and acquire acolytes.

As Christianity is an exclusive religion, it was considered important to destroy pagan sanctuaries. There are many accounts of this in Norway and Sweden, and it probably also happened in Denmark. Adam of Bremen tells a story about the pious Bishop Adalward, who did missionary work among the Svear in Sigtuna around 1060. He agreed with Bishop Egino from Skåne that they would travel together to Uppsala to destroy the temple there, for 'if it was torn down, or preferably burned, the conversion of the whole nation might follow'. But Sweden's Christian king, Stenkil, who had invited Adalward to Sigtuna, dissuaded them from their plan by explaining that it would result in their condemnation to death by the Svear, his own exile and the relapse into paganism of those who were already Christians.

The two bishops then travelled among the Götar and 'broke up idols and thereafter won many thousands of pagans to Christianity'. The Christian faith had already gained a sound foothold there, so the risk of revenge was not as great.

THE INTRODUCTION OF CHRISTIANITY

The Saxon Widukind provides us with an almost contemporary account of how Harald Bluetooth and Denmark were converted

THE INTRODUCTION OF CHRISTIANITY

The Saxon Widukind provides us with an almost contemporary account of how Harald Bluetooth and Denmark were converted around 960 – the exact year is unknown. The priest Poppo (who does not appear to have been sent from the Hamburg-Bremen archbishopric) performed a miracle which demonstrated that Christ was greater than all the other gods: he carried a large piece of red-hot iron in his bare hand without coming to any harm. 'After this trial the king was converted, decided to worship Christ as sole God, commanded his pagan subjects to reject the idols and accorded from then on due honour to the priests and servants of God.' Harald's motives, however, must also have had a practical, political basis – a desire to strengthen his royal power and to avoid conflict with the German realm.

The change of religion came about peacefully, as far as we know. King Harald's large Jelling monuments, which combine pagan and Christian structures in a magnificent unity, imply that there was a gradual and tolerant transition. The date and significance of all the Jelling monuments are not clear, but one of the oldest must be the small rune stone raised by King Gorm

Plan of the Jelling complex, Jutland, Denmark. The contour lines indicate a height difference of 0.5 m. There have been many excavations here and many interpretations have been put forward over the years.

A Bronze Age mound. B and C rows of large standing stones found under the South Mound. D and E small excavations where standing stones or traces of stones were found (approximate locations). F six large stones, possibly standing on the original ground level. G burial chamber. H North Mound. K South Mound, the x indicating the post in the centre of the Mound. L traces of roof-bearing posts in the earliest building below the present church. M King Harald's rune stone. N outline of the present church. O King Gorm's rune stone, whose original location is not known. P the extent of the churchyard in 1861. Q the extent of the churchyard today. R area excavated inside the mound during large-scale investigations in 1942. King Harald's rune stone stands at the mid point of a line (S) connecting the centre of the burial chamber in the North Mound and the post in the centre of the South Mound.

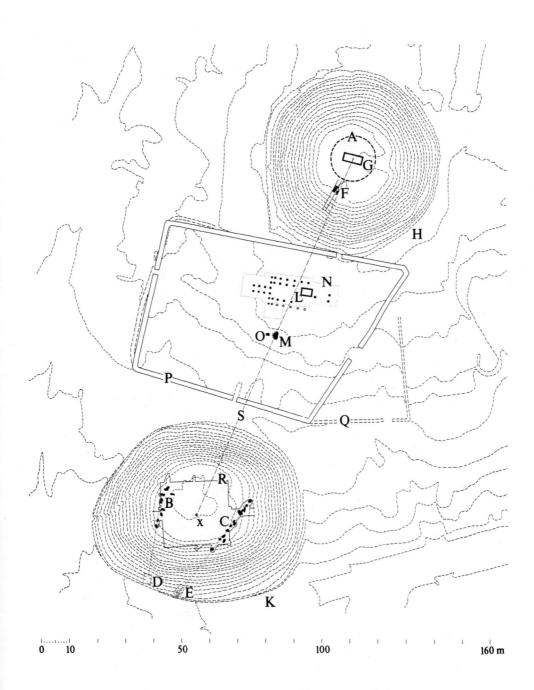

Plan of the Jelling monuments, Denmark.

mound, raised over King Gorm, today stands some 8.5 m high
and 65 m across. Dendrochronology has dated the timbers from
the burial chamber to 958 or 959.

The south mound is even larger than the north mound but
does not contain a grave; its purpose is unknown. It lies above
the southern part of the stone setting and presumably destroyed
it. It was built in the 960s, according to dendrochronology, at the
very end of the pagan era or the beginning of Christian times. It
may have been a memorial mound, or public functions may have
been performed on its large flat top. It was certainly a symbol of
power. Mounds are traditionally regarded as pagan, but this may
have been an exception.

After the introduction of Christianity, the Jelling complex was
radically altered. Precisely half way between the centre of the
two mounds King Harald raised the most magnificent of all
known rune stones, in memory of his parents and himself (see
p. 12 and Pl. 18). His conversion of the Danes to Christianity
is mentioned in an inscription below a large figure of Christ.
Immediately north of the stone he had a large wooden church
built, at least 30 m long and 14 m wide, with an important grave
at the eastern end of the nave.

Excavations in 1976–9 revealed that the grave contained most
of the bones of a man who had first been buried elsewhere, as
well as gold threads and two exquisite strap-mounts from the
cloth in which the loose bones had been gathered. It is very likely
that the skeleton is that of Gorm. Harald must have had his
father's remains transferred from the pagan burial mound to the
new church, both to Christianize him and to create retrospective
continuity. The burial chamber in the north mound did not
contain any human bones when it was examined in the nineteenth
century. It was clear that the chamber had been disturbed a long
time before, but the hole in the ceiling had been carefully repaired,
so it could hardly be a case of common robbery. Furthermore,
the two strap-mounts from the grave in the church are very
similar in style to objects found in the mound (Plate 20).

In the church there was room for another grave alongside the
one that has been found. Harald presumably intended to be buried
here himself, in a family sepulchre on a par with royal mausoleums
in churches abroad, but as mentioned earlier, Harald died after a

revolt led by his son Svein Forkbeard and was buried in Roskilde, in the first church built on the site of the present Roskilde cathedral. Kings are buried here even today. Jelling lost its importance, but a church still stands between the mounds, the fourth to be built on the site.

Norway's first Christian king was Hákon Aðalsteinsfostri. He grew up and was baptized in England and remained a Christian after he became king of his native pagan country c. 935. According to the scalds, he did not destroy sanctuaries, but he brought priests from England and churches were built in the coastal area of western Norway. Further north and in Trøndelag Christianity did not take root. When Hákon was killed c. 960 he was interred in a mound in traditional pagan fashion; the scald Eyvind describes his last great battle, his death and his reception in Valhalla in the poem Hákonarmál. Ironically, this poem about a Christian king gives some of the best information about Odin's realm of the dead.

Olaf Tryggvason became the next Christian king of Norway when he returned home c. 995 with much silver after many years abroad. He had also been baptized in England and brought clerics back with him. A systematic and ruthless process of conversion was initiated in conjunction with efforts to unify the realm. The greatest success was in western and southern Norway and around the year 1000 Olaf was responsible for the conversion of Iceland, probably under threat of reprisals. Shortly after this he was killed in battle.

The conversion of Norway was completed during the reign of Olaf Haraldsson. He had also become a Christian on expeditions abroad and his baptism is said to have taken place in Rouen in Normandy. On his return to Norway in 1015 clerics were again in the royal retinue, among them the bishop Grimkel, who helped Olaf mercilessly impose Christianity on the people. The old sanctuaries were destroyed, people had to choose between baptism and strife, and Christianity was made obligatory at the Moster Thing, possibly in 1024, when edicts prescribing the Christian way of life were issued.

The battle of Stiklestad, where Olaf met his end in 1030, was not caused by religion but by his equally ruthless attempts to unify the kingdom. He was acclaimed as a martyr, however, and his body was taken to Trondheim a year later. He became the primary saint of the Vikings and was worshipped over an area that stretched from Russia to Ireland, and the church in which he was buried in Trondheim had become a centre of pilgrimage as early as the second half of the eleventh century; he remained a popular saint throughout the Middle Ages.

The political situation in the eleventh century meant that ecclesiastical influence in Denmark and Norway came largely from England, to the chagrin of the archbishops of Hamburg-Bremen.

The conversion of Sweden is poorly documented. The year or an event which marks the change of faith is not known. The new faith gradually penetrated the country, first in Västergötland, where Skara became the seat of a missionary bishop around 1020. Besides the mission from the Catholic archbishopric of Hamburg-Bremen, the Orthodox church probably had some influence for a time. As in the rest of Scandinavia in the late Viking Age the Swedish kings supported Christianity, although we know that a local chieftain was active in the conversion of Jämtland, between Sweden and Norway, in the eleventh century. He had a stone raised in memory of his good deeds on the small island of Frösö, named after the god Frey. The inscription reads: 'Östman, Gudfast's son, had this stone raised and this bridge made and he had Jämtland made Christian. Åsbjörn made the bridge. Tryn and Sten cut these runes.'

The first Christian king of Sweden was Olof Skötkonung, king of the Götar and the Svear at the beginning of the eleventh century. His successors were all Christians, but the old and the new faiths coexisted for almost a century. Paganism flourished, especially in the lands of the Svear, even in the time of Adam of Bremen, but at the same time there was a large group of Christians, who raised most of the many rune stones in the area. It is not known when the cult in Uppsala was abandoned, but Sweden must have been predominantly Christian by the beginning of the twelfth century.

Christianity brought completely new rituals, beliefs and rules of conduct, such as baptism, church services, bell-ringing, burial in consecrated churchyards without grave-goods, a belief in one God (or the Trinity), very strict regulations about marriage with relatives, while exposing unwanted children, eating horseflesh and worshipping the old gods were prohibited.

In many parts of the countryside, however, the old peasant traditions and sites associated with fertility in the house, field and stables lived on, either in secret or in a Christian guise. It took several generations before a network of churches, parishes and bishoprics covered Scandinavia. The acceptance of Christianity was epoch-making, but its implementation took a very long time.

Östman's rune stone on Frösö in Jämtland, Sweden. Part of the inscription reads: 'he had Jämtland made Christian'. The stone was raised in the middle or second half of the eleventh century, and is the most northerly rune stone in Sweden.

ART AND POETRY

The art of the Vikings was full of vitality, imagination and self-confidence. Decorative and pictorial art as well as poetry flourished throughout Scandinavia and had a character all their own.

As an art form, poetry survived the longest. Even in the first half of the thirteenth century it was treasured in court circles in Scandinavia. Icelanders were particularly skilful poets then, and Snorri Sturluson's book about the art of poetry, *Edda*, written around 1220 gives a key to understanding the complicated conventions of scaldic poetry. Without Snorri's explanations, much of it would be incomprehensible today.

There is no such key to the equally complicated conventions of decorative and pictorial art, so although we can appreciate them visually, we only rarely understand the meaning. Having said that, much of the art was presumably purely decorative, fascinating in its elegant interplay of lines and its forcefulness.

DECORATIVE AND PICTORIAL ART

Viking Age art was flamboyant in its use of contrast and colour, yet formal. Great care was lavished on details as well as the overall design. On high-quality pieces the ornamentation is often so minute that it can only be seen at close quarters.

Ornamentation survives mainly on a wide range of functional objects: clothes, brooches, ships, weapons, sledges, harnesses, buildings, memorial stones, wall-hangings, cups and much else. Three-dimensional art occurs most often in the form of heads, usually animal heads embellishing objects of varying sizes, such as wagons or caskets. The most common materials must have been textiles and wood but very little of these survives. The pictorial tapestry and the many carved wooden objects from the Oseberg grave, together with the wood carvings from the second half of the eleventh century, re-used in the mid-twelfth-century church at Urnes in western Norway (Plate 23), demonstrate what has been lost. Apart from those on Gotland, memorial stones were not decorated until after the middle of the tenth century, probably taking Harald Bluetooth's Jelling stone as a model. There are quite a number of decorated stones from the late Viking Age, some in Denmark and Norway, but most in Sweden. Plenty of small decorative metal objects survive, especially in graves and hoards, from throughout the Viking Age and from nearly all of Scandinavia. Gold and silver items were obviously greatly treasured and presumably set the fashion, but carvings in walrus ivory, whale bone and elk horn were also prized. The most magnificent examples of such carving are the Bamberg and Cammin caskets, which were further embellished with gilt bronze mounts and survived as reliquaries in churches in Germany and Poland. The large, house-shaped Cammin casket disappeared during the Second World War, but descriptions, photographs and good casts survive. Bone and amber, as well as jet from the north-east of England, were also carved.

The effects of relief, of contrasting materials and colours, and of the interplay of light and shade on blank and decorated fields were exploited. A piece of jewellery, for example, might be made of gilded bronze with details in silver and niello; an iron stirrup might be decorated all over with patterns of silver and copper contrasting with the black iron.

Traces of paint on shields, furniture, tent poles, rune stones and building timbers have been found so often that most large objects of stone and wood must have been painted, often to emphasize decoration that had been incised or carved in low relief. Painting is also mentioned in scaldic poetry and other written sources, such as inscriptions on some Swedish rune stones which record that they were once painted. The usual colours were black, white and red, but brown, yellow, blue and green were also used. The surviving colours are faded and partly dissolved, but those that can be reconstituted come up strong and bright. Garments and household textiles were often dyed.

The dominant motifs of Scandinavian art are stylized animals, some of which can be traced back to the fourth and fifth centuries, the end of the Roman period, and continued to be adapted throughout the Viking Age. Snakes and birds, ribbon plaiting and interlacing were also used. Plant ornament was rare until the mid-tenth century, but flourished in the next century under the influence of European art.

Very few representations of people survive, but, unlike the highly stylized animal and plant ornament, they are often semi-naturalistic. They occur primarily on memorial stones, such as the Gotland picture stones, where the scenes probably have religious significance (Plate 15), as with the Oseberg tapestry. A popular motif in the rich pictorial world of Gotland is a ship under full sail, with shields along the gunwale and manned by warriors, perhaps on the journey to the underworld. Other scenes show a horseman welcomed by a woman offering a drinking-horn – perhaps his reception in the underworld – and a battle between men with drawn swords. The scenes can rarely be identified today with any certainty, but a few from the pre-Christian pantheon, and from legends of great heroes, have been identified with the help of surviving literature. This is the case with the god Thor's fishing expedition (p. 151), and the exploits and downfall of the hero Sigurð Fáfnisbani (slayer of Fáfnir). Christ, of course, is easily recognized by his cross halo and his stance with outstretched arms.

When deciphering complicated animal ornament it is best to start with the head and follow the curves of the body and limbs. In tracing the development of art through the three centuries of the Viking Age various styles can be distinguished. Most are named after the place where a good or famous example of the style was found. Apart from the Borre and Jellinge styles, which were virtually contemporary, they developed from and succeeded one another.

Work is in progress to refine definitions of styles and their dating, and to established foreign influences, how Scandinavian artists created innovations and the interaction between art in Scandinavia and that in its colonies. A number of questions about

The story of the hero Sigurð Fáfnisbani carved on the rock at Ramsund
in Södermanland, near Eskilstuna, Sweden, in the eleventh century.
The runic inscription mentions bridge-building and the monument
was raised by a woman named Sigrið. The pictures illustrate scenes
from the legend: at the bottom, Sigurð kills the dragon Fáfnir, whose
body forms the rune band. Above stands his horse Grani; to the left
Sigurð cooks Fáfnir's heart. He has got some dragon-blood on a finger,
which he puts in his mouth – by tasting dragon's blood he understands
the song of the birds. These sit on the tree on the right and warn him
that Regin the smith is treacherous. He lies on the far left with his
tools but minus his head, for Sigurð has listened to the birds and killed
him.

art in the early Viking Age, where there are only a few certain
datings, are still open to discussion, but most scholars agree on
the main features.

Style E is the name given to the art of the late eighth century
and part of the ninth. This style developed out of the pre-Viking
Age animal styles A–D, all part of the so-called Style III. Wood
carvings from Oseberg, including one of five posts with a three-
dimensional animal-head terminal, and twenty-two small cast
gilt-bronze bridle mounts from a man's grave in Broa on Gotland,
are some of the finest examples of Style E.

Style E is characterized by long, at times almost ribbon-shaped,
animals or birds, with small heads in profile and large eyes; their
curved bodies widen evenly, and intertwining limbs dissolve at
the junction with the body into open loops with tendrils. Fre-

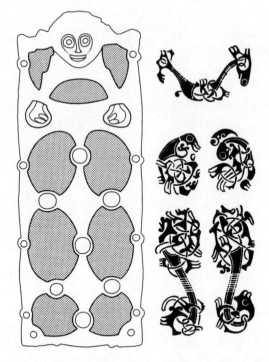

Cast gilt-bronze bridle mount from Broa on Gotland, Sweden, with typical Style E ornament. Height 9 cm. Left: the mount's outline and its division into fields. Right: the complicated animal ornament which fills the fields. National Antiquities Museum, Stockholm.

quently a framework is imposed on the animal's harmonious, flowing lines, which divides the surface into fields. One variant of the Style E animal is more compact, and a completely new motif, the gripping beast, makes its appearance in Scandinavian art with Style E. It is a vigorous, well-fed, fairly naturalistic animal or person, with the head seen full face, its feet gripping everything within reach. This motif has European predecessors but it so appealed to the Scandinavians that it remained popular for 200 years.

The Oseberg finds are probably from the first half of the ninth century, but they have not yet been precisely dated by dendrochronology. The many decorated wooden objects have been divided into several groups, each with its own artistic character, probably because they are the work of different, and not necessarily exactly contemporary, artists. The master of another of the five posts with animal-head terminals introduced innovatory features such as a multitude of animals and birds of equal importance, instead of one main motif. Some scholars think that this is a significant enough development of Style E to justify giving it its own name: the Oseberg style.

In southern Scandinavia there was a contemporary variant of Style E known as Style F, probably short-lived. This was inspired by Anglo-Frankish art disseminated on the Continent by Anglo-Saxon missionaries, and flourished around the mouth of the Rhine, among other places. Style F shows that the Scandinavians had connections with Western Europe even before the first documented Viking expeditions. The animals of this style are generally small, compact and coherent, with the motifs covering the entire surface within delineated fields.

Gilt-bronze mounts from the excavated mound at Borre near Oseberg belong to the succeeding style, the Borre style (see Plate 19), whose motifs are considerably easier to decipher than those of Style E. The Borre style probably developed in the second half of the ninth century at the latest and survived until the end of the following century. A completely new and characteristic motif was the compact ribbon interlace with inset geometric figures, known as the ring-chain. This consists of a pair of two-strand plaits which where they overlap are covered by a lozenge-shaped motif alternating with a grooved cross band. The ribbons frequently terminate in a small animal head viewed from above. Another important Borre motif is a single, contorted gripping beast, with a long curved neck and a long thin body which twists back across the neck at a point just below the head. A third important motif is a compact, semi-naturalistic animal.

A typical Borre ornament thus has a compact composition of ribbon and animal shapes. The flow of the lines is often emphasized by additional lines; geometric shapes are common and filigree and granulation, or cast imitations of these, were now popular on jewellery and other decorative objects. The Borre style was the first Scandinavian style to be used in the Viking colonies, as finds from Iceland, the Isle of Man, England and

Russia demonstrate. The Scandinavians were becoming established here by the time the style matured in Scandinavia in the late ninth century.

The Jellinge style overlaps with the Borre style but again it is not known when the style began. It was flourishing by the mid-tenth century but may be quite a lot older. It died out before the year 1000. The animals on the silver cup, only 4.3 cm high, from the burial mound at Jelling are a good example of this style (Plate 20). Two s-shaped ribbon animals are symmetrically intertwined, their heads are seen in profile, and each has a long pigtail and a lip-lappet. The animals of this style are often surrounded by or intertwined with ribbon interlace, and foliage-like shoots may sprout from them. Two strap-mounts with animal heads found in the grave in Jelling's first church are also in the Jellinge style. As with the Borre style, filigree and granulation, or cast imitations, were often used. The Jellinge style is also known from Russian and English finds, and an interesting Anglo-Scandinavian style arose in northern England with strong Borre and Jellinge elements.

Ornament on the small silver cup found in the burial chamber in the North Mound at Jelling (see also Plate 20). National Museum of Denmark, Copenhagen.

The Mammen style is splendidly represented by the ornament on an axe buried with a rich man in Mammen, central Jutland, in 970 or 971 (Plate 21). The axe has a powerful bird on one face, and a vigorous tendril ornament on the other in silver wire inlay. This style is clearly a development of the Jellinge style and it is sometimes difficult to differentiate the two, although in the Mammen style animals and birds are given bodies, and the plant ornament is given new significance. There is no symmetry here but unprecedented vigour and movement. The style is a magnificent synthesis of Scandinavian and European art, the latter inspiring the often semi-naturalistic animals and plants. It must have arisen around the mid-tenth century and flourished until *c.* 1000.

The main monument decorated in this style is the huge rune stone at Jelling, which features a great rampant animal entwined by a snake (Plate 12). Other fine examples are the Cammin and Bamberg caskets mentioned above and a cross in Kirk Braddan, Isle of Man (p. 219), but the style was not much used in the British Isles, perhaps because of the political circumstances at the time.

The Ringerike style, which succeeded the Mammen style around the turn of the century, is full of speed and movement (Plate 22). Western European influence increased, for example from the Winchester style, which flourished in southern England under Cnut the Great, and plant ornament became ever more important compared to birds and animals. The main motifs are a large animal in a dynamic pose (presumably a development of the animal on the Jelling stone), snakes and ribbon-animals, masses of tendrils and foliage sprouting vigorously from the animals or growing on their own. Most Ringerike-style works are composed around an axis and small tendrils are often arranged in groups. The style is named after a group of fine memorial stones made of sandstone from the Ringerike area north of Oslo.

A superb example of the Ringerike style is the weathervane from Heggen in Buskerud, Norway, which depicts a large animal on one side and a blazing, feathered bird on the other. A stone slab inscribed with runes from a grave in the churchyard of St Paul's, London, is another fine example. Several other finds decorated in this style come from southern England but it is better known in Ireland, where it became so popular that it developed independently. It was even used for Irish church art and survived longer there than in Scandinavia, where it flourished until the mid-eleventh century.

The Urnes style is the last phase of the long development of Scandinavian animal ornament (Plate 23). This seems to have developed shortly before the middle of the eleventh century and was popular for a century, that is into the early Middle Ages.

After a final phase where it gave rise to details or influences in Romanesque art, now predominant in Scandinavia, it died out completely around the year 1200. Many other forms of Viking Age culture followed the same course.

The vigour and vitality of the Ringerike style gave way to this sophisticated, elegant, indeed almost decadent, style. It is named after the exquisite wood carvings that were re-used in Urnes church in western Norway: a portal and a door, two wall planks, a corner post and two gable ends, one complete (Plate 23). A far more ordinary example of the style is a carved and painted plank from Hørning church in Jutland, dated by dendrochronology to the late eleventh century. The large, four-legged animal is still one of the main motifs, but it has become as slim as a greyhound. Snake-like animals with one foreleg, snakes and thin tendrils sometimes ending in a snake's head are also featured. The designs characteristic of this style form open, asymmetric patterns, creating an impression of an undulating interweaving of animals and snakes. The large loops are often figures-of-eight and the shapes grow and diminish evenly; there are no abrupt transitions. The style is also used with virtuosity on large numbers of rune stones in central Sweden, where the undulating ornament follows the shape of the stone and the long bodies of the snakes are used as rune bands. In Sweden the name 'rune-stone style' is therefore often used instead of Urnes style. A few examples of the style have been found in England, and in Ireland it became as popular as the Ringerike style.

The development of Viking art has been outlined with reference to great works of art which are often executed in costly materials, but the same aesthetic ideals can be seen on much more ordinary objects made of all sorts of cheaper materials. The art styles, perhaps with the exception of the Mammen style, were common to the whole of Scandinavia and to all levels of society. Together with language, religion and much else, they must have contributed to a feeling of Scandinavian identity.

The great works of art and the innovations of style must have been produced by craftsmen working for kings, chieftains and, in the late Viking Age, the Church. Innovation spread rapidly, presumably because many craftsmen travelled to markets and trading stations, or served the aristocracy for a time and came across foreign art abroad or through imported goods. Copying was an accepted and widespread practice, and it was technically easy for artist-craftsmen to produce a series of almost identical objects in bronze, silver or gold, such as oval brooches for women's garments and jewellery with filigree ornament.

Craftsmen and artists were both known as *smiðr*, sometimes compounded with the word for the material or object with which they worked, for example *trésmiðr* (tree-smith, carpenter). Skilled weapon-smiths and 'ship-smiths' were highly regarded, but the status of jewellery-smiths and most other craftsmen is not known. The only people who signed works of art in the Viking Age were rune-stone artists, and mainly in the Mälar region of Sweden in the late Viking Age. Some have an impressive output to their name and worked in quite a large area. Åsmund Kåresson's signature appears on more than twenty stones, Fot signed eight stones, and Öpir around fifty. Stylistic details of a large number of other rune stones indicate that Öpir or other named rune carvers were responsible for them too.

Besides the formalized art, a number of graffiti pictures have survived. As with graffiti of all ages, they are swiftly incised on any suitable material or object, just like rune jottings. They give lively and impressionistic sketches of what touched the heart and the mind – elegant ships are a frequent motif.

POETRY

In many other parts of this book, poetry has served to illuminate historic events, religion, ethics and much else. This section gives a short introduction to the transmission of the poems, their social framework and formal features. Metre, style and vocabulary are what make the impatient reader shy away from eddaic poems and scaldic verse, but they enchant and enrapture those who penetrate their formal and conceptual world and learn to hear the steady rhythm of alliteration.

Scandinavian Viking Age poetry can be divided into three categories according to their transmission and contents: rune poems, eddaic poems and scaldic verse. The rune poems are preserved on rune stones and a few other objects from various parts of Scandinavia, especially Sweden; they date from *c.* 970 to 1100. They are usually brief poems praising named men, composed in a simple metre and style. A stone in Hällestad in Skåne from *c.* 1000 bears this common formula: 'Äskil placed this stone in memory of Toke, Gorm's son, his gracious lord'. Then follows the poem:

Saʀ flo œigi	He fled not
at Upsalum	at Uppsala.
Sattu drœngiaʀ	'Drængs' set up
œftir sinn broður	after their brother
stœin a biargi	the stone on the rock,
støðan runum.	stayed with runes.
þœir Gorms Toka	To Toke Gorm's son
gingu nœstir	they marched closest.

In metre and style, but not content, most rune poems resemble the eddaic poems. These are about ancient Germanic or Scandinavian heroes and their deeds, or about pagan gods, and are preserved in a few manuscripts from the thirteenth and fourteenth centuries written in Iceland (p. 13). The authors are anonymous and it is difficult to tell whether many of them are from the Viking Age or later. Where they originated is also uncertain. They do, however, allow us to identify stories portrayed in some of the Viking Age pictures. This is the case with the story of Sigurð Fáfnisbani, which is about courage, great deeds, gold, treachery, love and fate, and the story of Thor fishing for the World Serpent. Such legends and myths were popular in the Viking Age.

The stanza form of the eddaic poems is also found among the rune poems and a unique rune stone, the impressive ninth-century Rök stone in Östergötland in Sweden, includes in its long inscription a superb stanza from a poem presumably about the ancient hero of central Europe, Þiðrik of Bern. All this implies that a corpus of poems about gods and heroes existed in the Viking Age, cognate with those in the Icelandic eddaic manuscripts, and with the same form, style and metre.

Most scaldic poems survive through the Icelandic sagas, written down at the end of the twelfth century and in the thirteenth century (p. 12–13). Here long poems are often split up into single stanzas and inserted in various places to support the prose narrative. As a result it is often difficult to establish the structure of the poem as a whole. The essence of scaldic poetry is public praise of named kings and chieftains, composed by named scalds on specific occasions. In contrast to the eddaic poems, scaldic poetry celebrates contemporary events which can often be placed in a historical context, so many of the poems can be dated fairly precisely and are thought to have been faithfully transmitted by word and memory, even though many years elapsed before they were written down. They usually have a complicated metre and are composed in an elaborate style that presupposes great knowledge on the part of the audience if they are to be understood. This, and the fact that scaldic poetry was regarded as the noblest of all art forms, has undoubtedly contributed to the preservation of so many stanzas. A single complete scaldic stanza survives in written form from the Viking Age, on the rune stone at Karlevi on Öland, dating from c. 1000.

From all this it appears that there was no strict distinction between rune poems, eddaic poems and scaldic verse. It must also be emphasized that most surviving verse was written down late in Iceland, and that many of the scaldic poems we know were composed by Icelanders, frequently in Norway. No Viking Age poetry from Sweden is preserved in medieval manuscripts. In Denmark, although such poetry is included in Saxo's Gesta Danorum (the exploits of the Danes) of c. 1200, it is translated into elaborate Latin, and sometimes even re-composed in hexameters and thus completely transformed.

In spite of the very uneven transmission, it does appear that poetry was part of the common Scandinavian culture: that content, structure, metre and diction were valued not only in Iceland and Norway but all over Scandinavia. Much of the rich store of poetry which survives in Icelandic tradition can thus be used to shed light on matters relating to the Scandinavian Viking Age. The poems illustrate the sense of form and stylistic ideals characteristic of the period. Some contain good accounts of history and prehistory, and the vocabulary is often archaic. Many Viking Age phenomena can only be described precisely in words with recourse to the old vocabulary in Norse poetry, and many features of warfare and navigation, for example, are best understood in the light of the diversity of expressions in the eddaic and scaldic poetry.

Poems were good entertainment. The origin of the Old Norse word for poet, *skáld*, is uncertain, but it was known already in the early Viking Age and it appears on a couple of rune stones. The art of poetry was not the sole prerogative of men, for we know that around 930 Jórunn Skáldmær (Jórunn poetry maid) was active in Norway. Scaldic poetry was by far the most difficult genre and, as mentioned above, was given particular respect. Many scalds were members of a king's or chieftain's retinue and were often highly trusted. Their task was to praise him, to preserve his memory and his deeds and to increase his fame by performing the poetic art for an audience – often at his great hall. The ability to improvise was an essential qualification; there are examples of a verse being composed in dramatic situations, such as on the battlefield.

Some of the eddaic poems may have been created by scalds. As experts in the art of poetry they might also have been asked to recite eddaic poems during an evening's entertainment at the court. In the saga of St Olaf, written *c.* 1230, Snorri Sturluson describes a somewhat different reason for declaiming an eddaic poem. In the early morning, prior to the fateful battle of Stiklestad in 1030 when King Olaf was killed, he asked his court poet Þormóð Kolbrunarskáld to recite a poem. This became the eddaic poem *Bjarkamál* about the great battle of the heroic king of ancient times Hrólf Kraki and his loyal men. Þormóð recited so loudly that the entire army awoke and many thanked him for the poem, which was so well suited to the occasion and boosted their morale. The poems of the eddaic genre, normally easily understandable, and often with exciting plots, were undoubtedly known outside court and warrior circles too.

Scandinavian poetry shares several features of Germanic poetry, including the frequent use of alliteration, but it differs in that it was divided into stanzas and there was usually a fixed number of syllables in each line. The ideal was to have only a few syllables to the line. These qualities of brevity and conciseness, and the particular metres and style of scaldic poetry, are not found elsewhere. The earliest preserved scaldic poems probably date from the end of the ninth century and much indicates that the most notable Scandinavian metres and the scaldic style were created in the early Viking Age.

The two main metres of the eddaic poems are *fornyrðislag*, 'the old words metre', and *ljóðaháttr*, which may mean 'the magic songs metre', even though only a fraction of the surviving poems deal with magic. *Fornyrðislag* is also used in nearly all the rune poems, for example in the stanza from the Hällestad stone mentioned above. It was used in some scaldic verse, but was not much favoured in this genre. *Ljóðaháttr* is very rarely encountered outside the eddaic poems.

Fornyrðislag has a stanza of eight short lines, each with two stressed syllables and a number of unstressed syllables (mostly two). Pairs of lines are linked by alliteration to make one long line. The alliteration in the first part is usually contained in two words, and in the second part in one word in the first stressed syllable. The stanza is divided into two halves, each of which forms a whole.

This metre will be demonstrated by the third stanza of the poem *Vǫluspá* (*The Song of the Sybil*). The stanza is about the era before the creation of the world and Ymir is a figure from pagan mythology. The alliterating words are printed in italics and the rules of alliteration are that consonants alliterate with similar consonants, while all vowels alliterate with one another. Snorri Sturluson recommends in his handbook for scalds that the alliterating vowels should preferably differ from each other.

Ár var *alda*,	When Ymir lived
þat er *Ymir* bygði	long ago
vara *sandr* né *sær*	was no sand or sea,
né *svalar* unnir;	no surging waves,
iǫrð fannz *æva*	nowhere was there earth
né *upphiminn*,	nor heaven above,
gap var *ginnunga*,	but a grinning gap
enn *gras* hvergi	and grass nowhere.

Ljóðaháttr has a pair of lines that alliterate according to the same rules, followed by a third line with two or three stressed syllables which alliterates within itself but not with the other lines. Normally a stanza consists of two sets of three lines. The most important differences between the two metres are that in *ljóðaháttr* the stanza has six and not eight lines, and that line three and line six alliterate only within themselves. All surviving examples of *ljóðaháttr* are in the form of direct speech. The poem *Hávamál* (*The Speech of the High One*) is a good illustration of this metre. A translation of some stanzas appears on p. 62f, including the stanza quoted here in Old Norse with the alliterating words printed in italics:

Deyr fé	Kine die,
deyia frœndr	kindred die,
deyr *siálfr* it *sama*;	every man is mortal:
en *orðztírr*	but the good name
deyr *aldregi*	never dies
hveim er sér *góðan getr*	of one who has done well

The metre most used in scaldic poetry is the *dróttkvætt*, 'the heroic metre'. The stanza is eight-lined, each line with six syllables. Three syllables in each line must be stressed, and the penultimate syllable of the line must be long as well as stressed, while the last syllable must be unstressed. The lines are linked in alliterating pairs as in the *fornyrðislag* and the first line of such a pair must have two alliterating syllables. All lines must have internal rhyme. A *dróttkvætt* stanza is thus very demanding metrically. It may be illustrated by one composed by the Icelander Egil Skallagrímsson *c.* 925 when he served the English King Athelstan:

> Hrammtangar lætr hanga
> hrynvirgil mér brynju
> Hǫðr á hauki troðnum
> heiðis vingameiði;
> rítmœdis knák reiða
> ræðr gunnvala bræðir
> gelgju seil á galga
> geirveiðrs, lofi at meira.

A *dróttkvætt* stanza falls into two parts, each of which is a unit, but the word order bears no relation to that of normal prose or speech, which does not make for immediate understanding. In prose the first four lines of this poem would read:

Brynju Hǫðr lætr hrammtangar hrynvirgil hanga mér á hauki troðnum heiðis vingameiði.

In addition scaldic poetry uses a great deal of circumlocution, based on myths of gods and legends of heroes, which often have the nature of riddles and can only be solved by a knowledgeable audience. Such conventions were integral to the art of scaldic poetry. This is why Snorri included stories of gods and heroes in his handbook for scalds, and he classified the two major forms of circumlocution as *heiti* and kennings. *Heiti* is the simpler of the two and can be found in poetry the world over. A synonym, often a rare and artful word, is used instead of a normal word; archaic words, or established synonyms for the names of gods, are typical.

Kennings are used far more extensively in scaldic poetry than in any other form of poetry and are the most characteristic feature of scaldic language. A kenning consists of two elements: a basic word and a determinant; the latter is either in the genitive or it forms the first element of a compound with the basic word. The determinant can itself be a two-word kenning, so a circumlocution can consist of four or five elements. Scaldic poetry has several thousand examples of kennings, among them 'the sea of the wound' or 'the sweat of the sword', meaning blood; 'the feeder of the raven' – warrior; 'the horse of the waves' – ship; 'the field of the golden rings' – woman; 'the flame of the Rhine' – gold; 'the burden of the dwarves' – the heavens. The last two examples can only be understood if it is known that the great gold treasure of the Völsungs, which Sigurð won from the dragon Fáfnir, ended up at the bottom of the Rhine, and that the heavenly vault was held aloft by dwarves.

Because of the complex metres of scaldic poetry, the abnormal word order and the many subtle and pregnant circumlocutions, it is impossible to be faithful to the art of scalds in translation. Besides, there are often several possible interpretations. In order to understand a typical scaldic verse, such as Egil's stanza cited above, it is important to know the background to how it came to be written. The stanza occurs in *Egil's Saga*, written in the thirteenth century. According to the saga Egil and his brother Þórólf had taken part in a great battle on King Athelstan's side, but Þórólf was killed. Afterwards at a feast in the king's hall Athelstan sat in the high seat and Egil in the place of honour in the middle of the bench opposite. Both men had their swords placed across their knees. Egil was very angry and full of grief. After a time the king removed a large gold ring from his arm, placed it on the point of his sword, got up and walked across the floor and proffered it to Egil across the hearth. Egil got up and walked over to it, pushed his sword into the ring, withdrew it and returned to his place. He put down the sword, received the drinking-horn and declaimed the verse.

Here is an almost literal translation of the stanza, with an explanation of the kennings in parentheses, but with the word order changed to that of normal prose, without regard to the metre:

Hǫdr of the mailcoat [the warrior, the king] lets the halter of the arm [ring] hang on my hawk-trodden [where the hawk sits] hawk-gallows [arm]; I know how to make the pin-string [arm-ring] of the shield-tormentor [sword; i.e. the gold ring] ride the gallows [sword] of the spear-storm [battle]. The feeder of the battle-hawk [warrior, the king] enjoys the greater praise.

In plain English the meaning of the stanza is: 'The warrior lets the ring hang on my arm; I know how to make the ring ride the sword; the warrior (Athelstan) enjoys the greater praise'. The kennings with their circumlocutions evoke the battle and the death which are the real reasons for Athelstan giving Egil the gold ring. Hǫdr in the first line was one of the gods and the brother and slayer of the virtuous god Baldr; the catastrophe is already glimpsed here.

It is unfortunate that justice cannot be done to the sophistication of scaldic poetry in translation. Nevertheless the poet John Lucas has captured much of the form and tone of Egil's poem in his free translation:

> It was the warrior's
> work, to hang this gold band
> round an arm where hawks ride
> ready to do my will.
> And see how I make my sword
> summon the ring to *its*
> arm. There's skill in this. But
> the prince claims greater praise.

THE EXPANSION

Stone cross in Anglo–Scandinavian style in Middleton Church, North
Yorkshire, England, tenth century. Height 106 cm. (Schematic
drawing with a reconstruction of the right arm of the cross.) The cross
was made after the major conquests and settlements of the Vikings. On
the stem is a warrior with a helmet and a belt round his waist in which
a large knife is fastened. On his left are a shield and an axe, and on his
right a spear. The reverse is decorated with a large ribbon animal in a
kind of Jellinge style. The cross is a good example of the widespread
rural art, which was not always of high artistic merit.

Background and Beginnings

The foundations of modern Scandinavia were laid in the Viking Age. Never before had so many decisive changes taken place in such a short space of time, and never before or since have Scandinavians played so great a role abroad. This lies at the heart of the Viking myth. They moved easily and with familiarity from Limerick in the west to the Volga in the east, from Greenland in the north to Spain in the south. They appeared in many guises: as pirates, traders, extortioners of tribute, mercenaries, conquerors, rulers, warlords, emigrating farmers, explorers and colonizers of uninhabited regions.

Good sailing ships and formidable seamanship allowed them to travel vast distances and assured much of their military success, based on surprise attack and mobility. They were familiar with many cultures, through long association with neighbouring peoples (Frisians, Saxons, Slavs, Balts, Finns, Lapps), and this must lie behind their exceptional adaptability. But what were the causes of this immense wave of outward activity?

Ever since the Viking Age the answers that have been given often reflect the cultural problems of the period and the circumstances in which the questions were posed. The cleric Dudo in Normandy, for instance, writing *c.* 1020, thought that the great Viking expeditions against his part of the world were the result of over-population in the homeland *Dacia*:

these people who insolently abandon themselves to excessive indulgence, live in outrageous union with many women and there in shameless and unlawful intercourse breed innumerable progeny. Once they have grown up, the young quarrel violently with their fathers and grandfathers, or with each other, about property, and if they increase too greatly in number, and cannot acquire sufficient arable land to live on, a large group is selected by the drawing of lots according to ancient custom, who are driven away to foreign peoples and realms, so that they by fighting can gain themselves countries where they can live in continual peace.

Half a century later Adam of Bremen wrote that Norwegians became Vikings due to poverty and he also boasted that Christianity had made the wild Danes, Norwegians and Swedes cease their Viking expeditions. Before that they could merely

in barbarism gnash their teeth, but have now long since learned to intone Alleluia in the praise of God. Behold that piratical people, by which, we read, whole provinces of the Gauls and of Germany were once devastated and which is now content with its bounds and can say with the Apostle, 'For we have not here a lasting city, but we seek one that is to come.'

In thirteenth-century Icelandic literature the idea prevailed that emigration from Norway *c.* 900 took place as a reaction to royal tyranny and Harald Finehair's efforts to unify the realm. It was in the thirteenth century, after all, that the king of Norway finally gained supremacy over Iceland, hitherto independent.

There is presumably some historical basis for the last explanation, for contemporary sources mention that chieftains, sons of kings or pretenders to the throne left their homelands because the opportunities were better abroad or because they were exiled. It is doubtful, however, whether Dudo's explanation contains any truth, and the cleric Adam's opinion that the Viking expeditions were caused by barbarism, which could be cured by Christianity, is of course merely wishful thinking.

Many Scandinavian scaldic poems and rune stones claim that honour and loot were the main driving forces for the Viking expansion. West European written sources indicate that the Vikings first sought easy money, and then in time trading bases and land to dominate and inhabit. Scandinavia was changing rapidly and many people cut their ties with their homeland and stayed abroad for varying periods. From the 840s armies wintered abroad and in many places bands of soldiers with a long Viking career behind them were the first to settle abroad, as in Normandy and England. Others eventually returned home with their acquired wealth and used it to build up power and status, as King

Harald Harðráði did in Norway. There were also expeditions based firmly in the homelands, for kings and chieftains needed good income in order to pay their followers and retain their power; or a king might send an expedition to back up his foreign policy, or to conquer a country, as when Svein Forkbeard invaded England in 1013.

The expansion must furthermore be seen against the background of Scandinavia's many connections with Europe even before the Viking Age. The whole of Northern Europe had seen great economic growth during the eighth century, including the establishment of trading centres along the coasts and rivers of Western Europe and England and in the Baltic regions, as well as the opening up of trade routes in Russia. By the year 800, when the Viking expeditions gathered momentum, there was a large network of trading centres such as Quentovic on the river Canche near Boulogne; Dorestad on the Rhine; Hamwih (the precursor of Southampton), London and York in England; Ribe, Hedeby, Kaupang and Birka in Scandinavia; and on the south and east coasts of the Baltic, Ralswiek in Germany, Wolin and Truso in Poland, Grobin in Latvia, and Staraja Ladoga in northern Russia on the route to the large eastern trading centres. Far more goods were being traded than before, which meant there was far more to plunder or demand as tribute, in Scandinavia as well as elsewhere.

The political structure of these areas was comparatively loose and unstable. Byzantium was a major power but the kingdoms of Western Europe and the British Isles underwent many changes. England was not united until 954, and Charlemagne's immense empire was divided among three of his grandsons in 843, twenty-nine years after his death, following a long period of unrest. These kingdoms changed several more times before the end of the century. In Russia a large stable realm was established some time during the ninth and tenth centuries under a Scandinavian dynasty. The Vikings were adept at exploiting the changing balance of power. Rumours of opportunities for obtaining gold and silver, quick profit and new land spread fast, and Scandinavia itself was as vulnerable as other regions.

In 1971 the English historian Peter Sawyer may have come close to the truth when he described the explosive outward activity of the Viking Age as an extension of what had been normal in the preceding era but had now become much greater and more profitable because of special circumstances. Besides the development of suitable ships, and the economic growth and exploitation of internal strife mentioned above, the expansion must have been fuelled by a spirit of adventure, self-confidence and fatalistic attitude engendered by social conditions in Scandinavia. Life was at stake and Viking expeditions and emigration became a way of life for many people.

A rune stone was raised *c.* 1040 at Gripsholm in Södermanland in Sweden to one of the many men who accompanied the Swedish chieftain Ingvar on his unsuccessful expedition east and south to Serkland (the land of the Saracens, which presumably means the Arab Caliphate). The expedition became legendary, although Ingvar is known only from rune stones raised in memory of other people, and from far later Icelandic annals and a saga. The inscription at Gripsholm reads 'Tola raised this stone in memory of her son Harald, Ingvar's brother,' and ends in a poem:

> They fared like men
> far after gold
> and in the east
> gave the eagle food.
> They died southward
> in Serkland.

A better fate was enjoyed by one Skarðe, in whose memory a stone was raised at Hedeby by King Svein Forkbeard around 1000:

King Svein placed this stone in memory of Skarðe, his household-man, who had fared westward [i.e. on an expedition to Western Europe or England] and now met death at Hedeby.

The man who carved this gleeful verse on a silver neck-ring some time in the late Viking Age may have got off scot-free:

> We went to visit the Frisian lads
> And it was we who split the spoils of war.

The neck-ring was hidden on the island of Senja, north of the Arctic Circle, with another neck-ring and two chains, one with a cross and the other with large Eastern pendants.

The violence of many Viking raids must not obscure the fact that the Vikings also enjoyed peaceful relations with the world around them, based on accepted norms for social behaviour and on special agreements. International trade, towns and trading centres flourished. Diplomatic contacts were established by official visits abroad, and foreigners visited Scandinavia, among them the missionaries. Many Viking armies maintained such tenuous contact with their homelands that no king or chieftain in Scandinavia could be held responsible for their actions, which probably explains why Alfred the Great, king of Wessex, was prepared to receive Ohthere from Hálogaland in Norway at his court c. 890, even though the Vikings still constituted a major threat.

Not all the Scandinavians who settled abroad came as conquerors with sword in hand. They settled in the uninhabited North Atlantic regions, and in other areas they were sometimes just one of a number of foreign peoples. Many Vikings joined the armies of foreign princes, and some chieftains achieved high rank. In Western Europe and the British Isles Christianity had to be accepted before any such office could be held and in order to marry a nobleman's daughter. Religion was the most important cultural distinction between Scandinavians and foreigners.

The Vikings' acts of aggression often had catastrophic results on a local level, but they have frequently also been blamed for disasters that were caused by strife between local lords and rulers. Rival Irish groups, for example, were just as capable as the Vikings of plundering and burning each others' monasteries. In fact, wherever there was internal strife one of the parties usually enlisted the support of the professional and mobile Viking bands, and several dissatisfied chieftains or pretenders to a throne joined a Viking army to fight the lawful ruler of their own country. In some areas the Vikings were only active for short periods, and they were not the only ones to intervene in the affairs of European countries: the Moors from Spain and the Magyars from Hungary both undertook military expeditions.

One of the reasons for an exaggerated view of the destruction caused by the Vikings is the estimated sizes of armies and fleets given in the documentary sources. They are normally given in round figures, and are often wildly exaggerated for literary reasons or because of nationalistic fervour. For example, the

Annals of St Bertin give an account of the expeditions of King
Horik of Denmark to the Elbe in 845, and maintain that 600 ships
were sent (one Scandinavian warship could probably hold around
fifty men); the priest Abbo relates that the Viking army outside
Paris in 885–6 consisted of 40,000 men, while the defenders of
the city numbered a mere 200, sometimes less; Regino's Chronicle
states that only 400 Vikings of a total of 15,000 returned to their
fleet after Alain of Brittany's victory in 890.

Many armies or *lið* probably consisted of 100–200 men, but
sometimes several armies gathered together to swell their
numbers, as must have happened in England in 865–80. The
armies which conquered the whole of England at the beginning
of the eleventh century were obviously huge, and in the 840s,
when the going got tough in many different places, vast numbers
of Vikings must have been on the move.

The Vikings were portrayed as exceptionally blood-thirsty and
cruel, but this must have been due to contemporary reactions to
their pagan religion. Plundering heathens who kill vast numbers
of people are mentioned in many contemporary Christian sources,
but Christians also plundered and killed each other with great
alacrity. Viking ferocity was greatly magnified in the Scandinavian saga literature and histories written in the Christian era.
The classic example of Viking cruelty is the practice of carving
the eagle on a victim's back, the 'blood eagle'. This was in fact
invented during the twelfth century, probably as the result of a
misinterpretation of a complicated scaldic verse, which says that
King Ælla was killed by Ívar (the scene was the Viking conquest
of York in 866). This developed into an exciting story to the
effect that Ælla had the figure of an eagle carved into his back.
In even later stories 'eagle-carving' develops into a pagan ritual
associated with Odin, in which the victim's back is cut open, the
ribs bent outwards and the lungs pulled out, so that it is remi-
niscent of an eagle. This literary pagan sadism has fascinated
many.

The Viking raids became a serious threat to Western Europe
and the British Isles at the end of the eighth century. The Anglo-
Saxon Chronicle relates that the first ships with 'Danish men'
(undoubtedly meaning Vikings) came to England in the days of
King Brihtric of Wessex (786–802). There were three ships and

when the king's reeve rode down to greet them and asked them to accompany him to the royal manor, thinking they were merchants, they killed him. By 792 King Offa of Mercia was organizing the defence of Kent against 'seagoing pagans with roaming ships'. In 800 Charlemagne inspected the defences he had built along the northern coast of the Frankish realm to the Seine, an area threatened by pirates.

In 793 came the attack which has traditionally been taken as the start of the Viking Age, the sack of the monastery on Lindisfarne, off the coast of Northumbria. The Anglo-Saxon Chronicle described it thus:

In this year dire portents appeared over Northumbria and sorely frightened the people. They consisted of immense whirlwinds and flashes of lightning, and fiery dragons were seen flying in the air. A great famine immediately followed those signs, and a little after that in the same year, on 8 June, the ravages of heathen men miserably destroyed God's church on Lindisfarne, with plunder and slaughter.

The learned Alcuin of York, who was in charge of Charlemagne's court school in Aachen, was shocked by this disaster and wrote letters to England with injunctions to lead a virtuous life in order to avoid divine punishment, which must have been the cause of the Viking attacks. He wrote to King Æthelred of Northumbria:

Lo, it is nearly 350 years that we and our fathers have inhabited this most lovely land, and never before has such terror appeared in Britain as we have now suffered from a pagan race, nor was it thought that such an inroad from the sea could be made. Behold, the church of St Cuthbert spattered with the blood of the priests of God, despoiled of all its ornaments; a place more venerable than all in Britain is given as a prey to pagan peoples.

By 795 the Vikings had worked their way round Scotland and reached the island of Iona, where they sacked the ancient monastery of St Columba, and all the way to Ireland. In 799 the monastery of St Philibert on the island of Noirmoutier at the mouth of the river Loire was plundered. In the period following, there was often interaction between Viking activities all over the British Isles and between these and the expeditions on the

Continent and colonizing expeditions to the North Atlantic islands and regions.

The settlement of Iceland began around 870. The Faroes may have been colonized rather earlier, while Greenland was not settled until *c*. 985, from Iceland. Vikings from Greenland reached America around 1000.

In the east, people from central Sweden and Gotland had settled on the east coast of the Baltic before the expeditions westwards started. During the ninth century Scandinavian communities were established in several parts of Russia and on the south coast of the Baltic. There were contacts with Byzantium and with the Caliphate, and expeditions to areas as far south as the Black Sea and the Caspian.

THE MAINLAND OF WESTERN
EUROPE

HISTORICAL EVENTS

The first recorded attack on the mainland of Western Europe took place in 810. It is mentioned in the Frankish Annals and was directed at Frisia, which was for many years a focus of Viking ambitions. This raid was undoubtedly a political move: in 808 Godfred had ordered the building of his border wall (see p. 135); (see p. 135)

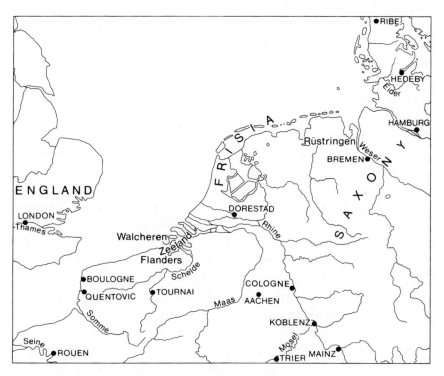

Western Europe

the following year negotiations had broken down, a Frankish fortress had been built on the border, and Charlemagne was planning a military expedition against Godfred. The size of the Viking fleet is given as 200 ships, Frisia was plundered and 100 lbs of silver was paid as a tribute. The emperor then gathered an army and camped by the river Weser, where he waited for Godfred and his army. But Godfred was killed by one of his own men and his successor made peace with the emperor. Charlemagne died in 814 and was succeeded by his son Louis the Pious.

The first recorded pirate attack (apart from the plundering of St Philibert's monastery on Noirmoutier in 799) took place in 820. According to the Frankish Annals, the fleet consisted of thirteen ships, which first tried their luck in Flanders but were repulsed by the coastguards. Then they attempted a raid at the mouth of the Seine but had to withdraw. Only when they arrived in southern France on the coast of Aquitaine were they able to seize good booty. The coastal defences, organized by Charlemagne, had proved effective.

Later on another form of coastal defence came into being: Viking chieftains were granted regions by the mouths of great rivers in return for providing protection against pirates, and becoming Christians. The prelude to this was when Harald Klak was granted Rüstringen, at the mouth of the river Weser, which formed the border between Frisia and Saxony, in fief in 826. Harald was one of three Danish kings at the time and had long been the Franks' man, but his position at home was insecure and Rüstringen was a place of retreat in case he was exiled. This did occur the following year, and soon he was one of several Viking chieftains exploiting the power struggles in the Frankish Empire.

Louis the Pious was in open conflict with his three sons Lothar, Louis and Charles. In 833 he was captured and deposed by them. They could not agree with one another, so their father regained formal supremacy but he did not manage to unite the nobility. The defences of the empire broke down and the Vikings streamed through: Dorestad was sacked in 834 and again in 835, 836 and 837. Dorestad, on one of the arms of the Rhine, was one of Northern Europe's greatest trading centres and an important link in the Scandinavian foreign trade network with connections with Hedeby and Birka. In 838 King Horik of Denmark sent diplomatic messengers to the emperor denying any responsibility for the sacking and making it known that he had captured and killed the leaders of the pirates who had committed the devastation. In return he laid claim to Frisia, but this was refused.

The rebellious Lothar and Harald Klak were no doubt the perpetrators of these and other raids in the area. Building fortresses to defend the empire certainly claimed much of Louis the Pious' time until his death in 840 and prevented the solution of other problems. The Annals of St Bertin record the following for the year 841:

To Harald [i.e. Harald Klak] who with the other Danish pirates for a number of years, to his [Lothar's] advantage, had done so much damage to Frisia and other coastal countries of the Christian world in order to harm his father [Louis the Pious], he gave for this service the Walcheren and the neighbouring places in fief ... A deed which certainly deserves every abhorrence that people who had brought evil on to Christians were placed in charge of Christian countries and people and of Christ's church.

This was a magnificent gift, since from the island of Walcheren, now in The Netherlands at the mouth of the great rivers Rhine, Maas and Schelde, an immense trade could be protected, controlled and exploited. Two years later, in 843, the great Frankish Empire was formally divided into three. Lothar was given a strip from Italy to Frisia; Louis the German got the East Frankish kingdom from Saxony to Bavaria; and Charles the Bald got the West Frankish kingdom.

By this time Viking expeditions had become a lucrative source of income for many people and the tide could not be stopped. The first recorded expedition to southern England took place in 835, a year after Dorestad was first sacked. Many followed and in Ireland the plundering escalated dramatically. The monastic community on the island of Noirmoutier, a trading centre for salt and wine from the Loire, fled to a safer place. In 841 the Vikings sailed up the Seine, extorted much tribute and plundered Rouen. The following year Quentovic, a centre for trade with England, was sacked. Nantes, on the Loire, was plundered on St John's day, 24 June 843. The date was well chosen, as the town was crowded with people gathered for the feast day and its large markets. It was rumoured that this attack was made in collusion with a rebellious count who rejected Charles the Bald as his overlord and wished to secure Nantes for himself.

Lothar and Louis the German probably also made agreements with the Vikings from time to time, in order to weaken their brother Charles. The year 843 is the first recorded occasion of the Vikings overwintering on the Continent, at Noirmoutier; the Annals of St Bertin describe how the Vikings acquired houses from the mainland and settled in as if they were going to stay for ever.

The Vikings in Nantes are described as *Westfaldingi*, that is, the men from Vestfold, in southern Norway. Other armies are spoken of as Danish, but there were undoubtedly men from Sweden among them. The expeditions were now of an international character with fleets operating between various places on the Continent and in the British Isles, depending on the political situation and local defences. Charles the Bald's West Frankish kingdom was the main focus of the attacks, but the other realms were not exempt and the Vikings also penetrated the Mediterranean.

The year 845 was a fateful one. The region around the Seine was plundered. Paris, including the town's fortified centre on the Île de la Cité, was conquered and looted on Easter Sunday, 28 March; Charles the Bald paid the Vikings 7,000 lbs of silver to withdraw – the first of many payments to them. The Vikings did not get much joy from their 'heavy-laden ships', however. Their leader Ragnar (who brought back a bar from the city-gate of Paris as a souvenir) and almost all the others died in an epidemic on the journey, or at home, 'a judgement of God with the darkness of blindness and madness'. King Horik of Denmark, who had had Hamburg destroyed that year, also thought that divine forces lay behind the epidemic, and offered to release all Christian prisoners of war, possibly also to hand back the stolen treasures. He may therefore have shared responsibility for the great expedition to France.

The epidemic did not halt the further advance of the Vikings, however, and a joint mission to King Horik from the kings of all three Frankish kingdoms in 847 was of no avail, even though they threatened war. In the 860s the monk Ermentarius of Noirmoutier gave a graphic description of the calamities the Vikings caused:

The number of ships grows: the endless stream of Vikings never ceases to increase. Everywhere the Christians are victims of massacres, burnings, plunderings: the Vikings conquer all in their path, and no one resists them: they seize Bordeaux, Périgeux, Limoges, Angoulême and Toulouse. Angers, Tours and Orléans are annihilated and an innumerable fleet sails up the Seine and the evil grows in the whole region. Rouen is laid waste, plundered and burned: Paris, Beauvais and Meaux taken, Melun's strong fortress levelled to the ground, Chartres occupied, Evreux and Bayeux plundered, and every town besieged.

Towns, churches, monasteries and their inhabitants all fell prey to the Vikings. The rural population also suffered to some degree, for many official ransoms were paid to the Vikings by imposing taxes on everyone, 'also the poor', and the Vikings took booty and many slaves. In some places they stayed, although we do not know how long for. In 845 they 'settled peacefully in the country' – in Aquitaine. In 850 they were given land to settle on after plundering along the Seine because Charles the Bald sought the raiders' help against Lothar's imminent approach.

During this period several Viking armies were active; in 861 King Charles promised a large sum to an army led by a certain Weland in return for driving out another army, which had lodged itself on an island in the Seine. The beleaguered army, plagued by hunger and misery, also gave Weland much gold and silver and the joint forces then dispersed and camped for the winter along the Seine. The next year Weland joined Charles and was baptized and the great fleet sailed away. But in 863 Weland was killed by another Viking and Charles the Bald's policy of playing off Viking against Viking was abandoned for a time.

At a national assembly in Pîtres, south-east of Rouen, in 864 the problems of the realm were underlined by royal edicts banning nobles from seizing the horses and property of free men and thus preventing them from undertaking military duty for the king against the Vikings. The sale of horses and weapons to the Vikings was prohibited under penalty of death. The most effective defences against them, however, were fortified bridges across rivers and the refortified town walls and new fortresses that

Charles and his successors had built throughout the country. The Vikings' long siege of Paris during 885–6, so vividly described by Abbo, eventually had to be abandoned, but Charles could not protect the mouths of rivers and coastal areas, so here the armies made their bases.

Some of the Vikings' most famous expeditions went as far as the Mediterranean. The first documented expedition to Spain took place in 844. Seville was conquered as well as other places, but the Moors soon put the Vikings to flight. The most illustrious expedition was led by the chieftains Björn Jarnsiða and Hasting, who left the Loire in 859 with sixty-two ships, it is said, and did not return until three years later, having visited Spain, North Africa, the Rhône valley and Italy and captured fine booty and many slaves. Much of it they lost on their way back, but tales of their exploits travelled far and wide and are recounted in the contemporary Annals of St Bertin, in Arab sources and in late Norman and Scandinavian stories. In his work on the rulers of Normandy Dudo writes that the two chieftains conquered the small northern Italian town of Luna with great cunning, in the belief that it was Rome itself. The story is entertaining, but these well-travelled Vikings would hardly have made such a mistake. We know, however, that they made a winter camp in the Camargue in the Rhône delta and from here plundered deep into the country, and that in Italy they looted Pisa as well as other towns, among them perhaps Luna, which is only 60 km to the south.

In the year 870 the northern part of the central Frankish realm was divided between the East and West Frankish kingdoms. Charles the Bald's realm now reached the coastal regions around the Rhine and he immediately entered into an alliance with the Viking chieftain Rurik, who had had a firm grip on Dorestad and Frisia for a long time, and who may have been Harald Klak's nephew.

The policy of Lothar and his successors had been to safeguard the inland regions by agreements with Viking chieftains who established their bases at the mouths of rivers: Harald Klak had been given the Walcheren area in 841; when Rurik had begun to make incursions along the Rhine in 850, Lothar, unable to contain him, 'received him with the promise of loyalty and gave him Dorestad and other counties'. In 855 Rurik and a kinsman, Godfred, gained power briefly in a part of Denmark but had to return to Frisia and Dorestad.

The political trafficking that went on between the Frankish realms, Denmark and the Viking chieftains along the coast is far from clear, but on several occasions Frisia certainly gave shelter to pretenders to the Danish throne. They amassed silver, held high office, and, like other nobles in the Frankish realms, enjoyed a high degree of independence.

The Viking chieftains could not, or would not, prevent all attacks on an area. After the first raids in 834–7, Dorestad was again sacked in 846, 847, 857 and 863. The combination of these attacks, changes in the river course and a large flood led to the town soon losing its importance. Other parts of Frisia were also plundered. In 867 Rurik was expelled by Frisia's inhabitants and it was feared he would return with Danish reinforcements. He is last heard of in 873.

Charles the Bald died in 877 and the following eleven years saw five different rulers of the West Frankish kingdom and much internal strife. The expeditions gathered momentum again, having subsided during Charles' last years, when many Vikings had been busy in England. They continued to operate along the coastline, but the inland areas in Flanders and along the Rhine now suffered a great deal too. In 880, for example, Tournai and monasteries by the river Schelde were sacked, and in 881 the region between the Schelde and the Somme was attacked. In 882 the famous chieftain Hasting from the Loire plundered the coastal regions, and other Vikings burnt Cologne and Trier and a great many monasteries deep in the country along the rivers Maas, Mosel and Rhine. Charles the Fat, who assumed the title of emperor, then entered into an agreement with the chieftain Godfred, who was baptized and was granted Frisia and the other fiefs once held by Rurik. To other chieftains he gave gold and silver, part of the rich treasures of churches and monasteries.

Godfred, however, had greater ambitions. His wife Gisla was the daughter of Lothar II, and her brother persuaded Godfred to rebel against the emperor. According to Regino's Chronicle, a reliable source, he was promised half Charles' realm if the plan succeeded. Godfred sent a message to the Emperor informing

him that he would only adhere to his oath of fealty and defend
the borders of the realm against his compatriots on condition
that he was also given 'Koblenz, Andernach, Sinzich and other
domains of the emperor, because of the amplitude of wine, which
was there richly available, while the land, which he had received
by the Emperor's munificence, did not produce any wine at all'.
The argument of wine-producing districts had been employed
on many other occasions in the drawing up of borders and
granting of land in the Frankish Empire but in this instance
Godfred's real purpose was to obtain bases inland, or, if the
request was refused, to provide an excuse for rebellion. A large
reinforcement army was to be called in from Godfred's native
country (presumably Denmark), but the plan was discovered and
Godfred was killed in 885. This was the last time a Viking chieftain
was entrusted with Frisia.

Viking raids continued but fortresses were being built and
defences improved, which meant that by the end of the ninth
century the golden years were coming to an end. In 890 a Viking
army attempted to exploit internal strife in independent Brittany
but finally suffered defeat and went northwards. In 891 they were
defeated by the German King Arnulf at the Dyle, a tributary
of the Schelde, and that year some newly built fortresses are
mentioned. These may very well have been some of the large
circular fortresses on the coast of what is now northern France,
Belgium and Zeeland in southern Holland, among them Souburg
on the island of Walcheren. After some successful raids in 892,
the army took their property and families to England, presumably
with the aim of settling there. The Loire chieftain Hasting did
the same. But King Alfred's defences in England were effective,
and in 896 the army gave up and dispersed. Some went to the
Viking realms in East Anglia and Northumbria, others returned
to the areas they knew around the Seine.

There is not much information about the Vikings on the
Continent in the subsequent period, but some presumably lived
as before. The last recorded payment was made to them by the
West Frankish King Rudolf in 926. In Brittany, where the Vikings
had had considerable power for some years, they were decisively
defeated around 937. But in Normandy they could not be ousted.
Probably in 911, and certainly before 918, King Charles the

Simple resorted to the old dangerous stratagem of setting Vikings against Vikings. The chieftain Rollo and his men were given the town of Rouen and the surrounding region as far as the sea and possibly some way up the Seine. Rollo was probably also baptized. This became the basis for the Duchy of Normandy.

Throughout the tenth century the Western European kingdoms grew strong and the balance of power shifted. Denmark's southern border was threatened several times and overrun by the Germans. At the end of the century there were a few Viking raids on their old, profitable target of Frisia, but most of their energies were directed towards England. The Viking Age in Western Europe was over, except in Normandy.

ARCHAEOLOGICAL EVIDENCE AND THE SIGNIFICANCE OF THE EXPEDITIONS

Without written sources we would know very little about Scandinavian activity on the Continent. Only in Normandy are there place-names of Scandinavian origin and a certain amount of Scandinavian influence on the language. The archaeological evidence is very sparse: only a gold arm-ring and finger-ring from Dorestad, despite extensive excavations there; a woman's grave, with a pair of typical oval brooches from Pîtres near Rouen; a chieftain's burial in a ship on the Île de Groix off the south coast of Brittany, about 100 km north-west of Noirmoutier. Apart from this there is the odd weapon, including swords found in rivers, a graffito of a Viking ship from the Seine region, and a possible fortress in Brittany.

The chieftain on Île de Groix was buried according to Norwegian customs, but the grave-goods were a mixture of Scandinavian and Western European objects, which suggests that he had been away from home on expeditions for a long time. He was laid to rest here in the first half of the tenth century or a little later, with another person of unknown sex. He must have been one of the last Vikings in the area.

The defences that the Vikings often built, when in winter camp as well as on expeditions and on the battlefield, can only rarely be identified today, and most of them have completely disappeared. But the fortress Camp de Péran in Brittany, near St Brieuc, was presumably used by either Vikings or natives in the battles of the period. Scientific dating demonstrates that it was destroyed around the 930s when the Vikings were finally expelled from Brittany, and a coin found there was minted between 905 and 925 in the Viking kingdom of York.

Because of the enduring fascination of the Vikings, in the past the number of Viking finds was considered larger than is the case. The carved ornaments from ships' prows found in the river Schelde cannot be dated to the Viking Age, although Vikings did sail on that river. A number of so-called Viking finds from Holland have turned out to be fakes, and of the many swords found in rivers, which were once ascribed to Vikings, only about ten can be accepted as such now. Future excavations in Normandy, the Loire region and Frisia may reveal settlements, bases, camps and trading activities, as has happened in England, Scotland and Ireland. Documentary sources are virtually silent on these subjects. Indirect evidence of the Vikings may be gleaned from the many defensive structures built to keep them at bay, but identification is usually impossible without precise dating.

The impact of the Viking expeditions on Western Europe is difficult to assess, as they cannot be isolated from the many other causes of changes. The violent attacks, raids, killings and abductions were, of course, catastrophic for many individuals and small communities along the coast and the great rivers, and many people had to contribute to the large ransoms. Churches and monasteries lost their treasures and several monastic communities had to seek safety elsewhere. Some bishoprics were vacant for a time, among them Avranches and Bayeux west of the Seine, and in many places ecclesiastical organization collapsed. The Vikings doubtless also contributed to the political disintegration of the West Frankish realm, but they were only able to operate there because it was already in disarray.

Stories about the devastation of large areas, however, date from a later period and may be attributed to the fast-growing Viking myth. Most people in Western Europe were not much affected by the Vikings and for those that were, it probably made little difference whether they were plundered by Vikings or by a local faction involved in the interminable power struggles. In

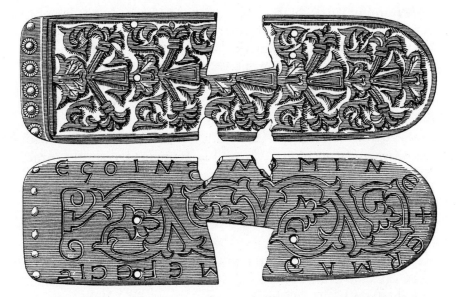

Frankish strap-end from *c.* 800, silver-gilt and niello, found on the island of Als, Denmark. The four drilled holes show that it had been made into a brooch. The Latin inscription on the reverse tells that the maker of the strap-end was a Christian by the name of Ermadus. Length 12.7 cm. National Museum of Denmark, Copenhagen.

Normandy, however, where a strong Scandinavian dynasty was able to extend and maintain its power, the Vikings had a decisive influence on political development, which was perpetuated by their descendants' conquests of southern Italy and England.

In Scandinavia the connections with Western Europe made a deep impact. There were many cultural influences, and many luxury goods, most of which were presumably acquired through trade. Belligerent activities are less visible there, even though the profits were immense and must have been of great significance. There is written information about official payments totalling 44,250 lbs of gold and silver during the ninth century. Other unrecorded payments must also be taken into account, as well as booty, the sale of slaves, and the ransom of prominent captives. A vast quantity of gold and silver must have been melted down and used for the many gold and silver objects made in Scandinavia, while more wealth must have been spent by the Viking armies in Europe.

A number of decorative silver mounts from Frankish sword equipment and other small objects have been found in Scandinavia, especially in Denmark, reminding us of the glorious expeditions in Western Europe, as do some rune stones. But the most magnificent testimony is the large hoard from Hon in southern Norway (Plate 6), which consists of 2.5 kilos of gold objects, a little silver and some beads. It includes a superb example of the art of the Frankish goldsmiths: a large trefoil mount with plant ornament in filigree, as well as Roman, Byzantine, Arab, Anglo-Saxon and Frankish coins, and other objects of native and foreign origin. The Hon hoard is thought to have been hidden in the 860s, when the expeditions were at their height.

NORMANDY

The chieftain Rollo and his descendants consolidated their power and extended their dominions in Normandy, a feat unmatched by other chieftains in Western Europe, and many Scandinavians settled in this rich and fertile country. Legends about the early rulers were written in the early eleventh century by the priest Dudo, but there are few facts. It is not even known whether Rollo was of Danish or Norwegian origin. Dudo says he was Danish, but later Norwegian-Icelandic literature claims he was the son of the Norwegian Earl Røgnvald of Møre, who was also the ancestor of the earls of Orkney. The fact that Rollo's daughter, Geirlaug, had a Norwegian name may indicate that he was Norwegian – the question has given rise to considerable debate.

The precise contents of the agreement with Charles the Simple, which Rollo is said to have entered into at St Clair-sur-Epte, and the underlying political circumstances are not known. But he was not given the whole of what was later to become Normandy. This was acquired in various wars in the tenth century and the dominion was subsequently confirmed by the Frankish king. The major conquests took place in 924 and 933. The first rulers are referred to as the Counts of Rouen. The first reliable evidence of the title duke occurs in 1006, during the reign of Richard II, Rollo's great-grandson.

The rule of the Rollo dynasty was far from secure in the first

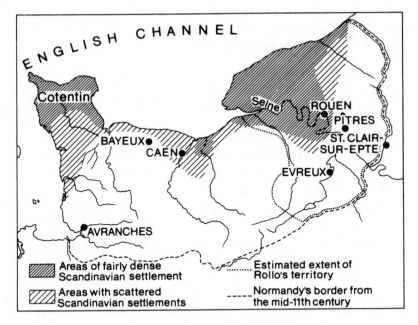

Normandy

century and a half. As in other Viking realms and fiefs, new bands of Vikings arrived seeking land and booty, and there were wars with the Frankish king as well as with neighbouring princes. The name Normandy (*terra Normannorum* or *Northmannia*), meaning the 'land of the Northmen', is not known before the beginning of the eleventh century. The border with France was clearly defined and fortified during the same century. The government became exceptionally strong and centralized and although the French kings had formal supremacy, Normandy retained a high degree of autonomy until it was conquered by the French king Philip August in 1204.

Rollo and his family must have seized a great deal of land in their new country, and the Vikings seem to have taken over and retained many of the existing Frankish institutions. The Archbishop of Rouen remained in office despite the many pagans who came to power. Rollo, and especially his son William Longsword, revived and strengthened churches and monastic communities with very large gifts. Both were buried in the cathedral in Rouen and it appears that most of the Vikings quickly became Christians. Rouen flourished, partly because trade was fuelled by Viking loot. The minting of coins was resumed here under William Longsword, with his name, not that of the French king, on the coins.

Actual Scandinavian influence is hard to establish. It was presumably strong at first but gradually decreased because of the powerful French framework. In the first half of the eleventh century interest in Scandinavian culture seems to have disappeared from the court in Rouen and command of the language too. Because French was chosen, the Scandinavian influence on the Norman language was therefore small and mostly relates to fishing and shipping. It is also significant that no ruler after Rollo had a Scandinavian name. Until 1106 they were called William, Richard or Robert, which became Rollo's Frankish name.

Place-names with Scandinavian elements reveal that Vikings came to Normandy from many areas: mostly from Denmark, but also from Norway, some Celtic-speaking areas and from England. Such place-names are found especially in the region between Rouen and the sea, which was the heart of the Norman area, along the coast and on the Cotentin peninsula. English Vikings, perhaps the group of men who went from England to France in 916, under the leadership of Earl Thurketil, established place-names around Bayeux, while the Celtic ones are concentrated in Cotentin.

There are a few place-names with the suffix -torp and some with the suffix -tot (= toft); the suffix -by is probably not present. Some place-names are purely Scandinavian but far more are compounds of a French and a Scandinavian element, especially the French suffix -ville and a Scandinavian personal name (nearly always a man's name) as the prefix. Quetteville is derived from Ketil, and Auberville from Ásbjørn. The most important function of the many new names appears to have been to demonstrate ownership. The Scandinavian words for natural features, such as brook, hill and grove, occur in a number of place-names; Etalondes, for example, is based on -lundr (grove). Such names help to show that many Scandinavian immigrants not only owned land but also got to know it and cultivate it.

Around 1020 the Normans began to involve themselves in the affairs of southern Italy and before the middle of the century they had become firmly established as rulers there. In 1066 William the Conqueror, Duke of Normandy (1035–87), became king of England, but he was a French Norman; the links with Scandinavia had been broken. Against the background of magnificent achievements, with powerful realms in Normandy, southern Italy and England, a literary image of the Normans as energetic, resolute and invincible conquerors, who ranged wide and had great organizational gifts, came to be created. This Norman myth has much in common with the modern Viking myth.

SCOTLAND AND THE ISLE OF MAN

Many of the Vikings who raided Lindisfarne, Iona and other places along the coasts of northern England, Scotland and Ireland at the end of the eighth century must have travelled via the Shetlands and the Orkneys, since these islands were on the route from Norway. The journey to Shetland from the west coast of

Scotland and the Isle of Man

Norway took about twenty-four hours with a reasonable wind. From there it was only a short way to the Orkneys and on to Caithness on the northern tip of the Scottish mainland. From here the route down the east coast of Scotland led to northern England, or the one along the west coast, the Hebrides and Iona led to the Isle of Man, Ireland and the west coast of England.

As in Norway, most of the route to the Irish Sea was in the lee of islands and skerries, where it was possible to disembark at night or in bad weather and to stock up with provisions. The journey from western Norway to Ireland was no longer or more difficult than the chieftain Ohthere's journey from northern Norway to *Sciringesheal* in Vestfold, which could be done in about a month. This means that Vikings could get as far as Ireland or northern England and back to Norway in a season, probably leaving in early May and returning at the end of September.

Norwegians settled on the Shetlands, the Orkneys, the Hebrides, the Isle of Man and other islands, as well as in several parts of the Scottish mainland. The land and climate were similar to those at home, but their interest in this area also lay in gaining access to Ireland and northern England, which became some of the Vikings' most profitable areas, as well as their links with Iceland. Merchant ships carrying many sought-after goods gave excellent opportunities for profit all along the route and there were also good raiding bases. The Orkneys occupied a strategic position and became the seat of a powerful dynasty of earls in the second half of the ninth century.

Apart from raids on Iona we have no certain information about when the Vikings reached Scotland and the Isle of Man or when they settled there. The inhabitants were all Christians, but they have left no surviving record of these events. Contemporary Irish and Anglo-Saxon sources give few details, while the earliest Scandinavian written sources date from the end of the twelfth century, more than 300 years after the events occurred; not surprisingly, they appear to be contradictory in several respects. *Egil's saga*, for example, from the first half of the thirteenth century, relates that many fled from Norway at the time of Harald Finehair and settled in uninhabited areas, among them the Shetlands, the Orkneys, Caithness and the Hebrides, whereas the late-twelfth-century Latin history of Norway, *Historia Norvegiae*, tells how the Norwegians had to defeat the inhabitants in the Orkneys. Archaeological investigations have confirmed that people did live there, and that their farms were often taken over and rebuilt by Vikings. This is unlikely to have happened peacefully and in Udal on North Uist in the Hebrides there are signs of unrest; several graves in Norway contain items of Scottish origin, which must have been acquired by plunder. We know that there were Viking raids in Iona in 795, 802 and 806, and by 807 the community in the monastery there had decided to move to Kells in Ireland. As Kells was situated a little way inland (north-west of Dublin), it was safer than the small island on the Vikings' sailing route.

Place-names and language show that the Scandinavians assumed total power in the Shetlands and Orkneys but it is not clear whether the native population was reduced to slavery or whether they merely lost what land and influence they had. It has also been suggested that they were exterminated or exiled, but finds from Buckquoy in Orkney show that this cannot have been the case everywhere.

Various Norse sources indicate that the dynasty of earls in the Orkneys came to power in the second half of the ninth century at the time of King Harald Finehair. But they also tell of Viking bases for raids both here and elsewhere, and the date for the formal establishment of the earldom is uncertain. *Orkneyinga saga*, from the end of the twelfth century, relates that Harald Finehair sailed westwards in order to chastise Vikings based in Orkney and Shetland who were plundering in Norway, and that on this expedition he subjugated not only these islands, but also the Hebrides and Isle of Man. On his way home he granted Orkney and Shetland as an earldom to Røgnvald, Earl of Møre, in western Norway. Røgnvald passed the title to his brother Sigurð, who extended his power over Caithness and several other areas on the Scottish mainland, and it later passed to Røgnvald's son Einar, the ancestor of the famed earls of Orkney. However, the saga no doubt projects many twelfth-century conditions back on to the ninth, and it is doubtful whether Harald Finehair ever undertook such an expedition. But the stories about the fate of Røgnvald's sons are excellent illustrations of how far the activity of a west-Norwegian chieftain family might have extended. According to the saga, Rollo won Normandy; Ivar was killed on Harald Finehair's expedition west; Einar gained the earldom of Orkney; Hallad, who had previously been the Earl of Orkney, failed to secure peace there and returned home; Þórir stayed at home and Hrollaug went to Iceland.

Many scholars have chosen to disregard the late written sources and believe that the Scandinavian settlement was established on Orkney and Shetland c. 800, and that the other Scottish areas and the Isle of Man were settled slightly later. The arguments supporting this view are the proximity of Norway, the need for a stepping-stone on the way to loot targets in northern England and Ireland and the contents of a possible grave on Arran. But, as mentioned above, these targets could easily be reached directly from Norway, and so far there is no archaeological evidence of a Scandinavian settlement this early. However, we do know that large numbers of immigrants, mostly from Norway, settled here in the ninth century. As elsewhere, there was a period of looting and the establishment of Viking bases before the farming settlements. The Pictish silver hoard, which was concealed in the early ninth century in a small church on St Ninian's Isle, off the south-west coast of Shetland, is presumably evidence of this. Many who lived here for a while went to Iceland or to other Viking colonies and settled there permanently.

There is a great deal of archaeological evidence of the Vikings' presence in Scotland and the Isle of Man, and Scandinavian influence here was strong and lasting. The original inhabitants spoke Celtic, except in south-east Scotland, where English was spoken, and the area was divided into several realms. There were Scots in Dalraida in the west; Britons in the south-west in Strathclyde; Picts on Shetland and Orkney and in the north and north-east of the Scottish mainland almost as far south as Edinburgh; Angles in the south-east, and Manx in Man. In the mid-ninth century the Scots extended their power eastwards, gaining dominion over the Picts, and later also southwards.

The distribution of Scandinavian place-names and graves, farms and hoards corroborates the later written sources and gives us a definite, though sketchy, picture of where the Vikings settled. It was primarily on islands and in coastal districts: Shetland, Orkney, Caithness, the Western Isles (more on the Outer than the Inner Hebrides), along the inlets of the west coast of Scotland and on the Isle of Man. There is even a grave on the small, remote island of St Kilda, west of the Hebrides. Many female graves, characterized by the typical bronze oval brooches, show that whole families settled.

There were no towns anywhere in Scotland or on the Isle of Man before the arrival of the Vikings and none developed there during Viking supremacy. The economic centres were York and Dublin, but there were important chieftains' and earls' seats. No coins were struck in the area during the Viking Age, apart from in the Isle of Man c. 1025–40, but many silver arm-rings have been found from the period c. 950–1050. They are of very simple design and weigh about 24 grams, which corresponds to the Scandinavian unit of weight, the *eyrir*. These were presumably used as 'ring-money' for trading in these communities, which had no coin economy. There are many hoards containing silver and some gold, but only a few date from the ninth and early tenth centuries; most are from the time when the Vikings were firmly established and Dublin had become the great trading centre of the West.

That Orkney was particularly wealthy is confirmed by the silver hoard from Skaill on the west coast of Mainland. This was hidden shortly after 950 and comprises large penannular brooches, splendidly ornamented in Scandinavian style, arm-rings, neck-rings, pins, bars, some hack-silver and twenty-one coins. The total weight of around 8 kilos (a little has been lost) is similar to that of the largest hoards known in Scandinavia.

The Orkneys are made up of some seventy islands and the Shetlands of around 100, though many are uninhabited today. Very few of the original Pictish place-names appear to have survived. Virtually all the names are purely Scandinavian: Egilsay (*Egils ey*, Egil's island), Westness (*vestr-ness*, west headland), Buckquoy (from *bygg*, barley, and *kví*, meaning a fold or pen). The language also became Scandinavian and the distinctive dialect, Norn, survived into the eighteenth century. Politically the Orkneys belonged to Norway right up to 1468 and the Shetlands until 1469, when they were given by King Christian I of Denmark and Norway to King James III of Scotland as security for the dowry of James's wife, the Danish princess Margrethe.

The islands have never been reclaimed, but Shetland's capital Lerwick (wick from the Scandinavian word *vík*) celebrates its Scandinavian background annually with a feast on the last Tuesday in January. This lasts the whole night and includes the burning of a large model Viking ship as a reminder of the burial of a heathen warrior. In its present form the celebration goes back to the end of the last century, but its roots are ancient.

Several Viking Age farms in Orkney and Shetland have been excavated. The classic example is Jarlshof, by a protected inlet on the southern tip of Shetland near Sumburgh. The splendid name, meaning earl's hall, does not go back to the Viking Age but was invented by Sir Walter Scott for his Viking novel *The Pirate*. The ruins are an impressive sight, with buildings from many periods, going back as far as the Bronze Age. The earliest Scandinavian farm was of the usual size, with a main building about 23 m long, a stable, a barn and some other outbuildings. Later it expanded.

The main occupation was agriculture, but in time fishing became more important here and elsewhere. Large fish-processing sites have been found in excavations in Freswick in Caithness. The vast quantities of fish landed here, among them cod of a size rarely found today, mean that it must have been a centre for commercial fishing, established while Caithness was Scandinavian, although it is not yet known whether it was during or just after the Viking Age.

In the late Viking Age Birsay on Orkney was particularly important. The Brough of Birsay is a small island in the Bay of Birsay; it is connected with the north-western coast of Mainland at low tide. There was a good view of the sea from the Brough and good protection against enemies. Excavations here have revealed that it was inhabited for a long period, but much has disappeared into the sea because of coastal erosion. Buckquoy lies on Mainland just opposite and both places had earlier Pictish buildings.

The Scandinavian farm complex on the island is extensive and comprises many large buildings. This may have been the seat of Earl Thorfinn, who died in 1065, and his immediate successors. *Orkneyinga saga* relates that Thorfinn ceased his piratical activities (this is not said of any of his predecessors) and around 1050 he made a pilgrimage to Rome. A bishop's see was established on

Orkney and after his return he built Christ Church as a cathedral in Birsay. The church ruins that can be seen on the Brough today, above the remains of an older church, have often been identified as Christ Church, but the ruined church probably dates from after Earl Thorfinn's time. It is possible that both Christ Church and the earls' seat were situated in Birsay on Mainland, not on the Brough. Less than 100 years later, however, the religious centre moved to Kirkwall on Mainland, where a large new cathedral, consecrated to St Magnus, the earl killed c. 1117, was commenced in 1136. Birsay was also abandoned as the seat of the earls.

It is not known precisely when the earldom of Orkney became Christian, for the saga account of King Olaf Tryggvason's forced conversion in c. 995 may not be reliable. It may have happened gradually here and elsewhere in Scotland, according to personal choice, during the tenth century, when pagan burial customs were abandoned (Plate 24) and Christian funerary monuments were adopted. For the aristocracy these may have been like the stone from Iona, decorated with a cross and inscribed with runes in a formula also well known in Scandinavia: 'Kali Ölvisson laid this stone over Fogl, his brother'. All the names are Scandinavian.

The Isle of Man occupies a highly strategic position in the middle of the Irish Sea. The island is only some 50 km long and 15 km across, but the wealth of Viking evidence here is unequalled in any other Viking colony. As with Scotland, there are hardly any written contemporary sources. *Chronicon Manniae et Insularum* (the Manx Chronicle), compiled in the thirteenth century, does not begin until 1066, with legendary accounts of Godred Crovan, who, having survived the fateful battle at Stamford Bridge, came to Man and by 1079 had consolidated a kingdom there. The Manx kingdom was later extended to include all the islands off the west coast of Scotland, including the Hebrides, and was officially under Norwegian supremacy until after the Battle of Largs in 1263. It was ceded to the King of Scotland in 1266 but has retained a certain independence within Great Britain to this day (one of the Queen's titles is Lord of Man). The island's own affairs are administered by its parliament, the Tynwald (the same word as the Icelandic *Þingvellir*). According to a tradition said to

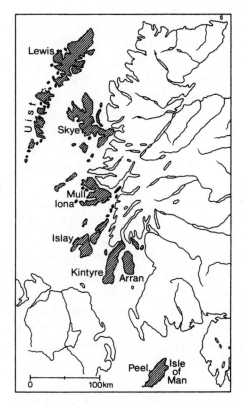

The Kingdom of Man, which at its height included the Hebrides and the other islands west of Scotland. The name of the bishopric of Sodor and Man is derived from *Suðreyjar*, the South Islands, which was the Scandinavian name for the Hebrides as seen from Norway. The bishopric came to have its seat on the small Peel Island on the west coast of Man.

go back to the Viking Age, the Tynwald sits annually on a man-made hill, Tynwald Hill, and is attended by the Crown's representative on the island and representatives of the Church. It ratifies the laws which have been passed during the previous year.

There is no definite evidence of when the Vikings reached Man, but when raids on Ireland began at the end of the eighth century, the island can hardly have escaped. More than twenty graves from the ninth century are known, so they must have settled here during the course of this century. In time a number of Scandinavians who had first lived in Ireland arrived; the island had many connections with Vikings there and was in some periods subject to them. Others probably came via England or south-western Scotland.

Only a few Viking Age buildings have been excavated on Man, but place-names show that there were many immigrants and that they dominated the island completely, for they gave new names to virtually everything (only Douglas and Rushen can be proved to be Celtic names pre-dating the Viking Age). Many of these Scandinavian place-names are in use today, for example Snaefell (*Snæ-fell,* snow-fell), which is the island's highest point; others are later Celtic names. Presumably many people spoke both Norwegian and Celtic, but in the Middle Ages Celtic prevailed.

The pagan Vikings respected the Christian faith to a certain extent, for some were buried in old churchyards, such as the chieftain interred in a ship with weapons in Balladoole. But both he and another chieftain in Ballateare had their graves marked by a mound and the latter was accompanied by a woman slave who had been killed – a violent blow had cut a piece off her skull. During the tenth century the Vikings must have become Christians, for there are very few pagan graves from this period but many beautifully decorated stone crosses. Runic inscriptions on several of them tell that sometimes there were very close relations between Vikings and the local population, for some sons had Celtic names. This can be seen on a stone in Kirk Braddan, raised by Thorleif in memory of Fiacc. His mother was presumably a Celt from Man or Ireland. However, there were also Scandinavian women in Man; one grave is certainly known, on Peel Island. The style of the runic script shows close links with Norway in this period.

The crosses are carved in low relief on soft slate. Though their shape was inspired by crosses from Ireland, the ornamentation is derived from Scandinavian art. The Borre and Mammen styles predominate, although elements of the Jellinge and Ringerike styles and a number of characteristic local features can be seen. The earliest crosses are thought to date from the first half of the tenth century and the latest from well into the eleventh century. An artist with the Scandinavian name Gaut has proudly signed two of the early crosses. On one in Kirk Michael he ended the inscription with the words 'but Gaut made it and all in Man'. On the cross in Kirk Andreas he tells us more: his name was Gaut Biørnsson (which confirms that he was the son of a Scandinavian)

Three sides of Thorleif's cross in the church of Kirk Braddan, Isle of Man, with Scandinavian-style animal ornament. On the fourth side is the runic inscription. The cross was raised in memory of Thorleif's son Fiacc, who had a Celtic name.

and he lived in Kuli, which is probably in Man. He may have been the great master-craftsman on the island, although many crosses were made after his time, among them Thorleif's, in Kirk Braddan, a fine example of the Mammen style.

The crosses on Man have some of the few known pictorial scenes from the Viking Age. Some of the motifs must be from pagan mythology and are interesting examples of the juxtaposition of paganism and Christianity at the time of conversion. Others are definitely scenes from the heroic legend of Sigurð Fáfnisbani (cf. p. 171). These are the oldest surviving pictures illustrating this cycle of legends, which was not written down until much later.

IRELAND

The Viking Age in Ireland started with the odd expedition in the 790s and ended with the conquest of Dublin by the English Normans in 1170. It is documented by many written sources, in particular the Annals of Ulster, and also by important archaeological finds and some Scandinavian place-names and loanwords.

Trade came to be the economic basis of the Scandinavian settlements in Ireland rather than ownership of land or farming, as elsewhere in Western Europe. Throughout the Viking Age many Scandinavians also made a good income as professional warriors, for, after the first great period of looting, Vikings and their fast fleets were often in demand among the many warring Irish factions; they were often heavily involved in power politics in the Irish Sea, in Scotland or in northern England. Sporadic income came from looting and from tributes imposed on Ireland and on other realms where supremacy had been established.

This traditional Viking economy survived much longer here than elsewhere in Europe because of the constantly changing balance of power in the region. The involvement in Ireland was to have great economic and cultural significance for Scandinavia, especially Norway and Iceland, and in the later Icelandic sagas it is imbued with a fabulous character.

THE VIKINGS IN IRELAND

The story of the Vikings in Ireland can be divided into four phases, which often ran parallel with, or were dependent on, Viking activities elsewhere. The interplay can seldom be clearly

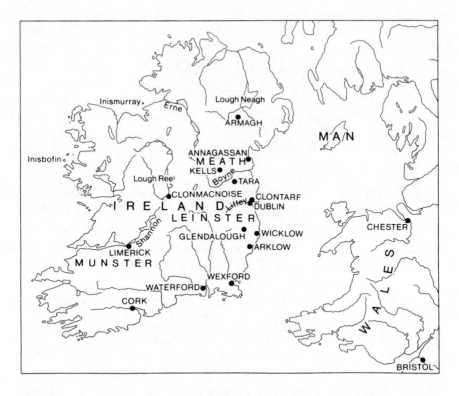

Ireland

defined, however, for the written sources only name a few of the chieftains involved which makes it hard to trace the activities of a particular Viking army or band.

During the first phase, from about 795 to the 830s, roaming bands of Vikings carried out swift raids on isolated monastic communities on small islands or coastal regions. In 795 Inismurray and Inisbofin on the north-west coast of Ireland were among those that suffered. By 812–13 at the latest the Vikings were attacking south-west Ireland and by the 820s they had worked their way round the entire island. The atmosphere in isolated monasteries at the time is captured by a monk who wrote a poem in the margin of a manuscript in praise of stormy nights when Vikings do not set out to sea. Three times in one month in 832 they plundered the large and wealthy monastery at Armagh, despite the fact that it lay a little inland. Its abbot was head of the

Irish Church. Defence against such lightning attacks was virtually impossible, but a couple of times the Irish did succeed in putting the Vikings to flight.

The Vikings concentrated on monasteries, not because they had a vendetta against Christian religious communities, but simply because they could get the greatest loot here. There were no towns in Ireland in the contemporary sense of the term, but several monasteries were like monastic towns: they were important economic and political centres, sometimes with many inhabitants, where much wealth might be accumulated or stored. They were so well organized that they could survive attacks and could thus be plundered again and again.

Ecclesiastical objects were not the Vikings' main target, as they were rarely made of precious metal. Usually only small ornamental mounts were made of gold and silver and many mounts were only made of gilt-bronze, though they might be richly decorated. A great quantity of such items, torn from reliquaries, sacred books and other church objects in Ireland (as in Scotland and northern England), ended up in graves in Norway. Some were no doubt taken home as souvenirs and given to wives and girlfriends and some were refashioned as jewellery. Fine secular objects of daily use were also of interest, such as the bucket with handsome mounts from Ireland or Scotland, which lay in the Oseberg grave, but it is impossible to tell whether this particular object was traded or stolen. What the Vikings sought above all was gold, silver, slaves and honour, here as elsewhere.

The Vikings were far from being the only people to commit acts of violence in Ireland. The Irish Annals record twenty-six attacks by Vikings in the first twenty-five years or so of their operations there, but in the same period eighty-seven were carried out by the Irish themselves. The Irish community was particularly pugnacious. It was divided into a multitude of small kingdoms with complicated dynastic rules. The kings were in almost constant conflict over such issues as who would be High King over a number of small kingdoms. Only the abbots of Armagh had authority at that time over the entire island and the balance of power fluctuated constantly. Because of the monasteries' special economic and political situation, and their very close links with the secular rulers, plundering and burning down monasteries was an integral part of Irish warfare. Wars between two monasteries, or between a monastery and the king, also broke out.

The second phase of the Vikings in Ireland runs from the 830s to 902. In the 830s the expeditions gathered momentum, as in the Frankish realms and England. Great tracts of land were now plundered and large fleets sailed inland along rivers such as the Erne, Shannon, Liffey and Boyne. In 839 a fleet was based on Lough Neagh in Ulster and the Vikings overwintered there in 840–41. In 841 they established fortified bases in Dublin and in Annagassan, just to the north on the east coast, and new fleets joined them. In 845 the attacks reached a climax and a further fortified base was constructed on Lough Ree, in the centre of the country. Many different armies were operating in various regions, apparently independently.

A certain Turgesius became the most famous Viking chieftain of this period. He was taken captive in 845 by the Irish King Máel Sechnaill and drowned in a lake. This is virtually all that is known for certain about him. His fame is due to a work of political propaganda, *Cogadh Gaedhel re Gallaibh* (The War of the Irish against the Foreigners), written some 250 years later. It relates dramatic stories of Turgesius's amazing exploits in order to glorify the deeds of the great Irish King Brian Boru and to enhance the prestige of his dynasty. This work portrays Turgesius as a sort of pagan super-Viking who operated far and wide and was the leader of all Vikings in Ireland. It claims he captured the monastery of Armagh, assumed the office of abbot and tried to convert the Irish to the worship of Thor, and that his wife Ota performed pagan rituals from the high altar in the monastery at Clonmacnoise!

The great wave of raids in the 840s was in time countered by several Irish kings, but the Vikings were now firmly established on the island. New fleets continued to arrive from Norway and also from Denmark, possibly via England or the Frankish kingdoms. Sporadic plundering continued and the Viking armies often fought each other. No regions of any great size were captured, but bases were established in many places along the coast, where the Vikings lived in small enclaves, of which Dublin was the most important. In many places, however, they were expelled for a time or for ever, and at the end of the ninth century the pressure on the Irish settlements became so great that some departed for other shores.

By the mid-ninth century they had become integrated into the life on the island. Their military professionalism and their superior weapons had made them useful in Irish wars and the growth of peaceful social and cultural relations is reflected in the number of Irish–Scandinavian marriages, and the fact that many second-generation Vikings were given Celtic names. Most also became Christians. On an artistic level the close contacts can be discerned in the way the large traditional Irish annular brooches or pins inspired the penannular brooches for men's cloaks, often made of silver, which became so popular in Viking communities in the West and in Norway. New types of small, bronze dress pins, inspired by Irish designs, also became fashionable. In return, the Irish learnt to produce better weapons, among other things.

It was presumably at this time that the Vikings established themselves as international merchants. The Irish had no tradition of foreign trade, nor of selling goods for silver, whereas the Vikings, with their close contacts with family and colleagues over vast parts of Europe, were used to trading in all sorts of goods. They also had the necessary ships. The hoards of gold and silver, the large penannular brooches and other objects demonstrate that a great deal of precious metal was introduced into Ireland, but so far there is little specific information about the peaceful economic transactions between the Scandinavians and the Irish. It may be that the Scandinavians acquired slaves and provisions among other things in return for weapons and luxury goods.

The base in Annagassan of 841 has been identified tentatively. Here high ground was protected by the curve of the rivers Clyde and Dee on two of its sides and by an earth wall on the third. No civilian Scandinavian settlements of this period have been found, nor has the large Dublin base been located, although we do know that it was not situated in the excavated parts of the centre of modern Dublin. It may have lain a little further up the river Liffey in the Kilmainham–Islandbridge district. In the nineteenth century the construction of a railway here went through a large ninth-century Scandinavian cemetery, where there were graves of men with weapons (about forty swords and thirty-five spearheads were collected) and of women with oval brooches. These grave finds and a few others confirm that Scandinavian families settled here alongside the mixed marriages, as in other areas of Viking settlement.

In 853 Olaf the White (a Norwegian) and Ívar (a Dane) came to Dublin and became kings there. The Dublin kingdom grew powerful, but Ívar's death in 873 was followed by many years of strife and in 902 the Vikings in Dublin were ousted by an Irish coalition. Many of them probably went to the Isle of Man and the Hebrides, to north-west England and Iceland. Others may have tried their luck in the remaining Viking bases on the Continent.

The third phase of the Irish Viking Age began in 914 and lasted until 980. Fleet after fleet arrived and a new wave of plundering swept the entire island just as in the 840s. Again it was the work of many different, uncoordinated groups. These Vikings probably came not from Scandinavia but mostly from the settlements in north-west England, the Isle of Man and Scotland. Others may have come from bases on the Continent, for Rollo's assumption of power in c. 911 in the Lower Seine region had reduced still further the opportunities for Vikings there. Some may also have left eastern England, where the kings of Wessex were systematically extending their dominion northwards, and one group is known for certain to have come from Brittany via Wales and western England, where luck had not been with them. Ireland was one of the few areas in Western Europe where opportunities still existed for Vikings and, although Irish kings made counter-attacks and were occasionally victorious, it took many years before the opposition was fully effective. It was presumably the many acts of aggression that encouraged the monasteries to build more churches of stone rather than inflammable wood, and to erect the characteristic circular, free-standing stone towers, which are mentioned for the first time in the Irish Annals in the mid-tenth century.

The Vikings again established many bases and in 917 the Dublin base was re-established. The kings now aspired to supremacy over all the Vikings in Ireland, but they did not succeed in this aim. Their greatest ambition, however, was to win the prestigious and profitable title of King of York, the wealthy capital of Northumbria. Much effort was expended on this and kings such

as Røgnvald, Olaf Godfredsson and Olaf Cuaran were successful
for a time. However, in 954 York came under English sovereignty
and the dream of the Dublin kings came to an end.

The excellent opportunities for trade led to the founding of
towns in Ireland like Wicklow, Arklow, Wexford, Waterford,
Limerick and (probably) Cork. Dublin was the most important
and here and in several other places the Vikings conquered the
hinterland. Some presumably farmed there but they nearly all
lived on the coast or a little way up the rivers.

By the mid-tenth century, Dublin was a flourishing international trading centre, and during the reign of Olaf (or Anlaf)
Sigtryggsson, who had the by-name of Cuaran, which means
'sandal' (c. 950–80), it ruled over a considerable part of the hinterland. But the star of this kingdom, as of other Viking realms,
was waning, in both the political and military spheres. Its political
independence was lost at the battle of Tara in 980, where Olaf
was defeated by Máel Sechnaill II, King of Meath (in eastern
Ireland, north of Dublin). From now on the Irish held supremacy
and the Vikings paid tribute to them, although they stayed on in
Dublin and in other towns, and retained their kings and their
control of the international trade, which the Irish appear to have
been uninterested in handling themselves.

In the last phase, until 1170, the Vikings were integrated into
the Irish community. The towns flourished and the large-scale
manufacture of all sorts of objects strengthened the economy of
Dublin, which so far is the only Scandinavian settlement in Ireland
to have had large-scale excavations. The culture increasingly
acquired an Hiberno-Norse character and the Irish kings gradually
became more involved in the affairs of the towns. Some assumed
the title of king there (in Dublin in 1052) and some took up
residence there. From 997 coins were minted in the town for many
years, modelled on English coinage, as were the contemporary
coinages in Denmark, Norway and Sweden.

Irish kings now aspired to the political supremacy of the whole
island and the legendary battle of Clontarf in 1014 was fought
by two rival Irish dynasties. The Munster realm (in south-west
Ireland) defeated Leinster (in eastern Ireland, south of Dublin)
and, as in so many other battles, Vikings fought on both sides; in
the Leinster army there were probably also men from the Isle of

Man and the islands to the north. The King of Munster, Brian
Boru, was killed and the battle was later the subject of Icelandic
sagas and Irish stories and histories. These describe the battle as
Brian Boru's decisive victory over the Vikings in Ireland, but
that had in fact been won at Tara thirty-four years earlier by the
King of Meath. Significantly, the King of Dublin, Sigtrygg
Silkenbeard, and his men did not take part in the battle of
Clontarf, which was fought only a few miles outside the town.
Not until the English conquest of Dublin in 1170 were the
descendants of the Vikings, with their Scandinavian-influenced
culture, finally overcome.

Far more hoards of precious metal from the Viking Age have
been found in Ireland than in Scotland, a clear indication of the
exceptional riches that came to the island. Hoards have been
found from the whole period, but most date from the tenth and
eleventh centuries. The most impressive is the gold hoard from
Hare Island in Lough Ree, where Viking bases were established
several times. It was hidden between the mid-eighth and the mid-
ninth centuries and consisted of ten broad gold arm-rings, with
a total weight of about 5 kilos – twice as much as the Hon hoard
in Norway, and the largest of all known Viking gold hoards.
However, it was found in 1802 and was soon melted down; only
some drawings and brief descriptions remain.

Most hoards consisted of silver arm-rings and other jewellery,
ingots, coins and fragments, as was normal in the Viking
economy. There are indications that many of them had come
into the hands of the Irish and were buried by them. Interestingly,
some written sources imply that large monasteries, such as Kells
in Meath and Glendalough in Leinster, became important centres
for internal trade in the tenth and eleventh centuries.

The different coins in the hoards show that trade with England
in the period c. 925–75 was conducted via Chester, directly across
the Irish Sea. It was superseded by another route round the south
coast of Wales to Bristol when trade with France was expanding.
Scandinavian place-names along the Welsh coast confirm this
later route.

In time the Irish adopted many Scandinavian personal names,
and vice versa. In Dublin and other towns the Scandinavian
language was in common use right up to the English invasion of

1169–70. The Irish language borrowed a number of Scandinavian words, for example *margadh* (Scandinavian *markaðr*) for market, but most were associated with seafaring. *Bád* (Scandinavian *bátr*) is still a usual word for boat. The number of Scandinavian place-names is not great compared with Scotland and the Isle of Man, and most survive in English forms, as that language came to be very important in Ireland after 1170. Wexford, for example, is probably from the Scandinavian *Ueigsfjǫrðr*, and Waterford from *Ueðra(r)fjǫrðr*. Limerick is a direct derivation from the Scandinavian *Hlymrekr*, while Dublin is pure Irish – *dubh* and *linn*, meaning black pool, refer to the estuary of the river Liffey around which the settlement grew up.

Many people must have spoken both Scandinavian and Celtic, and some, like a certain Þorgrím, wanted to make sure that they were remembered by both peoples. His cross stands in Killaloe near Shannon, a little north of Limerick, and the inscription is written both in runes and in the old Irish alphabet, ogham.

Apart from the Scandinavian graves in Kilmainham–Island-bridge, only about a dozen have been found in the whole of Ireland – far fewer than in Scotland or the Isle of Man. This was presumably because Christian rites were adopted more quickly in the Irish trading centres, and Scandinavian settlements outside them were very limited. The first church on the site of Dublin's present cathedral, Christ Church, was the Church of the Holy Trinity, built around the year 1030, and in various places in Ireland churches were dedicated to St Olaf.

THE EXCAVATIONS IN DUBLIN

Extensive excavations from 1961 to 1981 in the centre of Dublin, especially around Christ Church and down towards Wood Quay and the river Liffey, have confirmed that the Vikings founded the Irish capital. This was where they settled when they returned after fifteen years' exile in 917. They chose a hillside on the southern bank of the Liffey, close to its junction with a tributary, and the area was soon divided up into plots and surrounded by an earth rampart. This was later repaired several times and around 1100 a stone wall was built. As time went by, however, the

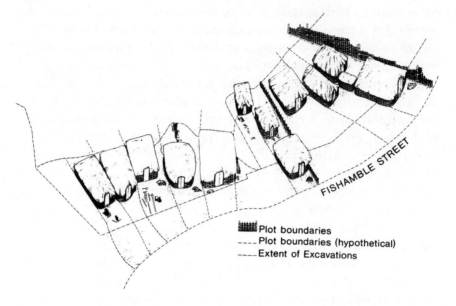

Reconstruction of plots and buildings along Fishamble Street, Dublin, from *c.* 1000.

northern part of the town and its fortifications extended further and further out towards the Liffey, which was then far wider here than it is today.

The town plan was not completely regular because of the topography, but the plots, enclosed by wattle fences, remained the same size throughout the Scandinavian period. How the town developed later is not certain, for the upper layers were destroyed in many places by the deep cellars of more recent buildings. Inside the fences the inhabitants could apparently build as they wished, for the sites of dwellings and outhouses often changed.

The houses were not impressive by today's standards, but they compared quite well with those in contemporary towns such as Hedeby, Birka and York. The normal house, however, has no direct parallels there and may have been of the Irish type, or influenced by local building customs around the Irish Sea. Nearly all buildings were of wattle, with internal roof-bearing posts; the ground plan was rectangular with rounded corners. The largest buildings were approximately 8.5 m long and 4.75 m wide and

16   Thor's hammer, Öland, Sweden   17   Cross from Trondheim, Norway

18   Christ on the Jelling stone, Denmark

A

B

C

19   Mounts from Borre and Gokstad, Norway

20   Cup and mounts, Jelling, Denmark

21   Axe from Mammen, Denmark

22   Stone from St Paul's churchyard, London

23 Portal from Urnes church, Norway

24　Viking burial at Westness, Orkney

25　Hogback grave stones from Brompton, England

26   Cuerdale silver hoard, England

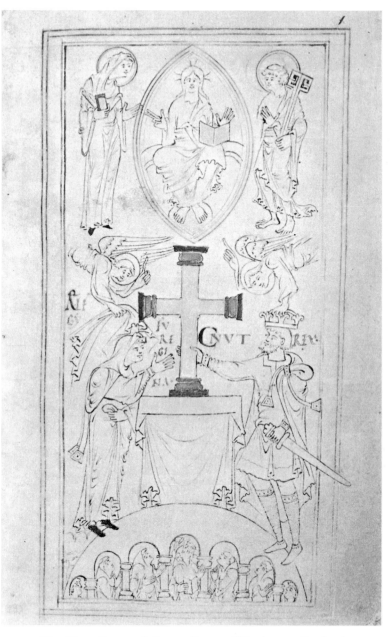

27   King Cnut and Queen Emma, Winchester, England

28   Brattahlíð, Greenland

Notes on the Plates

16   Thor's hammer, the symbol of Thor's power, here in the form of a silver pendant, from Bredsätra on Öland, Sweden. Height 4.6 cm. National Antiquities Museum, Stockholm.

17   Cross-shaped pendant from a silver hoard hidden *c.* 1030 in Trondheim, Norway. Christ, as was usual at the time, is depicted as a proud, victorious god, here with an elegant moustache. Height 7 cm. University Museum, Trondheim.

18   The depiction of Christ on King Harald Bluetooth's large rune stone at Jelling, Jutland, Denmark. Below the picture is the end of the long inscription 'and made the Danes Christian'. The runes, pictures and ornament stand out against the background blackened with soot. The stone's other picture face can be seen in Plate 12. Jutland, Denmark.

19   Borre style. Three cast gilt-bronze mounts: A and C are from Borre while B is from Gokstad in Vestfold, Norway. They show the style's characteristic motifs: A ring-chain; B gripping-beast with its body twisted backwards; C compact, semi-naturalistic animal. Height: A 5.1 cm; B 2.3 cm; C 2.9 cm. University Museum of National Antiquities, Oslo.

20   Jellinge style. Silver cup with traces of gilt and niello from the chamber grave in the north mound at Jelling, Denmark. Height 4.3 cm. Two silver-gilt strap-mounts from the grave in Jelling's earliest church. Length 2.8 and 7.4 cm. National Museum of Denmark, Copenhagen.

21   Mammen style. This axe from the grave at Mammen in Jutland, Denmark, decorated with a large bird in silver wire inlay. On the other side of the axe is tendril ornament. Length: 17.5 cm. National Museum of Denmark, Copenhagen.

22   Ringerike style. Limestone slab from a box-sarcophagus from St Paul's churchyard, London. It is decorated in Scandinavian Ringerike style with one of the style's main motifs: a large animal entwined with a smaller snake-like creature. There are traces of colour on the stone and part of a runic inscription on the edge. Length 57 cm. The Museum of London.

23   Urnes style. Carved portal and door re-used in the mid-twelfth

century in the present church in Urnes, Sogn og Fjordane, Norway. The decoration consists of elegeant sinuous plaitwork of slender, anaemic animals, snakes and plant tendrils.

24 Scandivanian grave from Westness, Rousay, Orkney, ninth century. The man was about thirty years old when he died and was buried in the pagan manner with various belongings: shield, arrow quiver, harvesting sickle, knife, scissors, comb, dress pin and twenty-five bone gaming counters.

25 Three house-shaped grave stones, known as hogbacks, in Brompton Church, North Yorkshire, England. The stone at the front is 128 cm long. The hogbacks have curved long walls and a curved roof-ridge, as was common in the large houses of the time. The front two have shingled roofs. The meaning of the large muzzled bears clasping the gables is uncertain.

26 Silver from the vast hoard found at Cuerdale, Lancashire, England. It weighs approximately 40 kilos and was hidden in a lead chest on the bank of the river Ribble in c. 905. It contains silver from all points of the compass: coins, jewellery and other objects, as well as many fragments. The British Museum.

27 Cnut the Great and his queen Emma donate a golden altar cross to the church of New Minster in Winchester. Cnut's right hand clasps the cross, his left his sword. The names of the royal couple are written above their heads. Above that of the queen is the name Ælfgyfu, which was her English name. Drawing on parchment in the church's memorial book of friends and benefactors, *Liber Vitae*, which was probably begun in 1031. This is the only surviving contemporary picture of Cnut. The British Library.

28 Greenland. Northern part of the Brattahlíð plain, looking north across Eiríksfjörð (Tunugdliarfik). Here are Viking Age and medieval ruins, along with modern buildings. 1 The medieval church and church-yard from c. 1300, which had a predecessor. 2 A contemporary dwelling. 3 Byres and barns. 4 Small turf-walled church, the ealiest known at Brattahlíð. 5 Building with slightly curved long walls, also of turf, which may have been one of the earliest dwellings here. The distance from here to the small church is distorted on the photograph and is only some 45 m. The house (5) may be that of Erik the Red, and the church (4) is probably þjodhilð's.

normally had a door in each gable wall. The interior was divided into a floor area with a central hearth and narrow, low benches along each side. At each end there were sometimes small cubicles. Many of these houses were presumably used both as dwellings and as workshops or stores. No stables or byres have been found in Viking Age Dublin and the animal bones confirm that meat must have come from outside the town.

The finds from the Dublin excavations are much more varied and of higher quality than those from any other Viking town, a reflection of Dublin's powerful economic position, particularly from the end of the tenth century. Imported goods included walrus ivory, amber, soapstone vessels and brooches from the North; pottery, swords, jet and metal ornaments from England; pottery and glass from the Continent; much silk from the East; and a number of coins and two gold arm-rings. There must also have been many goods which have decayed, such as furs and wine. Written sources describe Dublin as a centre of the slave trade and slaves, hides and textiles were probably the major exports from Ireland. Many crafts also flourished there. Traces have been found of carpentry, ship-building, wood-carving, comb-making (using red deer antler), bone-carving, wood-turning, coopering, shoe-making and other leather work, bronze-casting and a great deal of iron forging. Amber and jet were also worked there, and probably silver, gold, tin and lead.

Some runic inscriptions on fragments of bone and other items confirm that Scandinavian culture continued to exist, but the main character of Dublin was now no longer purely Scandinavian. The craftsmen tended to produce art objects that appealed both to Scandinavian and Irish taste, developing local variations of Scandinavian styles. This is particularly evident on the 'motif pieces' – pieces of bone or stone on which artists or apprentices have tried out various motifs. They have been found by the hundreds. Many splendidly decorated wooden objects were also found in the excavations.

Examples of the Borre style are comparatively rare, both on motif pieces and on other objects, while the Jellinge style does not appear on the motif pieces at all. Both the Ringerike style and Urnes style, however, became highly popular, in particular in their Irish versions, but still easily recognizable. They were even used to decorate church objects, such as the abbot's crosier from Clonmacnoise and the cross of Cong, and had a much longer life than the main styles in Scandinavia.

ENGLAND

England came to be one of the Vikings' best sources of income, and here more than anywhere they gained honour and prestige. They looted, extorted tribute (Danegeld) and acted as mercenaries and traders. They also settled, cultivated the land and had a significant impact on the development of towns. This was the one place where they conquered well-established kingdoms and assumed the title of king – in several of the minor realms which existed in the ninth century, as well as over the whole of England in the early eleventh century. From 1018 to 1042 (apart from a period of five years) England and Denmark were ruled jointly by one king. The deep Scandinavian involvement in England throughout most of the Viking Age was of the greatest importance both there and in Scandinavia.

The source material is exceptionally rich and extensive: many written sources (the most important of which are the various versions of the Anglo-Saxon Chronicle), archaeological finds from many parts of the country, innumerable place-names, as well as personal names and other linguistic evidence. This explains why so much interdisciplinary research has been carried out into the English Viking Age.

EXPLOITATION, CONQUEST AND SETTLEMENT

Apart from the attack in southern England and the precautions taken against pirates there shortly before the year 800 (see p. 192), and the destruction of Lindisfarne monastery in 793, the only record of Vikings in England before 835 concerns the plundering of the monastery *Donemuthan* in the kingdom of Northumbria

in 794. This monastery was presumably situated near the mouth of
the river Don, in south Yorkshire, or may have been Tynemouth
monastery; it is unlikely to have been the famous monastery of
Jarrow. These Viking bands are thought to have come from
Norway and during the following years they may have found
better opportunities in Scotland and Ireland.

In 835 the Viking expeditions really got under way on the
Continent and were escalating in Ireland. That year the Vikings
resumed their activities in England, and the Anglo-Saxon Chronicle tersely notes: 'In this year heathen men ravaged Sheppey'.
This was the real beginning of more than two centuries of heavy
Scandinavian involvement, in which the Danes were particularly
active. The course of military events can be followed almost year
by year in the Chronicle, but there are also other written sources,
such as Asser's history of King Alfred the Great of Wessex.

In the first years it was particularly southern and eastern
England which suffered, including the great towns of Hamwih
(Southampton) and London. England at this time was divided into
several kingdoms: Northumbria north of the Humber, Mercia in
the centre, East Anglia to the east and Wessex in the south. They
were not unified until 927 and again in 954. Celtic-speaking Wales
remained an independent realm until well into the Middle Ages.
There were flourishing towns (though not yet very many) and
the nobles owned great wealth, so, as on the Continent, it was
not only monasteries that were plundered.

To begin with Viking involvement followed the same pattern
as elsewhere: quick raids on islands and various coastal regions
from bases on the Continent, in Ireland or directly from the
homelands. The first mention of them overwintering in England
is 850–1, when they camped on the island of Thanet on the east
coast of Kent. A few years later they made their first winter camp
on Sheppey, at the mouth of the Thames. Reports of expeditions
inland soon followed and in 865 an army encamped on Thanet
and made peace with the people of Kent in return for money.
This was the first of many English payments of Danegeld.

Then things started to gather momentum. In 865 a 'great
heathen army' came to England. Its size has been much debated,
but it is thought to have numbered 2–3,000 men. They took
up winter quarters in East Anglia, obtained horses and made

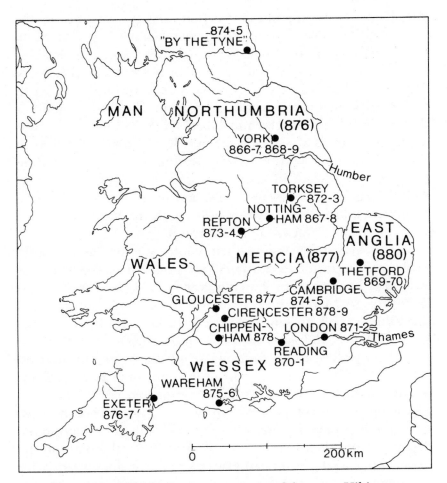

England. The bases and winter quarters of the great Viking army during the years 865–79 are marked with black symbols. The dates indicate the year the army shared out land and settled in each of the kingdoms.

peace with the people. The following year the army moved to Northumbria (where a civil war was in progress), captured the capital, York, on 1 November, made peace with the Northumbrians, placed a puppet king on the throne and wintered there. It was probably also about this time that Whitby monastery, on the east coast, was plundered and destroyed. A number of mounts have been found there which were probably torn off ecclesiastical objects during the destruction, and place-names in the district indicate that church lands were taken over by Vikings. In 867 the army went to Mercia, took up winter quarters in Nottingham and made peace with this realm. In 868 it returned to York and stayed there for a year. In 869 it rode through Mercia to East Anglia, established winter quarters in Thetford, conquered the whole of East Anglia and killed King Edmund, who was soon venerated as a saint and martyr. In 870 it was the turn of Wessex. The army made its base in Reading and in 871, according to the Anglo-Saxon Chronicle, nine great battles were fought, as well as many minor engagements, and nine Danish earls and a king were killed. Wessex made peace with the Vikings and that year Alfred the Great ascended the throne.

This pattern of changing their winter quarters and making many peace agreements continued for a time. In 871–2 there was a camp in London, the following year in Torksey in Mercia and in both years Mercia made peace with the army. But in 873–4 the Vikings took up winter quarters in Repton, drove out the king of Mercia, and put a renegade on the throne.

Repton proved to be a turning point. In 874 the great army divided. Halfdan went with part of it to Northumbria, made his winter quarters by the river Tyne, conquered the country the following year and plundered to the west and north. According to tradition the monastic community of St Cuthbert on Lindisfarne departed from their exposed island in 875 to seek safety on the mainland. They moved from place to place for some years, with the relics of St Cuthbert and others, and apparently without coming to any harm, although Northumbria was teeming with Vikings. In 876 the Chronicle contains the statement: 'And that year Halfdan shared out the land of the Northumbrians, and they proceeded to plough and to support themselves.' The Vikings had taken land to settle on. Halfdan himself probably died the following year.

The other part of the army left Repton in 874 under the leadership of the kings Guthrum, Oscetel and Anwend, and went to Cambridge where they remained for a year. Then the army moved into Wessex, the last independent kingdom, and King Alfred had to make peace. In 875–6 they encamped in Wareham and the following year in Exeter. During the harvest of 877, 'the army went away into Mercia and they shared out some of it and gave some to Ceolwulf' (the Vikings' puppet king). But not all settled. There was a base in Gloucester and just after the New Year the army returned to Wessex, to Chippenham, and took charge of most of the realm. King Alfred fled with a small company into the marshes and entrenched himself in Athelney. During the spring of 878, however, he succeeded in gathering an army together and won a decisive victory over the Vikings at Edington. When peace was concluded the Vikings promised to leave Wessex and their leader Guthrum agreed to be baptized. King Alfred acted as godfather for Guthrum, and he and thirty nobles were given many baptismal gifts and courteous treatment. In 878–9 the army took up winter quarters in Cirencester and then went on to East Anglia. For the year 880 the Chronicle records that it settled and shared out the land, although a group of Vikings sailed to Ghent, in present-day Belgium, and there were many raids there in the following years.

After fifteen years of roaming England the army had now conquered three of the four kingdoms and had got land to live on and to cultivate. Guthrum soon broke his treaty with King Alfred, but made another, whose text survives, in 886 or soon afterwards. This established the border between Alfred's and Guthrum's realms (the borders with the other Viking realms are not mentioned) and set down a number of rules for peaceful relations between the two peoples. The border followed the river Lea from where it joins the Thames (a little east of London, which Alfred had captured in 886) north-west to its source and from there to Bedford and onwards along the Ouse to Watling Street, the old Roman road between London and Chester.

Until the army finally settled in England the population around the bases and winter camps was no doubt obliged to feed the soldiers (and was probably only able to do this for a year at a time). The many 'peace agreements' presumably involved handing over treasure, supplying provisions and perhaps winter quarters for the army, exchanging hostages, swearing oaths and other special agreements. The meaning of the term for 'peace', friðr, must however have been closer to 'make agreement' than to 'make peace'.

A number of silver hoards from these years are evidence of the troubled times and the army's passage around England. One of the many valuable objects that the Vikings captured in the ninth century can be identified with certainty. This is a magnificent illuminated manuscript of the gospels in Latin, the *Codex Aureus*, made in Kent in the eighth century. In the margin of the gold-ornamented page where the Gospel according to St Matthew begins its account of the birth of Christ, a note in Anglo-Saxon records that the ealdorman Ælfred (he was probably from Surrey) and his wife Werburg bought the book from a heathen army in return for gold, so that it should not remain in heathen hands, and that they donated it to Christ Church (presumably Canterbury Cathedral). Ironically, by a tortuous route this book ended up among Scandinavians: in the seventeenth century it was purchased for the Royal Library in Stockholm.

But the most dramatic evidence of the conquering army comes from excavations of the winter camp of 873–4 in Repton, where several kings of Mercia had been buried in the eighth century. The army fortified an area of about 1.5 hectares in an elevated position by the river Trent with a semicircular ditch terminating at each end of the church of St Wystan, thus making the church into a kind of gate tower. Several Viking graves have been found near the church, and the grave-goods include coins, a sword and a Thor's hammer.

A little outside the defensive ditch are some burial mounds, one of which was erected over a man's grave surrounded by huge numbers of human skeletal remains, which had clearly first been buried elsewhere. Unfortunately the mound was 'excavated' in the 1680s and the central grave no longer exists; according to a description of 1727 it contained a giant, nine feet long, in a stone cist! The other bones belong to at least 249 people, of whom about 80 per cent were men: robust persons whose bones in only a few instances carry traces of unhealed wounds, so most of them were apparently not killed in battle. This burial also contained coins and it may well be that they were members of the Viking army who died during the winter from epidemics and were individually buried, subsequently exhumed and reburied together around the dead chieftain. His identity can only be guessed at, but he was buried in the delapidated remains of a very grand, rectangular building. The floor level was a little lower than the surrounding ground and the low mound which covered it was almost rectangular, not circular, as was the norm.

If this interpretation of the excavations is correct, it is likely that a winter of such misery, resulting in the death of more than two hundred people, contributed to the Vikings tiring of their nomadic life. We know that they began to settle down two years later in England. They do not seem to have considered returning to Scandinavia in any numbers and no significant amount of English ninth-century objects has been found in Denmark. In Norway there are more but they mostly came from Northumbria and are not necessarily connected with the plundering of this particular army.

On the Continent, however, many were still employed in traditional Viking fashion. But times became hard and in 892 'the great Danish army' came from Boulogne to England, and Hasting came with his army from the Loire (p. 202). They brought everything with them and were apparently ready to settle, like their fortunate colleagues before them. The army was given support from the Viking realms in England, but King Alfred had organized effective defences with inland fortifications, armies which could be called out at any time, and ships which had been specially constructed for fighting against Viking ships. When the Danish army sought refuge in Chester in 893, King Alfred's army destroyed everything edible in the surrounding area, and when it took up a fortified position two years later by the river Lea, Alfred timed his arrival to coincide with the harvest to prevent the enemy laying its hands on the grain. He was the victor of many battles and epidemics ravaged the country, resulting in the death of many animals and people. The Anglo-Saxon Chronicle paints a gloomy picture of this roaming Viking army and in 896 it gave up. Some Vikings went to Northumbria, others to East Anglia, and 'those that were moneyless got themselves ships and went south across the sea to the Seine'.

THE SCANDINAVIANS IN ENGLAND

Alfred the Great died in 899 and was succeeded by equally competent children and grandchildren. The Vikings continued to be a problem on the Continent, in Ireland and in England, but

Wessex gradually extended its power northwards and consolidated it by means of a network of fortified towns and fortresses, *burhs*. By 917–18 King Edward (899–924) had conquered the whole of the region south of the Humber and in 920 he was formally accepted as supreme lord of Northumbria. This, however, did not last; power in the area alternated between English and Viking kings right up to 954.

Northumbria and York had English puppet kings until about 880; they were followed by a series of kings of Scandinavian origin but with vastly different backgrounds. From the second decade of the tenth century kings of the Danish dynasty in Ireland played a particularly prominent role and justified their title to the throne by their descent from the fabled Ívar, who had come to Dublin in 853, died in 873, and was said to be the brother of Halfdan. One grandson, Sigtrygg, married a daughter of King Edward, but died soon afterwards in 927. Olaf Godfredsson, who died in 941 after one or two periods as King of York, was a great-grandson of Ívar. He and his Scottish allies were defeated in 937 by King Edward's son Athelstan (924–39) at the great battle of Brunanburh (the place has not been identified). Many kings and earls were killed and the battle became famous in both English and Scandinavian literature. Olaf survived and went back to Dublin, only to return in 939. The last Viking king was Erik Bloodaxe, who had been exiled from Norway. He came to York for two brief periods before he was exiled by the Northumbrians in 954 and was killed at Stainmore. The English king Eadred then became the ruler of all England.

Very little is known about the political development in the Viking realms, but, as in the English realms, power was based on fortified towns and fortresses, *burhs*, new as well as old. There were two kingdoms, East Anglia and Northumbria, while the region in between, which included the Five Boroughs (Lincoln, Nottingham, Derby, Leicester and Stamford), had a different structure. The Scandinavians are often mentioned as armies associated with certain *burhs*.

The Danelaw, which today is often used as a blanket term for the whole region, never became a political entity. The word simply means 'the law of the Danes'. After the English kings gained power over the Viking realms, they let the Scandinavian

England

part of the population decide their own laws, which were undoubtedly influenced by Danish, or rather Scandinavian, ones. The term 'Danelaw' applied to specific geographic areas is first known from eleventh-century documents. The areas which these and later documents mention as observing Danish law correspond quite well with those which are known to have been dominated by Vikings and with the distribution of Scandinavian place-

names. But it is also very likely that legal peculiarities in these
areas, bounded to the south by the ancient Watling Street, were
thought to be Danish in the eleventh and twelfth centuries, though
they might in fact have had a completely different background.

The Vikings came to have a great impact, both direct and
indirect, on the development of towns in England. Many of the
fortifications which King Alfred and his successors established
against the Vikings developed into towns, as they quickly
acquired additional functions. In some places, such as the ancient
Roman town of Winchester, there were already churches and a
royal residence; now the walls were repaired and a new town
plan laid out. Nearly all the Viking *burhs* also developed into
towns. As well as the Five Boroughs mentioned above, there
were Cambridge, Bedford, Northampton and others. Most of
these localities had some centralized functions when the Vikings
arrived, such as an important church or a lord's residence, and
many presumably only became towns after the English assumed
power. However, excavations have demonstrated that important
urban structures in the two largest towns of the Danelaw, Lincoln
and York, came into being during the Scandinavian period.

The development of Lincoln gathered force around the year
900, when a new network of streets and a new settlement were
created within the old Roman walls. At the same time trading
connections were established with all England and with the Rhineland and even more distant regions. Finds include Oriental silk
as well as remains of the town's own crafts and industries. Many
street names with the suffix -*gate* (street), for example Flaxengate,
where large excavations have been carried out, bear witness to
the Scandinavian period, as does the lay-out of the town.

York was also founded by the Romans. The many large stone
buildings and the town walls fell into disrepair after the Roman
withdrawal from England in the fifth century, but an Anglo-
Saxon royal residence was soon built there. When the king of
Northumbria adopted Christianity in the seventh century a
church was built in the Roman military headquarters, some of
whose ancient buildings were still standing when the Vikings
captured the town in 866. By then York had also developed into
a flourishing trading centre, but this probably lay outside the
Roman walls to the south-east, on the other side of the river Foss.

The Vikings called the town Jorvík instead of the Anglo-Saxon Eoforwic. Under their rule the trading settlement was re-established on the promontory where the Ouse and Foss joined, which was protected partly by the rivers and partly by the old Roman ramparts and walls. These were now repaired and the old town plan was revised to meet new needs. As in Lincoln, many streets were given new names with the Scandinavian suffix -gate. The excavations in Coppergate, which probably means the street of the cup- and bowl-makers, give a particularly vivid insight into the development, the life and culture of Viking Age York, which acquired a marked Scandinavian stamp – it became Anglo-Scandinavian, just as Dublin became Hiberno-Norse.

The Coppergate area had been abandoned since the Roman period but came into use again at the time of the arrival of the Vikings. Around 935 it was parcelled out into long, narrow, typical urban plots, divided by wattle fencing, which remained the same right up to modern times. On the plots houses were built of wattle with a framework of posts. Their gables faced the street, which lies below present-day Coppergate and therefore could not be excavated. The houses were on average about 4.4 m wide and more than 6.8 m long (the gables facing the street projected beyond the excavated area).

In the four properties which were excavated, many kinds of metalwork were carried out. Lead, iron, bronze, silver and gold were worked and lots of everyday objects were produced, such as knives and jewellery, which imitated the grand fashions of the time in cheap materials. Iron dies for the striking of coins and lead die-trials were also found, which means that coins were either minted in Coppergate itself or the craftsmen manufactured the dies there and tested them before delivery.

There is nothing that marks the year 954, when the last Scandinavian king was ousted, but who could have known that this year was to be the end of a political era? The balance of power had changed so often before and the unity of England was far from consolidated. York continued to have a strong Scandinavian character. Around 975 a new type of house was introduced in Coppergate. These buildings had floor levels slightly below the ground outside and timber walls. On two of the plots there was another building a couple of metres behind the main houses. The finds indicate that the latter were workshops, while the buildings, which still had a gable projecting beyond the excavated area on to the street, were used as dwellings and no doubt also as shops. The craftsmen of this period mainly produced amber jewellery and turned wooden objects, including bowls, which may be how the street came to have its name.

The Coppergate excavation also showed that York was a centre for international as well as regional trade; apart from objects produced in England, there were things from Scandinavia, Ireland and Scotland, from many parts of north-west Europe (such as wine), from Byzantium (silk) and from the Middle East (a small decorative cowry shell only found in the Red Sea and the Gulf of Aden). It distributed luxury goods from all over the world, all sorts of objects produced in the town itself, and no doubt many products from the surrounding area as well. Life in Coppergate, however, was not luxurious. The craftsmen lived in surroundings which were normal for towns of the period: they were infested with fleas and lice and analyses of the contents of cesspits have shown that virtually everybody had intestinal worms (Plate 5).

The nobles about whom we read – Halfdan, the Dublin kings, Erik from Norway and the later earls with their families and men – must have lived much more grandly. The residences of the aristocracy have not yet been excavated, but place-names indicate that the Scandinavian kings, and later on the earls, lived in or near the eastern gate of the Roman fort, not far from Coppergate, and a little way outside the west wall of the old Roman fort. Here Earl Sigvard, who died in 1055, had a church built dedicated to St Olaf.

The Viking kings' interest in trade led to their minting of coins. Guthrum of East Anglia, for example, had coins minted in his short reign from 880 to 890, using the coinage of Wessex as a model. Shortly before 900 coins were also minted in the Five Boroughs and in York, and many coins from the first half of the tenth century, especially those from York, carry unique pictorial representations such as a sword, a banner, a bird or Thor's hammer.

A town like York, which is estimated to have had well over 10,000 inhabitants in 1066, required large supplies of foodstuffs as well as raw materials for its crafts. The rural population and the aristocracy would come here to acquire manufactured articles for everyday use and luxury goods. Very little is known about the life of the Scandinavians in rural areas, and so far it is uncertain whether Scandinavians or Anglo-Saxons lived in the two Viking Age farms excavated in Yorkshire: Ribblehead and Simy Folds.

The strong Scandinavian influence on the English language and the many Scandinavian place-names imply that the settlers arrived in considerable numbers. This must have been partly due to continued links with Scandinavia and with the other Viking settlements on the British Isles and because immigrants continued to arrive from there after the armies of 865 and 892 had settled down.

There are around 600 loan-words thought to be of Scandinavian origin in modern English, most of which are everyday words, such as 'cast', 'knife', 'take', 'window', 'egg', 'ill', 'die' (Old Norse *kasta*, *knífr*, *taka*, *vind-auga*, *egg*, *íllr*, *deyja*). In addition a number of important grammatical elements, such as the plurals 'they', 'them', 'their' (from Scandinavian *þeir*, *þeim*, *þeirra*) were introduced. English dialects contained thousands of Scandinavian loan-words, including many relating to agriculture, for example 'lathe' (Old Norse *hlaða*, barn), 'quee' (*kvíga*, heifer) and 'lea' (*lé*, scythe), but they are now disappearing together with the dialects. The strong linguistic influence resulted from the similarity of many Old English and Old Norse words, so from the beginning the two languages were intelligible to some extent, and a mixed dialect may soon have arisen in the Danelaw. The linguistic evidence also shows that many Scandinavians cultivated their own land and tended their own animals, unlike the Norman conquerors after 1066. The many Scandinavian loan-words relating to seafaring, which were quickly adopted, presumably reflect the Vikings' technical superiority in this field.

In many parts of eastern and north-western England the number of Scandinavian place-names is immense and their distribution gives us a good impression of where the Vikings settled. There are several hundred place-names with the Scandinavian suffix -*by*, which was given to many different types of settlement – for example, Derby, Holtby, Swainby, Slingsby and Ormesby – and many have the suffix -*thorp* – for example, Towthorpe, which has the Scandinavian man's name Tove as a prefix, and

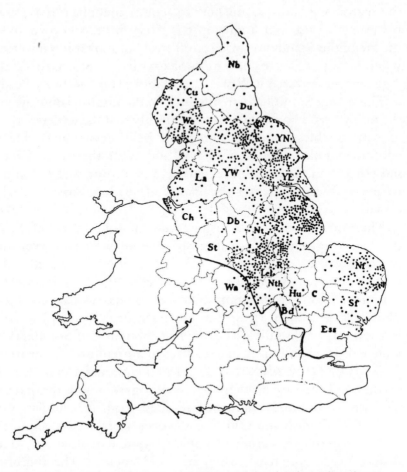

Parish names of Scandinavian origin in England. Their distribution
gives a good impression of where the Scandinavian settlements were
most dense. The border of the Danelaw is marked with a thick line.
Physical features such as uninhabitable marsh or bare uplands partly
explain the scarcity of Scandinavian place-names in some areas of the
Danelaw. Modern county divisions are indicated by dotted lines.

Wiganthorpe (Wigan from Viking). Place-names with a Scandinavian personal name as a prefix and an English suffix are also
quite common – Towton comes from Tove- and the suffix -ton –
and imply that an English settlement has been partly renamed. In
some cases the pronunciation of the English name was merely

changed a little, so that it came more easily to the Scandinavian tongue, for example Shipton became Skipton and Chesswick became Keswick. Others were translated, for example Churchton became Kirkby.

The naming process has been much discussed, but today it is generally agreed that many of the estates, farms and villages which the Viking leaders 'shared out' and the armies took over retained their names. There is much to indicate that the majority of Scandinavian place-names, certainly those with a personal name as a prefix and -by as a suffix, came into being somewhat later, when the large estates were split up into smaller units and given to individuals as their private property. The men who benefited from the estate divisions named their property after themselves. Some new farms with Scandinavian names were also established on marginal land, which had not been in use for some time, but these were relatively rare, for suitable soil was normally exploited. However, since Scandinavian language and Scandinavian personal names came to influence the language and naming customs within the Danelaw, some Scandinavian place-names were obviously formed a long time after the initial Viking settlements. This is especially the case with the names of fields and those based on Scandinavian loan-words for natural features.

The place-names also tell us that the Scandinavian settlements in the eastern part of the country were primarily Danish, which confirms the documentary accounts of the large armies, although some were Norwegian. From c. 900 there were also Scandinavian settlements in north-west England and the place-names demonstrate that both Norwegians and Danes settled there. Many of them presumably came via Ireland, Scotland, the Isle of Man or eastern England.

Perhaps the most important Viking Age find from north-west England is the immense silver hoard, weighing about 40 kilos, which was buried c. 905 in a lead chest on the banks of the river Ribble in Cuerdale, Lancashire (Plate 26). This is the largest of all known Viking hoards. Some of it must have been amassed in Ireland, possibly by one of the men driven out of Dublin in 902, for among the hack-silver there were penannular brooches and arm-rings like those current in Ireland. The hoard also included around 7,500 coins from different parts of the world. Most were from the English Viking realms, particularly from York, but some were from the independent English kingdom and from the Continent and Hedeby, and some were Islamic coins which arrived via Russia. There were more than 1,000 other pieces of silver: fragments of jewellery and ingots, and a few complete objects. The hoard is thought to have been worth about £300,000 in modern terms.

Pagan Viking graves have been found in twenty or thirty sites in the Danelaw area, singly or in groups. They confirm that here, as elsewhere, the settlers included women. There are relatively few graves, given the number of immigrants, but presumably many adopted Christianity quite quickly, especially in East Anglia, where the first Viking king, Guthrum, was baptized as early as 878. He had his Christian baptismal name, Athelstan, stamped on the coinage during the 880s, while coins commemorating St Edmund, whom the Vikings had killed in 869, were minted in East Anglia c. 895. Shortly after the turn of the century the written sources cease calling the Vikings from southeast England heathens, so by this time Christianity was presumably generally accepted here.

In northern England the picture is more complicated. Godfred, who became king of York in 880 or 881, was a Christian and a good friend to the monastic community of St Cuthbert. There were also archbishops in York throughout the period of Scandinavian rule, although some of the kings were pagan. But the Church in the north of England seems to have had its difficulties. People appear to have been buried with grave-goods, hence according to pagan rites, in churchyards for a time, many churches probably decayed, and we know that a number of monasteries were abandoned, among them Lindisfarne and Whitby. Some of the York coinage from the first half of the tenth century has Thor's hammer on one side and St Peter's name on the other, which shows that both religions were practised. However, even the Scandinavian countries were in the process of abandoning the old faith and many Scandinavians in northern England were undoubtedly Christians before the middle of the tenth century. The others followed quickly.

The art of stone carving flourished as a result of the conversion, giving rise to some of the most distinctive and interesting visible traces of the Scandinavians in England. Before their arrival, stone sculpture was almost exclusively found in monasteries; the Scandinavians, especially those in northern England, became greatly interested in stone memorials, but they required new forms and some new motifs, in keeping with their own needs and taste.

By far the majority of stone sculptures from this period, primarily the tenth century, are crosses and house-shaped grave stones. The latter have been called hogbacks, after their curved roof ridge, which, like the curved long walls, were characteristic of the large secular buildings of the time (Plate 25). In Yorkshire alone there are remains of more than 500 crosses and hogbacks. Many are decorated in Scandinavian, or rather Anglo-Scandinavian, style, especially the Borre and Jellinge styles and their derivations. Some carry motifs from popular heroic legends or Scandinavian mythology. The great hero Sigurð Fáfnisbani, for example, is depicted on a cross at Halton in Lancashire, while a stone in Gosforth church in Cumbria depicts Thor fishing for the World Serpent. The pictures on the most splendid of all crosses, the slender reddish cross which stands 4.42 m high in Gosforth churchyard, probably juxtapose pagan mythology and Christianity. The motifs on many stones cannot be understood today, but there is no doubt that these are Christian monuments, even though their decoration may include pagan elements and some motifs appear to be purely secular. The latter is the case with two warriors on horseback on a grave stone in Sockburn, and a warrior in full battledress, with helmet, shield, sword, spear, axe and large knife, carved on a cross in Middleton (p. 185), the reverse side of which is decorated with a limp ribbon-shaped animal in a sort of Jellinge style.

The number of stone monuments and the greatly varying quality of the carving indicates that they were commissioned by a relatively wide section of the community – and presumably also by the English. Some of the finest grave stones come from the Viking Age cemetery at York Minster, while many sculptures from village churches are rather rough works, on which the decoration was sometimes laid out using templates. The guidelines for motifs and ornaments might also be transferred on to the stone by means of small drilled holes – a principle used in Anglo-Saxon book illustration but not in pure Scandinavian art. On many stones, irregularities and cutting errors were hidden under a layer of plaster and all stones were presumably then painted in strong colours, for many paint traces have been found, as on rune stones in Scandinavia.

The art of scaldic poetry seems to have been highly valued in York, at least in the time of Erik Bloodaxe. The Icelander Egil Skallagrímsson declaimed a grand poem in his hall, according to *Egil's saga*; previously he had also composed in the hall of the English King Athelstan, though probably only a few of those present understood his art. After Erik's death a scald composed *Eiríksmál*, a grandiose memorial poem.

NEW EXPEDITIONS AND CONQUESTS

Throughout much of the tenth century many Scandinavians slaked their thirst for silver in Eastern Europe, and the efforts of the Scandinavian kings to extend and stabilize their realms involved a great number of warriors. Viking expeditions to Western Europe and England were unlikely to succeed, so these areas enjoyed a comparative respite from raids.

Around 970–80 the picture changed. Changes in Russia (see p. 285) meant that the influx of Islamic silver ceased around 970, causing profound problems in Scandinavia. And in 978 Edward, King of England, was murdered in mysterious circumstances. His brother Æthelred, who was only about ten, succeeded to the throne, and internal conflicts plagued the regime. Vikings reappeared in 980 and raided the south and west coasts of England, returning in 981 and 982. The attackers were few in number for the time being: the Anglo-Saxon Chronicle relates that seven ships plundered Southampton in 980 and three looted Portland in 983.

Some of these bands may well have come from Ireland, but from 991 large Scandinavian fleets entered the fray. In that year, according to the Chronicle, Olaf Tryggvason (who was not yet king of Norway) came to south-east England with ninety-three ships. He plundered far and wide, killed the courageous ealdorman Brihtnoth at the battle of Maldon in Essex, which was commemorated in a grand poem. It was decided that the victorious army of 'Danish men' should receive a tribute of 10,000 lbs of silver in return for ceasing the destruction. From then until 1016, when Cnut the Great became the sole ruler of England, the Chronicle contains almost annual accounts of great calamities caused by Viking armies and records a stream of acts of treachery, instances of cowardice, poor organization, wrong decisions on the part of Æthelred and his men, and serious ill fortune on the English side. To a large extent these were actual events, but it was also the apology of posterity for England being totally overrun. These sections of the Chronicle were not written until after the final conquest, with the bitterness of defeat.

In 994 Olaf Tryggvason attacked again, this time in company with Svein Forkbeard, king of Denmark, and ninety-four ships. They tried, unsuccessfully, to capture London and then proceeded to harry the environs until it was agreed that they should receive 16,000 lbs of silver, and provisions. The army took up winter quarters in Southampton. A separate agreement was made with Olaf: he was confirmed in the Christian faith, received royal gifts and promised never to return to England with warlike intent. The Chronicle stresses that he kept his promise, but does not mention that this was probably because he returned to Norway with his booty, took the Crown there, and was killed in battle against his old comrade-in-arms Svein Forkbeard in c. 1000. Shortly after Olaf and Svein returned home, they and the Swedish King Olof had coins minted, which, for the first time in Scandinavia, were modelled on the familiar and valued English coins (see illustration p. 113).

From 997 'the Danish army' was again on the offensive in England. There was a lull in the year 1000, perhaps because many men had returned home to take part in Scandinavian wars, but the Chronicle relates that the army was in Normandy that year and that King Æthelred himself plundered heavily in north-west England and the Isle of Man, presumably in order to crush the Scandinavian peoples there. The Viking army returned the following year and in 1002 they were paid 24,000 lbs of silver. In the same year Æthelred forged family links with the ruling dynasty in Normandy by marrying Emma, sister of Duke Richard, and he ordered all Danish men in England to be killed on 13 November. This plan probably did not include all those

who were of Scandinavian extraction and whose families had
lived in the country for a long time, but many lost their lives,
among them Svein Forkbeard's sister and his brother-in-law
Pallig, who had been in the service of Æthelred, but had betrayed
him in 1001 by joining the attackers.

In 1003 and the following year Svein harried large areas of
south and east England, presumably as an act of revenge. In 1005
the fleet returned to Denmark because of a great famine in
England. It returned in 1006 and the following year was paid
36,000 lbs of silver. In 1009 the mighty Danish chieftain Thorkel
the Tall and several other chieftains arrived with large fleets. They
were at once given 3,000 lbs of silver by the people of eastern
Kent and carried on to the Isle of Wight, which, as so often
before, became a base for plundering southern England. The
army moved on, raiding and pillaging and in 1011 Æthelred and
his advisers decided to pay up again, but before they could do so
the Vikings plundered Canterbury and captured the archbishop.
He would not allow himself to be ransomed (a slightly later
source says that 3,000 lbs of silver was demanded), which enraged
the Vikings so much that they killed him. The Chronicle describes
vividly how it happened: the Vikings had been drinking wine
and were very drunk; they had the archbishop brought before
their evening meeting, pelted him with bones and the heads of
cattle, and one of them struck him on the skull with the back of
an axe, 'and so he sent his holy soul to God's kingdom'. When
the huge tribute of 48,000 lbs of silver was paid soon after Easter
1012, the army dispersed, but forty-five ships under the command
of Thorkel went into English service and promised Æthelred to
defend the country.

The expeditions against England had followed the almost classic
course: small bands and scattered attacks were succeeded by large,
mobile armies which overwintered and extorted fast-increasing
payments – from 10,000 lbs of silver in 991 to 48,000 in 1012; and
finally Viking chieftains were engaged to keep others away.
However, in 1013 Svein Forkbeard sailed from Denmark to
conquer the whole of England. He took with him his son Cnut,
not yet twenty years old. Some of the ships must have looked
like Skuldelev 2 and 5. About twenty-five years later the fleet
was magnificently described in a work of literature (p. 88). It

landed at Sandwich, in Kent, and within a few months the country had been conquered. The army first moved to the Danelaw, which submitted and avoided being plundered. It then harried the areas to the south and west before moving northwards again. When all the English kingdoms submitted, Æthelred, Emma and their sons sought refuge in Normandy. Svein, as king of England, demanded tribute and provisions for the army. Thorkel the Tall did the same for his own army, which lay in the Thames, and had not joined Svein.

Svein Forkbeard, however, died on 3 February 1014. The army elected young Cnut king, but the English summoned Æthelred. An English army was organized and Cnut and his army were ousted. On their way back to Denmark the ships laid in at Sandwich in Kent and disembarked the hostages Svein had been given at the peace agreements; their hands, ears and noses had been cut off. Thorkel the Tall's army was given 21,000 lbs of silver by Æthelred, who obviously thought he might soon need it again.

In Denmark Cnut's brother Harald had ascended the throne. He helped reorganize the returned fleet, presumably because he was uncomfortable having an ambitious brother with a large army in his kingdom, and in 1015 Cnut set off again for England. The scald Óttar the Black says in *Knútsdrápa*:

> But a boy, you ship-batterer,
> when you launched your boat,
> no king younger than you
> yet cast off from his country:
> helmed one, you hacked
> the hard-cased ships,
> risked all, with the red shield
> raged along the shore.

This time the English defences were under the command of Æthelred's energetic son Edmund, who had succeeded his father in April 1016. The country was still weakened by acts of treachery, however, and Cnut was victorious at the great battle of Ashingdon. The Anglo-Saxon Chronicle says that 'all the nobility of England was there destroyed'. Edmund and Cnut agreed to divide the country, but before the year 1016 was out, Edmund had also died, leaving Cnut the sole ruler.

It was an impressive achievement to conquer England, but the armies of Svein and Cnut were probably organized on the same basis as the other Viking armies operating abroad: a number of *lið* (troops of warriors), each with its leader, who obeyed the king (pp. 67, 140). In this case the number of *lið* must have been very large. Both Svein and Cnut set out with a clear objective and must have had exceptional qualities as military leaders.

They would have found it easy to gather people for expeditions to England in 1013 and 1015, for by then everybody in Scandinavia knew that England's wealth was almost inexhaustible and not difficult to seize. The armies included men from all over Scandinavia, as had probably been the norm since 991. Olaf Haraldsson, later King of Norway and St Olaf, was, for example, in Thorkel the Tall's army of 1009–12. Many performed great deeds in England and returned home with silver, honour – and an inexhaustible fund of good yarns. In Sweden it was the fashion to raise rune stones at the time of the expeditions to England as well as later, when the veterans died, and many had their participation recorded on stones. The memorial inscription of Ulv from Yttergärde in Uppland ends thus:

> And Ulv took in England three gelds.
> That was the first which Toste paid. Then
> Torkel paid. Then Cnut paid.

Toste may have been a Swedish chieftain. Torkel is Thorkel the Tall and Cnut is Cnut the Great. Those who were given a memorial stone in Valleberga in Skåne with the following inscription may have been Cnut's men after he became king of England:

> Sven and Thorgot made this monument
> in memory of Manne and Svenne. God
> help their souls well. And they lie in
> London.

Some did not get that far. On a rune stone in Husby-Lyhundra in Uppland four men commemorated their brother Svein: 'He died in Jutland. He was on his way to England.' The mere fact

of having been on one's way to England was apparently worth
recording on a stone.

CNUT THE GREAT AND AFTERWARDS

In Cnut's first years as king of England there was much to be
done. The country was divided into four earldoms based on the
old kingdoms. Cnut kept Wessex, Thorkel the Tall got East
Anglia, Earl Erik, from the mighty Norwegian family of the
earls of Trøndelag, got Northumbria; the English renegade, the
ealdorman Eadric Streona, who had changed sides again and
again, got Mercia, but Cnut had him killed within a year, 'rightly',
says an English source. Other English nobles were also killed,
among them Æthelred's son by his first marriage, Eadwig, and
some were exiled. In 1017 Cnut married Æthelred's widow
Emma, whose two sons remained in Normandy, thus becoming
related to English royalty. Emma bore him two children, Harthacnut and Gunhild, or Kunigunde, although he also had another
woman, Ælfgifu (or Alfiva) of Northampton, by whom he had
two sons, Harald and Svein.

The great army was still in England, but by 1018 the conditions
there had become so stable that it could be dissolved – after an
unprecedented tribute of 72,000 lbs of silver, plus 10,500 from
London alone, was defrayed. Forty ships – the famous *þing-lið*:
loyal, splendidly equipped and disciplined Scandinavian warriors – remained with Cnut. Many probably still regarded him
as the Viking conqueror and he based his power on these warriors.
He also created a new English aristocracy, beholden to him for
their prosperity. In all the battles since 991 many English noblemen had died heroically, had been killed by the kings on suspicion
of betrayal, or had gone into exile. Cnut retained the main
structure of English royal power, but his men were new. They
had not served Æthelred, and as a result many lands were redistributed and the rule of the realm changed.

In 1018 King Harald of Denmark died and in the winter of
1019–20 Cnut went back in order to secure his hold over
Denmark, entrusting the government of England to Thorkel the
Tall. From Denmark Cnut sent a letter to the English people,

which was presumably proclaimed throughout the realm, giving
an account of his achievements in safeguarding England from
Danish threats, and emphasizing his role as a Chrstian king of
England and his authority there. Later Thorkel the Tall probably
became Cnut's representative in Denmark, together with young
Harthacnut. In the 1020s Cnut began to lay claim to Norway and
in 1028 he captured the country from Olaf Haraldsson. It was
then governed by Ælfgifu and her son Svein. In 1027 the king of
Scotland submitted to Cnut. That year, during his great journey
to Rome, Cnut sent another letter to the English people, in which
he calls himself 'king of all England, and of Denmark, of the
Norwegians, and of part of the Swedes'. In Rome he witnessed
the coronation of the German Emperor Conrad and was treated
with great honour. He also entered into practical agreements
that benefited the English and the Scandinavians and arranged a
marriage between his daughter Gunhild and Conrad's son Henry,
who later became emperor. The marriage took place in 1036, but
Gunhild died two years later.

Cnut became above all an English king. He went to Scandinavia
when problems arose there or (as he implies in his letters) to
prevent more Viking attacks on England. He brought peace to
the country, which had been ravaged for so long; there is no
evidence of internal revolt either. The price paid for peace was
tribute to his *þing-lið*, but this was presumably seen as both
cheaper and pleasanter than plunder and payment of Danegeld
to harrying enemies.

Cnut set great store by the English laws of former times and
he was a great benefactor of the Church. In many respects he
became almost more English than the English, and in a shower
of publicity he did penance for old Viking sins. In order to atone
for the martyrdom of King Edmund of East Anglia in 869 he
built a large church for the monastery in Bury St Edmunds; for
the murder of the Archbishop of Canterbury in 1012 he had his
body transferred with great ceremony from London to Canterbury; for the bloody battle of Ashingdon in 1016 he had a
church built on the battlefield. Many churches received large
gifts. The ceremony at which Cnut and Emma presented a golden
cross for the altar of the New Minster in Winchester was immortalized *c.* 1031 in a drawing in the church's commemorative book,

Liber Vitae (Plate 27). Cnut's right hand grasps the cross, his left his sword. Cnut and Emma were often in residence in Winchester and he was buried there in the Old Minster when he died in 1035, aged about forty. The young Viking had turned into an exemplary English king. One could wish to believe a much later description of him in *Knytlinga saga* from the mid-thirteenth century:

Knut was exceptionally tall and strong, and the handsomest of men except for his nose which was thin, high-set and rather hooked. He had a fair complexion and a fine, thick head of hair. His eyes were better than those of other men, being both more handsome and keener-sighted. He was a generous man, a great warrior, valiant, victorious and the happiest of men in style and grandeur.

Cnut's death meant the end of stability and the great 'empire' at once split up. Harthacnut was in Denmark and, in spite of much resistance from Emma and others, Ælfgifu's son Harald became king of England. Alfred, one of Emma's two sons by Æthelred, came over from Normandy, but was killed, and Emma had to flee. When Harald died in 1040 Harthacnut and Emma returned to England. Harthacnut imposed an immense tax to pay for his sixty ships and died two years later: 'he was standing at his drink and he suddenly fell to the ground with fearful convulsions', says the Chronicle. According to another version, 'He did nothing worthy of a king as long as he ruled.'

All Cnut's four children died without issue and Emma's other son by Æthelred, Edward (later known as Edward the Confessor), ascended the throne in 1042, which meant that Emma, having been the queen of two kings, saw a son by each of her husbands on the throne of England. In the reign of Harthacnut she commissioned a monk in the monastery of St Omer in Flanders to write a history of Cnut and his deeds, *Encomium Emmae Reginae*. It goes on to describe her two surviving sons, who are depicted in the book, together with their mother and the monk presenting her with the work. This work also contains vivid descriptions of Svein's and Cnut's fleets departing from Denmark in order to conquer England (p. 88). The problems of Æthelred's reign are not mentioned. Emma died in 1052 and was, like Cnut and Harthacnut, buried in the Old Minster in Winchester.

Edward the Confessor married Edith, daughter of the mighty Earl Godwin, who was by family and career connected with the Danish royal house, but Edward, who had been brought up in Normandy, allowed Norman interests to prevail over Scandinavian, and in 1051 he abolished the tribute, *heregeld*, which had financed contingents of Scandinavian mercenaries ever since Thorkel the Tall went into the service of Æthelred in 1012. All the soldiers were now sent home.

When Edward died without issue in 1066, Edith's brother, Earl Harold Godwinsson, was elected king. Others had their eye on the throne, however, and in September the king of Norway, Harald Harðráði, sailed for England. Like Svein Forkbeard before him, he wanted to begin his conquest in northern England, where the Scandinavian element in the population was strongest. He was defeated and killed by King Harold, together with a large part of the army, on 25 September 1066 at the battle of Stamford Bridge, 12 km east of York. Duke William of Normandy landed in southern England on 28 September, also with a view to conquest. Harold Godwinsson marched southwards in record time. At the battle of Hastings on 14 October his army suffered defeat, he was killed, and on Christmas Day 1066 William the Conqueror, a Viking descendant, was crowned king of England. The decisive battle of Hastings and the background to it was pictured about a decade later in the 70-m-long tapestry which came to be housed in Bayeux Cathedral in Normandy.

William introduced a completely new administration and a French-Norman aristocracy. There were several revolts against him; in 1069 a big uprising in northern England was suppressed and punished in an exceptionally brutal fashion. The large Viking fleets which arrived in 1069, 1070 and 1075, under the command of members of Danish royalty, made no significant inroads. In 1085 King Cnut of Denmark organized an immense fleet with the intention of reconquering the country over which his great-uncle had ruled. William transferred huge armies from Normandy to England, but Cnut's fleet never got under way. He was detained by problems on his southern border and in the late summer the fleet dispersed. His officials punished those who had returned home with such violence that it provoked a rebellion and in 1086 King Cnut was killed in the church of Odense dedicated to the English St Alban. The dream of seizing the English throne eventually made Cnut Denmark's first royal saint. This was the last time a Scandinavian conquest of England was attempted.

For nearly a century Scandinavia had had a decisive influence on the balance of power in England. Svein, Cnut and Harthacnut had been kings there. Many others had participated in the government of the country and even more had served in the royal fleets. There was no real immigration in this phase of the English Viking Age, but the new Scandinavian aristocracy made a certain impact on art and culture, especially in southern England, where most of them lived.

Famous scalds composed poems in praise of Cnut the Great, among them the Icelander Óttar, who also made poems about St Olaf of Norway and Olof Skötkonung of Sweden. Scandinavian taste is clearly reflected in the ornamental arts, including objects manufactured in England. The predominant style in the period of joint rule was the Ringerike style, which was itself influenced by English art and was therefore close to English taste and the abilities of English artists. One of the most magnificent surviving examples of this style can be seen on a stone from the churchyard of St Paul's in London (Plate 22). This is decorated with a great beast in an animated pose, entwined by a smaller, snake-like creature. The motif is undoubtedly inspired by the animal picture on King Harald's large rune stone at Jelling in Denmark, and the representation is closely related to the beast on the gilt weather-vane from Heggen in Norway, which once graced the prow of a Viking ship. Traces of paint on the stone from St Paul's show that it was originally painted in strong colours: the animals were blue-black with white spots, while the tendrils and the frame were red and the background whitish. On the edge part of a runic inscription, which must have continued on other stones making up the memorial, can be seen. It reads, 'Ginna had this stone laid and Toki'. We do not know the name of the deceased, but Ginna and Toki are Scandinavian names and they may all have been members of Cnut the Great's *þing-lið*.

Objects decorated in the Ringerike style have been found in Winchester and many other parts of southern England. The style was quite widespread and is occasionally used for ecclesiastical manuscripts. The Urnes style, which succeeded the Ringerike style in the mid-eleventh century in Scandinavia, also occurs in England. It appears on stone carvings in churches, such as Jevington in Sussex, Southwell Minster in Nottinghamshire and Norwich Cathedral in East Anglia, as well as on various metal objects, including a bishop's crosier from Durham. A certain taste for Viking art survived into the twelfth century, but the Ringerike and Urnes styles never came to dominate English art or to influence it, as the earlier Scandinavian styles had in northern England a century earlier.

For Scandinavia these English adventures were of immense importance. There were now closer links with Norway, Sweden and Denmark than there had been in the ninth century, and people from all the Scandinavian countries took part in the expeditions. Those who survived got a share of the huge amounts of silver paid as Danegeld and *heregeld* right up to 1051, and of the booty seized between 991 and 1016, although the leaders probably took the lion's share. Millions of English coins were paid out, of which more than 40,000 have been found so far in Scandinavia, and their number is still increasing. There are about 3,300 in Norway, 5,300 in Denmark and 34,000 in Sweden, but the relative numbers probably reflect the economic systems of the different countries rather than the numbers of people who travelled from each of them to England and the size of their profits. It is not surprising that Scandinavian coins were modelled on English ones for a long time after 995.

Many other objects from this period have also been found in Scandinavia, but of course much could have been acquired by trade. An English source from *c.* 1000, for example, says that York was a rich town because of the many treasures brought there by merchants who came from all parts and especially from Denmark.

English ecclesiastical influence was particularly strong in Norway and Denmark. English clerics were appointed to church offices; English saints became popular, and English church vocabulary was incorporated into the Scandinavian languages. The earliest Scandinavian stone architecture also displays English influence. It was undoubtedly commissioned by the aristocracy who had spent half their lives in England. In the time of Cnut the Great, England, Norway and Denmark were in many respects one cultural region, where the most influential figures regularly travelled from country to country with large retinues. The English adventures made Scandinavia internationally orientated to an extent never seen before.

Iceland, the Faroes, Greenland and America

===

Iceland, the Faroes and Greenland were colonized by Scandinavian farmers in the Viking Age and remain part of Scandinavia today. These islands were uninhabited, except, perhaps, for some Irish hermits in Iceland and the Faroes; there were no people at all in the parts of Greenland which were settled, as the Eskimos lived further north at this time. Here there was nothing to loot or conquer, only new land to live on and live off. Those who ventured here brought families, livestock and chattels, and succeeded in building up entirely new communities, although in Greenland the conditions stretched a peasant economy to the limits, and the Scandinavian communities here foundered at the end of the Middle Ages. But large numbers of present-day Icelanders and Faroese are direct descendants of the Viking Age settlers.

One of the great achievements of the Viking Age was that Scandinavians were the first Europeans to set foot in America. Those who reached North America were farmers from Greenland, though it is unlikely that they built farms, as the land was already inhabited.

The settlers in these new lands were predominantly Norwegian, and although the climate and conditions may seem harsh, in many ways they resembled the conditions in much of Norway. Besides, the soil was fertile and unused. As at home, the economy was essentially rural, with a mixture of livestock, fishing, hunting birds and animals of land and sea, and gathering berries; the cultivation of cereals obviously played a very minor role under these northern skies. As in northern Norway and Scotland, no towns or international trading centres were established. The lack of forests with good supplies of timber meant that the only sources

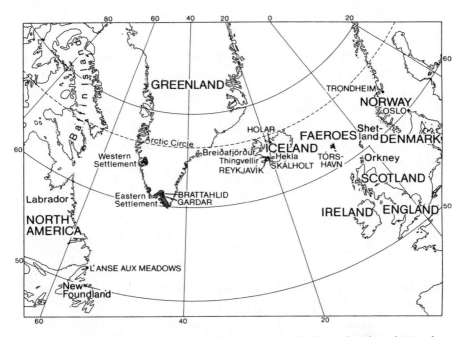

The North Atlantic region, the Faroes, Iceland, Greenland and North America in relation to Scandinavia and the British Isles.

of wood were scrubland, small trees or driftwood. Though this was excellent for many purposes, it was not good for building the flexible ships of the Viking Age.

The reason that the settlers chose to live in isolated communities at the edge of the known world must have been above all a desire for good land, so that they could support themselves and their families better than at home, where the soil may have been poor or become impoverished, or may have fallen into other hands by inheritance. A spirit of adventure and political factors probably also played a role; according to Icelandic literature, the desire for liberty was an important incentive: many Norwegian chieftains departed in order to avoid subjection to King Harald Finehair. None of the North Atlantic pioneer communities had a king or an earl, and they remained republics of farming magnates with a certain democracy and a high degree of independence until long after the Viking Age. The structure in Iceland is often described as an oligarchy. In some periods, the emigration from certain areas must have amounted almost to a mass movement. The new lands offered great opportunities, and many people proved themselves capable of coping with pioneer life.

Good ships and competent sailors were essential for the North Atlantic expeditions, both when setting out to colonize new land and to maintain connections with the old world, which were imperative for the survival of the traditional peasant economy and the deep-rooted Scandinavian culture. The North Atlantic was no place for narrow, light warships; what was needed were solidly built cargo ships which could stand up to long voyages on the high seas, in rough and stormy weather, and could transport people with their livestock and chattels to the colonies; later they had to be loaded with quantities of import and export goods. The settlers and their immediate descendants presumably used ships resembling the cargo ship Skuldelev 1. Despite the quality of the ships and the outstanding seamanship, there are many accounts of shipwreck, people washed overboard, ships driven far off course by bad weather, or striking land some distance from their goal because of the lack of accurate means of navigation.

The settlers must have sailed from their homelands in groups of households with their slaves, and with a leader in charge. The ships would be loaded with essential objects of daily use and raw materials unobtainable where they were going. In addition there would be the animals needed to form new herds of livestock, principally sheep, goats, cows and horses, and some dogs. Some seedcorn and vegetable seeds may also have been taken. Until the livestock became sufficiently numerous, and the plants had been harvested, the settlers must have lived by fishing, hunting, gathering wild plants and berries, and making dairy products. The conditions must have been very primitive, just as the settlers in America found in the eighteenth and nineteenth centuries.

The class structure was to a certain extent the same as that at home, and it was the group leaders who claimed large areas of land and formed the ruling elite of the new countries.

No contemporary written sources tell when and how the Faroes, Iceland and Greenland were first colonized. The Viking Age sources that we have contain very little information about these areas. Adam of Bremen's description of c. 1075, for example, says little more than how far away they seemed from the Continent. Adam wrote of the Icelanders:

They make a living only by raising cattle and clothe themselves with their pelts. No crops are grown there; the supply of wood is very meagre. On this account the people dwell in underground caves, glad to have roof and food and bed in common with their cattle, passing their lives thus in holy simplicity, because they seek nothing more than what nature affords.

A misunderstanding of the volcanic activities must lie at the root of his statement that 'the ice on account of its age is so black and dry in appearance that it burns when fire is set to it'. On the subject of Greenland he states that 'the people there are greenish from the salt water, whence too, that region gets its name'. He further tells that the Archbishop of Hamburg–Bremen, who was head of the Icelandic and Greenland churches, had sent letters to the people there, promising to come and visit them soon – presumably an empty promise.

Most of the immense literature that survives was first written down in the twelfth and thirteenth centuries or later, and was composed by the leading circles of Icelandic society. It consists of sagas, historical works, laws and a few poems. The large cast of characters and the many dramatic events that are now a colourful part of the history of these regions first appear in these stories, which naturally express the interests, the conception of history and the literary traditions current in the period when they were written down. Some were partly based on speculation about place-names and natural phenomena and theories about existing settlements or ruins. Direct links between this literature and archaeological finds from the Viking Age can rarely be established, which is not surprising, given that sometimes 300 or 400 years intervened. The stories of Erik the Red and his family in Greenland or of Leif the Lucky's visit to America may contain only a small kernel of historical fact, so they must obviously be read chiefly as literature, not as eye-witness accounts.

THE SETTLEMENT OF ICELAND

Iceland is a volcanic island of 103,500 square kilometres, about 500 km wide from east to west. Its northerly regions touch the Arctic Circle but the climate is relatively mild because of the Gulf

Stream. The island lies about 570 nautical miles (c. 1050 km) west of Norway and the journey involves crossing large expanses of open sea. Landfall could only be made on the Faroes, or on the Shetlands if a more southerly route were taken. Iceland must have seemed an alien country because of earthquakes, hot springs and geysers, to say nothing of the volcanoes, many of which were active. However, the indented rocky coasts, large glaciers (*jǫkull*) and barren mountain areas were familiar from Norway, there was good pasture for the animals and many birds, as well as fish in the sea and rivers, and whales and seals. There were also forests of dwarf birch and willow as well as scrub, and along the coasts there was masses of driftwood for house-building and carpentry.

The discovery and much of the earliest history of Iceland are shrouded in legend. The most important source is Ari Þorgilsson's famous work *Íslendingabók* (*The Book of the Icelanders*), written c. 1120–30. Ari, also known as Ari Fróði, 'the learned', was a member of Iceland's educated and cultivated elite, who clearly engaged in serious reflection about the history of the island. It is a brief work with a strict chronological framework. About the period of colonization Ari wrote:

Iceland was first settled from Norway in the days of Harald the Fairhaired [Finehair], son of Halfdan the Black, at the time – according to the opinion and calculation of Teit my foster-father, the wisest man I have known, son of Bishop Isleif, and of my paternal uncle Thorkel Gellison who remembered far back, and of Thurid daughter of Snorri Godi who was both learned in many things and trustworthy – when Ivar, son of Ragnar Lodbrok, caused Edmund the Saint, king of the English, to be slain; and that was 870 years after the birth of Christ. A Norwegian called Ingolf, it is told for certain, went first from there [i.e. from Norway] to Iceland when Harald the Fairhaired was sixteen winters old, and for the second time a few winters later. He settled south in Reykjavik.

According to Ari by 930 the land was completely settled. The settlements must have been on the coast, the plains in southern Iceland and open valleys in other areas. The interior was always uninhabitable, apart from an area to the south. Pagan graves from the end of the ninth century or the tenth century have been found in many places, and correspond well with Ari's account.

Landnámabók (*The Book of the Settlements*), a large work going back to the twelfth century which survives in later editions, gives a detailed account of the discovery and colonization of Iceland. About 430 leaders of individual settlements as well as their ancestors and descendants are mentioned. The real purpose of the work was probably to establish a register of the landed properties and to support the land claims of the families who were in power in the twelfth century.

It also tells that a certain Naddoð, who went off course at sea, reached Iceland before Ingolf. Garðar Svarvarsson and Flóki Vilgerðarsson are also said to have set foot on Iceland first. It is even possible that Iceland was discovered much earlier. Various written sources from the fourth century onwards mention an island called Thule, said to lie far north of Britain, where the sea to the north is frozen. Thule also appears in a geographical work written around 825 by the Irish monk Dicuil. He refers to Irish hermits who had moved to Thule; it was so light there in midsummer that one could catch fleas at night as easily as in daylight. The descriptions of Thule may well apply to Iceland, and Ari also tells of Irish monks who hastily left the country when the Norwegians arrived, but no archaeological traces of settlements earlier than the Scandinavians' have been found, despite much effort. It is possible that Ari's information is actually an explanation of some ecclesiastical objects he had seen, which had in fact come to Iceland with Vikings from Ireland.

Although the sources agree that the majority of the immigrants came from western and northern Norway, they also relate that considerable numbers came from the Scandinavian settlements in the British Isles, especially from Scotland and Ireland. Some of them had Celtic wives and others may have brought Celtic slaves with them. There are even some place-names with Celtic prefixes, such as Brjánslækr (from Brian), and personal names such as Njál, the main character in *Njáls saga*, written down around 1280, in which the battle of Clontarf near Dublin in 1014 is mentioned.

Among the 300 or so pagan graves of the Viking Age known from various parts of Iceland, some are presumably those of the first settlers, although no named person has been identified. Nor have any farms been excavated which can be dated with certainty to the very first period of settlement, although Hvítárholt in southern Iceland is certainly Viking Age and excavations have demonstrated that the settlement in Reykjavík is certainly very old. At present there is much uncertainty over the dating of a farm called Stöng and other farms excavated in 1939 in the large valley of Thórsárdalur in southern Iceland. For a long time it was thought that these were destroyed by ash from an eruption of the volcano Hekla in 1104 and then abandoned, and that they were built in the late Viking Age. New investigations indicate that they were also inhabited after 1104.

Ingolf settled in Reykjavík, which offered a good harbour, large areas of pasture, many birds, breeding grounds for seals, an abundance of fish in the rivers, lakes and sea, as well as whales. There were also hot springs. Barley could be cultivated and thus ale brewed. According to Ari Þorgilsson, the Kjalarnes Thing or Assembly, the earliest Icelandic social institution we know of, was established near Reykjavík. Ingolf's son Þorsteinn and other chieftains in the area set it up *c*. 900, according to Ari. As at home it was a public assembly of free men who, under the leadership of chieftains, decided the laws, resolved legal disputes and settled matters of common interest. Ari relates that the Kjalarnes Thing was the direct precursor of the Althing, established on *Þingvellir*, the Thing Plain, a little east of Reykjavík some years before 930. This became the Thing for the whole of Iceland. Here the chieftains and their people met for two weeks at midsummer. Current laws were declaimed, new laws passed, solutions to disagreements were sought by law, agreements were entered into, politics were discussed and markets were held. The Althing gave the scattered population of the island an opportunity to meet and hence also fulfilled social and cultural functions.

In order to contain disagreements within a more limited area, the island was later divided into quarters, each of which had three or four local Things. These were led by three officers known as *goði* (*goðorð* was the office), who were the heads of local chieftain families and whose public functions were primarily connected with the Thing. Many believe it is possible to glean much information about Iceland's earliest social organization, the judicial system developed in the tenth century, and cultural and historical matters in general, from the large collection of laws, known unaccountably as *Grágás* (grey goose), which contains many twelfth-century provisions preserved in late thirteenth-century manuscripts.

Throughout the Viking Age, Iceland had many links with the outside world, chiefly with Norway and the British Isles. According to *Landnámabók* it took seven days to sail to Norway and five to Britain, presumably in fair weather. Greenland, which was colonized predominantly by Icelanders, was also visited regularly as were other regions. Many people were very widely travelled. Some had been on trading expeditions to fetch essential goods – Iceland's exports were chiefly woollen cloth, but falcons were also in demand and goods from Greenland were traded in due course. Some travelled abroad as warriors or to visit the courts of great kings (the Icelandic scalds were a special category), while others had to leave their home country to sort out their inheritance or to make political agreements with the Norwegian kings, who soon became interested in the large free state in the Atlantic.

Christianity was accepted by the Althing, with some modifications, in the year 1000 (or 999) after strong pressure from Olaf Tryggvason. During the reign of Olaf Haraldsson, who is known as 'the Fat' in Icelandic literature, missionary bishops were sent out to organize Christian life on the island. The first Icelander to become a bishop was Ísleif, whose son was consulted by Ari Þorgilsson. Ísleif was consecrated in Bremen in 1056 and it is related that he had first visited the Pope in Rome and the German Emperor Henry III, whom he presented with a unique rarity, a polar bear from Greenland. At the end of the eleventh century the first permanent bishop's seat was established in Skálholt in the south, followed by a second in Hólar in the north in 1106.

From the eleventh century onwards, treaties with Norwegian kings regulated various matters of mutual interest; in 1262–4 the Icelanders acknowledged the formal supremacy of Norway and consequently became liable for taxation. This was the end of the free state. From 1380, Iceland, as part of the Norwegian realm, had Danish rule. In 1944 Iceland chose to become an independent republic once more.

THE FAROES

The Faroes are the summits of a submarine mountain ridge which connects Iceland with Scotland. The eighteen islands and many islets and skerries stretch 113 km from north to south and cover 1,399 km². The climate is tempered by the sea and the Gulf Stream and the islands have good pasture and rich birdlife, while the sea teems with fish and whales. When the land was settled there was also extensive scrubland and lots of driftwood on the coast.

There is no firm evidence of when the Faroes were colonized but, given their location, it was probably before the settlement of Iceland and perhaps contemporary with or shortly after the settlement of Shetland and Orkney by Scandinavian farmers. In 825 the Irish monk Dicuil wrote that by then Irish hermits had lived for almost a century on a group of islands north of Britain, where there were innumerable sheep and many kinds of seabirds and that they had now departed because of Scandinavian pirates. Although Faroes means 'sheep islands', it is not yet known whether these are the islands Dicuil describes. As in Iceland, no archaeological evidence of pre-Viking activity has been found. Farms and graves from the Viking period have been excavated but they are usually very difficult to date precisely and many of the earliest farms have no doubt disappeared into the sea because of the rise in sea level and erosion. At Kvívík, for example, only the upper end of a Viking Age farm remains. The settlement at Toftanes in Leirvík does seem to be early, probably dating from the tenth century or before, so this does cast light on how the first islanders lived.

Information about the Faroes in the Viking Age is scattered and often unreliable. *Færeyinga saga*, most of which is set in the decades around the year 1000, relates that Grim Kamban was the first man on the islands and that he arrived there in the days of Harald Finehair. It tells the story of the glittering hero Sigmund Brestisson, who brought Christianity to the islands, and his adversary Þrandr of Götu, and mentions the relationship with the Norwegian kings and much else. But the saga was not composed until the thirteenth century, probably around 1220. Some place-names and some linguistic and other evidence, however, suggest that a number of Scandinavian immigrants here came from

Celtic-speaking areas (Grim's surname of Kamban is also Celtic), as the *Færeyinga saga* relates, although the majority probably came from Norway. Later foreign connections must also have been primarily with Norway and the British Isles, and many people must have stopped off at the Faroes on their way to or from Iceland. The chief export was presumably wool or woollen cloth.

Like Iceland and the Scandinavian settlements in Scotland, the Faroes came under Norwegian dominion, probably in the eleventh century. In 1380 the islands devolved to the Danish crown together with Norway, and since 1948 the Faroes have been a self-governing community under the Danish crown.

COLONISTS IN GREENLAND AND TRAVELS TO AMERICA

The Scandinavian colonization of Greenland is far better documented than that of the Faroes. The most important written sources are Ari Þorgilsson's *Íslendingabók* (based on what Ari's uncle was told by someone who had accompanied Erik the Red to Greenland) and *Landnámabók*. There are also two colourful sagas, *Grænlendinga saga* (the *Saga of the Greenlanders*), and *Eíriks saga rauða* (the *Saga of Erik the Red*), which are about the earliest settlements but chiefly about the journeys to Vinland (America). However, they were not composed until the early thirteenth century and are often fanciful, as is much other literature of that genre, and contradict each other in places. Where they agree, we presumably come close to the oral traditions on which they are based, as the two authors probably did not know each other's work. In addition, the Viking Age in Greenland and America is illuminated by archaeological excavations.

Most of Greenland is covered with ice and snow but its southern tip lies far south of Iceland, on the same latitude as the Shetlands, Bergen and Oslo. Along the deeply indented coast of south-west Greenland there is a fair amount of pasture. The areas most suited to the Scandinavian peasant economy lie far down the fjords, not far from the inland ice fields, and it was there that the first Scandinavians settled around 985, under the leadership of Erik

the Red from Breiðafjörður in north-west Iceland. According to
Íslendingabók, Erik called the land Greenland because the name
would encourage people to go there.

Greenland is said to have been discovered by a man named
Gunnbjörn, whose ship had gone off course (a common way of
discovering new land in the North Atlantic). The sagas claim that
it was thoroughly explored by Erik the Red before he and his
followers went there to settle, which must be true. Twenty-five
ships departed from Iceland, according to *Landnámabók*, but only
fourteen are said to have arrived – some were wrecked and others
returned home. Erik and his wife Þjoðhild took the best fjord,
which they called *Eiríksfjǫrðr*, and built the farm Brattahlíð near
its head (in present-day Qagssiarssuk, just opposite the airport
Narssarssuaq) (Plate 28). Along one side of *Eiríksfjǫrðr* (Tunugdliarfik) there is much good pasture and Brattahlíð lies on a large
plain that is one of the most fertile in Greenland, with another
large green valley behind it. From Brattahlíð it is not far to
Garðar (Igaliko), another of Greenland's best agricultural areas
and from about 1125 the seat of the country's bishop. Both the
Eastern Settlement (the area around present day Qaqortoq or
Julianehåb) and the Western Settlement (around Nuuk or
Godthåb) were presumably established quite soon.

The agricultural economy was based on sheep, goats and cows,
and Greenland's main attraction was undoubtedly that it had
better pasture than Iceland – after about a century of heavy
exploitation, the land in Iceland had probably become very poor
or had even been destroyed. In Greenland the soil was fresh and
uncultivated, as farmers had never lived here. The climate was
probably a little milder than today, and, as on the Faroes, part of
the fertile, low-lying land has now disappeared into the sea. There
was probably also quite a lot of driftwood at that time.

The settlers also exploited the rich resources of fish, seals and
whales, and hunted reindeer, bears and birds. The essential
imports – metals, chiefly iron, timber, grain – and luxury goods
could be paid for with goods which were highly prized in Europe:
the pelts of polar bears and arctic foxes; hunting falcons; walrus
tusks, narwhale tusks and whalebone for works of art; rope from
walrus hide; baleen (from whales) for sewing into garments to
stiffen them and give them shape; and, the most exotic export of

all, live polar bears. Many of these things could only be found on perilous journeys to the far north.

The Greenland community was very vulnerable if there were epidemics among animals or people, failures of pasture, long periods of bad weather and even small climatic changes, and in fact it died out at the end of the Middle Ages, so far without any demonstrable reason. However, in the Viking Age things seem to have gone well and there were many links with the outside world. Christianity was introduced around the year 1000, though the sources disagree as to how it happened, and whether it came from Iceland or Norway, the countries with which Greenland had most contact.

A tiny church has been excavated at Brattahlíð, with thick walls of turf, measuring 2 × 3.5 m inside. This is probably Greenland's earliest church, built in the days of Erik the Red or shortly afterwards, perhaps by Þjóðhild, as the *Saga of Erik the Red* relates. The saga adds that the church lay at some distance from the houses, as Erik was against Christianity, but this may only have been the writer's theory, for excavations show that the church lay close to a building which may have been the main dwelling at that stage, though at some distance from the house and church in use at the time the saga was written. Presumably everything about the earliest house had been forgotten, whereas the site of the earliest church was still remembered.

There were 155 people buried around the church: sixty-four men, thirty-seven women and thirty-four children, and twenty adults whose gender could not be established. Twelve of the men were buried in a communal grave with a ten-year-old child; they had presumably perished elsewhere and were later brought here for burial. Several of the pioneers from the period of colonization, and perhaps some of those immortalized by the sagas, must be among those buried in the churchyard. They were tall, sturdy people: the average height of women was 5 ft 3 in, that of men 5 ft 8 in and several men were as tall as 6 ft $\frac{1}{2}$ in.

This fits well with the figures we have from other parts of Scandinavia and the same applies to the average lifespan (cf. p. 31). Seventeen of the fifty-two men buried in individual graves reached the age of between twenty and forty and twenty-three were between forty and sixty; it is not clear when the remaining twelve died. Of the thirty-seven women, fourteen reached an age of between twenty and forty, twelve were between forty and sixty, and three were more than sixty years old, while eight died at an indeterminate age. None seemed to have suffered from dental caries, though their teeth were very worn down. Most of the older people suffered from osteo-arthritis. Several would have stooped and been stiff-legged, but this was not confined to the Viking Age population in Greenland. Pagan Scandinavian graves have not been found, and the only known evidence of pre-Christian religion is a small Thor's hammer incised on a soapstone object found in Brattahlíð.

The sagas relate that America (Vinland) was discovered when ships went off course during one of the long sea journeys to Greenland from Iceland or Norway. The *Saga of the Greenlanders* attributes the discovery to Bjarni, son of Herjolf, who had emigrated with Erik the Red, although Bjarni did not actually land, while the *Saga of Erik the Red* says that the discovery was made by Leif the Lucky, Erik's son. Discovery of new lands was of course highly prestigious. One saga describes four visits to America by the other two, but they agree that Leif was there, and that another expedition was led by the Icelander Þorfinn Karlsefni.

There has been much discussion as to which parts of the long east coast of North America were designated Vinland (Wine Land), Markland (Wood Land) and Helluland (Stone or Rock Land). These were presumably Newfoundland, and possibly in Labrador and Baffin Island to the north. The only firm evidence of a Scandinavian Viking Age settlement in America has been found on the northern tip of Newfoundland, at L'Anse aux Meadows: large buildings with turf walls, like those in Iceland and Greenland, and a couple of Scandinavian objects, among them a ringed-pin of a type first made by the Vikings in Ireland, and a soapstone spindle whorl. Here all the resources a pioneer community could wish for were available: fertile agricultural land, a good climate, hunting and fishing grounds, as well as iron, which was smelted from local bog-iron ore, and a plentiful supply of good timber for ships. However, these lands were inhabited, and the local Indians or Eskimos, whom the Norse Greenlanders called *Scrælings*, were hostile. This, coupled with the vast distance from friends and relatives, was undoubtedly the reason why the journeys to America were only expeditions and did not give rise to permanent settlements. The sagas seem to be correct in this respect. The journeys continued into the Middle Ages, to obtain important raw materials.

The buildings at L'Anse aux Meadows were thus only used for short periods, and even though they have been dated to the era of the famous expeditions of the sagas, it is quite possible they were not built by the people we know of. Some scholars believe that L'Anse aux Meadows was a transit station for expeditions further south and that Vinland itself was in the south, but apart from a Norwegian coin from King Olaf Kyrre's reign (1066–80), found on an Indian settlement in the state of Maine, there are no traces of Viking Age or medieval Scandinavians further south.

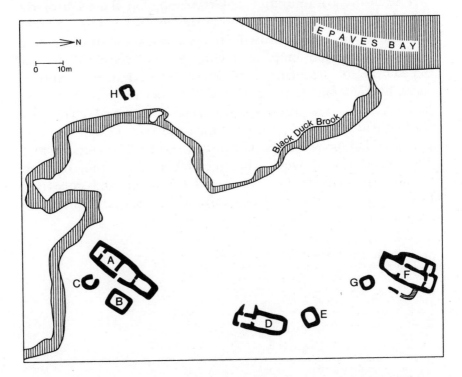

Plan of L'Anse aux Meadows, Newfoundland, the only known Viking Age settlement in America. Buildings and other structures which were only in use for a short period have been excavated here. A–G houses and other buildings. H smithy.

Some medieval finds from Eskimo settlements in Arctic Canada demonstrate that there was some contact between the two peoples, unless the objects were taken from shipwrecked or murdered Greenlanders, or picked up in their seasonal camps in the far north.

The Vinland journeys captivate the imagination: it is remarkable that Scandinavian people travelled so far and discovered America before Columbus. Enthusiasts have even imagined that the Vikings explored the entire American continent and in various places there are fake rune stones (the Kensington Stone) and other fake Scandinavian objects. Several ancient Scandinavian objects taken to America in more recent times have also caused a stir, and structures and art across North America, in Mexico and even in South America have been misidentified as Viking.

The Norse communities in Greenland, 'on the edge of the world', accepted Norwegian supremacy in 1261 and in 1380 they accrued to the Danish crown. In 1712, centuries after the links were broken, the king of Denmark and Norway sent an expedition to Greenland with Pastor Hans Egede to nurture the Christian faith among the Viking descendants, but none had survived. The Eskimos, the ancestors of today's Greenlanders, had long since penetrated the country to its southernmost point, and these were the Greenlanders that Hans Egede met. The expedition, however, became the starting point for new connections between Greenland and Denmark, and since 1979 Greenland has been a self-governing community under the Danish Crown.

THE BALTIC REGION, RUSSIA, BYZANTIUM AND THE CALIPHATE

The Vikings' adventures to the east and south of Scandinavia were fundamentally different to their colonial achievements in the North Atlantic. Eastwards and southwards lay the cultural and economic centres of the known world, the Byzantine Empire and the Islamic Caliphate; in Russia, too, there was great wealth and vast resources of coveted goods such as quality furs and slaves.

These regions were within reach of Scandinavia after only a short journey across the Baltic. A number of large rivers flow into the Baltic, giving access to Europe's interior, and trading centres grew up near the river mouths, such as Wolin on the Oder and Truso on the Vistula. Some rivers led to trading centres such as Staraja Ladoga near the head of the Gulf of Finland, 12 km south of where the river Volchov flows into Lake Ladoga; Novgorod near the Volchov's source in Lake Ilmen; Kiev on the Dniepr; and Bulgar on the bend in the Volga where the Volga and the Kama merge. Along these waterways the Scandinavians moved freely. Those who travelled in Russia were mostly from the eastern part of Sweden.

Some, travelling via the Black Sea and the Caspian Sea, got as far as the fabulous city of Byzantium, the capital of the Eastern Roman Empire, or even reached the Caliphate and Baghdad, which was for a long period the residence of the Caliph, and which displayed even more splendour and greater ceremony than Byzantium. Russia, Byzantium and the Caliphate were sources of vast quantities of silver, gold and magnificent artefacts for the adventurous, who also won undying fame. The journeys along the rivers were hazardous, however, as in many places the ships had to be dragged across land to reach another river or had to negotiate dangerous stretches with rapids, rocks and strong currents. Travellers were also vulnerable to attack by people who lived along the rivers. They presumably used fairly small, light ships, which could easily be dragged across land and were manoeuvrable on rivers.

The large area of Eastern Europe in which the Vikings travelled was inhabited by many different peoples and tribes. The West Slav tribes lived south of the Baltic; their lands bordered Saxony and Denmark in the west. Balts and Finno-Ugric peoples lived on the east coast of the Baltic up to the Gulf of Finland, and other Finno-Ugric peoples further north in Finland and towards the east. Poland became a kingdom in the tenth century and adopted Christianity in 968, but the other tribes along the Baltic did not become Christian until the twelfth and thirteenth centuries.

The East Slav tribes lived to the south and east of the West Slavs and the Balts. They came to have a ruling dynasty of *rus* origin from Scandinavia (cf. p. 287). In the tenth century their realm, with its capital in Kiev, became a major power in Eastern Europe and in 988 they adopted Christianity. They gave their name to Russia. In the south-east the Turkish Khazars ruled from the Aral Sea in the east to the Dniepr in the west, and from the Caucasus in the south to the bend of the Volga in the north. Their capital was Atil, at the mouth of the Volga. The Khazars officially professed Judaism but many other religions were also practised. The realm foundered in the second half of the tenth century. The Volga Bulgars, also Turkish, who adopted the Muslim faith in the 920s, had their capital at Bulgar, which was one of the most important fur-trading centres of the period. Fine pelts were brought from the cold regions in the north to meet the demand for them in Byzantium and the Caliphate, and traders came from as far as Arabia and the Orient along rivers and caravan routes. Large amounts of silver changed hands here.

The disparate documentary sources about the many peoples of Eastern Europe and about the activities and impact of the Vikings are quite different in many respects from those which record the situation in Western Europe. They are written in widely different languages and are often difficult to interpret, for the Scandinavians were only one of many groups of travellers in Eastern Europe, and the ethnic designations are not always clear. The difficulties are compounded by the fact that few West European scholars have had the opportunity to study Scandinavian archaeological finds in the Soviet Union, and strong nationalistic feelings have influenced the interpretation of such material, particularly in relation to the formation of the old Russian state. In recent years the discussions have become more balanced, however.

The most important documentary source about Russia is *The Russian Primary Chronicle* (also known as 'The Chronicle of Nestor', or 'The Tale of Bygone Years'), collated in Kiev in the first two decades of the twelfth century. There is also information in Arab geographical works (including the account of Ibn Fadhlan mentioned on pp. 34, 157) and in Byzantine sources and Western European annals and accounts. The latter concentrate on the West Slav tribes. Rune stones, nearly all from the eleventh century, found in Sweden record expeditions to Eastern Europe and Byzantium. Scaldic poems also mention exploits in the East, and the later Icelandic sagas imbue the expeditions to these exotic realms with a romantic glow.

ACROSS THE BALTIC

Long before the beginning of the Viking Age people from what is now Sweden had settled on the southern and eastern coasts of the Baltic. Scandinavian graves from c. 650 to 850 have been examined in Grobin in Courland, Latvia. Scandinavian graves from the Viking Age and back to c. 700 have been found in Elbing on the Gulf of Gdansk, at the mouth of the Vistula. In both places much typical Gotlandic jewellery has been found, as well as other Scandinavian objects, which indicate that people from the Swedish mainland settled there too.

Grobin may well be Seeburg, the town mentioned in Rimbert's *Life of Ansgar*. This includes an account of an unsuccessful Danish military expedition, and a successful Swedish one, against the Courlanders around 850, the time of Ansgar's second mission to Birka. It also relates that the Courlanders had previously been subject to the Svear. Tributes were now imposed by Olaf, King of Birka, who led the victorious expedition and captured not only Seeburg but also Apulia. This may be Apuole, about 40 km south-east of Grobin; the similarity of the names makes it likely, and we know that a large fortification here was in use in the Viking Age. The trading centre Truso, which the merchant Wulfstan visited after an uninterrupted sea voyage of seven days and nights from Hedeby, presumably lay at Elbing. His account of his journey is included in King Alfred's edition, made in c. 890, of Orosius' *History of the World*.

Throughout the Viking Age written sources contain sporadic information about trading and military expeditions from Scandinavia to the Baltic lands, and about extortion of tribute, political alliances and mercantile interests there. None of these written sources come from the area itself, but in many of the trading centres on the southern and eastern coasts of the Baltic there is archaeological evidence of contacts with Scandinavia, and even of some Scandinavian settlement. The Scandinavians remained a minority of the population, although they did hold political power for a time in some places. There is no evidence of Scandinavian rural settlements along the Baltic. They came to trade, as did people from many other regions who sought to profit from the flourishing Baltic trade by acquiring the local goods such as salt, amber, wax, honey, hides, furs and slaves. In c. 1075 Adam of Bremen wrote that Jumne (which must be Wolin, at the mouth of the Oder) was the largest town in Europe (a slight exaggeration) and that it was inhabited by Slavs and other peoples, Greeks (i.e. people from Byzantium), barbarians and even by Saxons, who were not allowed to display their Christian faith in public. It may well be that some of the Vikings who lived and died in these trading centres were mercenaries in the employ of local princes, as in many other parts of the world. Many trading centres were undoubtedly looted by Scandinavians during the Viking Age, even though this is rarely mentioned in contemporary written sources.

From west to east the trading centres included Oldenburg and Alt-Lübeck; Reric, whose precise location is debated but Mecklenburg is one possibility; Ralswiek on the island of Rügen, and Menzlin near the mouth of the river Peene, all in Germany; Wolin, Kołobrzeg and Truso in Poland; Wiskiauten (Višnevo) and Grobin in the Soviet Union. Staraja Ladoga, near the head of the Gulf of Finland, controlled a large part of the trade with Russia. In all these places and many more there is archaeological

The Mervalla stone in Södermanland, Sweden. The inscription begins at the head of the snake with the name of Sigrid, who raised the stone.
The stanza commemorating her husband begins in the band to the right of the snake's tail with the word *hn* (he); after the tail it continues with the word *knari*.

evidence of contacts with Scandinavia; and Hedeby and Birka were part of this great trading network.

In many parts of Sweden rune stones were raised in the late Viking Age in memory of men who took part in fighting and trade along the east coast of the Baltic. The stone in Mervalla in Södermanland, for example, was raised by Sigrid in memory of her husband Svein, who was given the following verse:

> He often sailed
> to Semgallen
> in dear-prized 'knarr' [ship]
> round Domesnäs.

Domesnäs is the dangerous northern tip of Courland, which had to be negotiated before sailing into the Gulf of Riga, and

Semgallen is the plain south of the lower Dvina, in Latvia. Many travelled along the Dvina to Russia. Other stones mention Samland (in the south-eastern corner of the Baltic), Vindöy (Windau, a harbour a little south of Domesnäs), Livland (between Semgallen and Estonia), Estland (Estonia), Virland (the north-eastern part of Estonia on the Gulf of Finland), Finland (presumably the south-western part of present-day Finland) and Tavasteland (a little further north in central Finland). Many archaeological remains also reveal close links between Sweden and Finland, but it was not until the thirteenth century that the great Swedish conquests and settlements took place there.

These connections made a great impact on Sweden, especially the east, where many imported luxury items have been found. There were also close links between the Danes and the West Slav tribes who were their neighbours. Quite detailed mention of these connections is made in West European written sources, though only when the West European realms had an interest in the matter. After the Frankish conquest of Saxony at the end of the eighth century, both the Danes and the Slavs became neighbours of the Frankish Empire and at the beginning of the ninth century the Frankish Annals record the alliance made between the Danes under King Godfred and the West Slav tribe, the Wilzes, on one side, and the Frankish Empire and another West Slav tribe, the Abodrites, on the other. In 808, the year Godfred had his border wall built against Saxony, he conducted a major military campaign against the Abodrites, with the assistance of the Wilzes, and subjected two-thirds of the population to tribute, destroyed the trading centre of Reric, which had provided him with a substantial income from tribute, and moved the merchants from Reric to Hedeby. The following year Thrasco, the ruler of the Abodrites, was murdered by Godfred's men in Reric, which had apparently survived. In 817 the Abodrites changed sides and entered into an alliance with the sons of Godfred, though after the next change of ruler they went back to the Frankish side.

In 983 a great alliance of Slav tribes and Danes joined forces against the German realm, which had expanded both eastwards and northwards, but was now decisively repulsed. Around this time marriages took place between Scandinavian kings and the daughters of West Slav princes. For example Harald Bluetooth married a daughter of the Abodrite prince Mistivoj. She raised a rune stone in Sønder Vissing in central Jutland in memory of her mother, whose name is not known; she called herself 'Tove, daughter of Mistivoj, wife of Harald the Good, Gormsson'. Svein Forkbeard also married a princess from the recently established Polish kingdom. She had earlier been married to the king of the Svear, Erik the Victorious.

From this time until well into the twelfth century West Slav influence in eastern Denmark and Sweden was strong and must have affected many things; today it can be seen mainly in pottery and jewellery. However, the techniques of bridge-building may have been learnt from the Slavs, who in turn learnt ship-building techniques from the Vikings. A number of Slavs probably settled on the southern Danish islands, where Slav place-names still survive, and during the eleventh century military power shifted in favour of the Slavs. After the death of Cnut the Great a long phase of Slav expeditions commenced, on land and at sea. One was halted on Lyrskov Heath near the Danish border by King Magnus the Good of Norway, who ruled Denmark from 1042 to 1047. According to later histories, the victory was due to assistance from his deceased father St Olaf, and the occasion was commemorated by the minting of a special coin in Hedeby with the picture of Olaf and his attribute, the axe. This is the earliest representation of him as a saint-king. The fact that Olaf and Magnus had been in exile in Russia illustrates that some Norwegians, as well as Swedes and Danes, went east.

TOWARDS THE GLORIES OF THE EAST

The written sources about the movements of the Vikings in Russia do not give a coherent picture of the development there – far too few are contemporary – but a basic outline can be drawn with the help of archaeological finds, among them the many silver hoards. The Scandinavian activities in the East were probably similar in many ways to those we know so well from Western Europe.

The earliest Scandinavian finds from eastern Europe are a few items from mid-eighth-century layers in Staraja Ladoga – the town's earliest phase; other finds show that Finno-Ugric, Baltic and Slav peoples lived there too. Much evidence of Scandinavians, including graves, from the second half of the ninth century and over the next hundred years or so has now been found here and elsewhere in central Russia, coinciding with the period when Staraja Ladoga, called *Aldeigjuborg* in the sagas, became a well-established trading centre on the route between Scandinavia and central Russia.

A hoard of Islamic dirhems, minted between 749 and 786, as well as single finds of eighth-century coins discovered in and around Staraja Ladoga show that the town developed partly on the basis of long-distance foreign trade, and Islamic silver was to provide the impetus for the expanding economies of Russia and Scandinavia for most of the Viking Age. Huge amounts reached Scandinavia between about 800 and 1015. Much was melted down and made into jewellery, but more than 85,000 coins, mostly from the tenth century, have been found there: more than 80,000 in Sweden, particularly in Gotland; about 4,000 in Denmark; and 400 in Norway. Although these figures reflect to some extent the degree of involvement of the various regions in the Baltic areas and Russia, they are, as far as Sweden and Denmark are concerned, also determined by the local economic systems: where it was more common to pay with silver and coins than with goods, the silver remained in circulation rather than being hidden as hoards, as on Gotland (cf. p. 112). The coins were obtained along the Baltic and in Russia in various ways.

Islamic coins reached Russia a little before the year 800. They came from the Middle East, from present-day Iran and Iraq, via the Caucasus and the Caspian Sea, and they were used in the realm of the Khazars, along the lower Volga and Don as payment for goods. From there they spread; the earliest Viking hoards containing Islamic coins found on the Baltic coast and in Scandinavia date from the early ninth century.

Hoards hidden in the ninth century and the early tenth century in these regions also contain quite a number of Russian silver neck-rings (so-called Permian rings) most of them were twisted into spirals so that they could be used as arm-rings. They have a fixed weight of 100, 200 or sometimes 300 grams, which correspond to $\frac{1}{4}$, $\frac{1}{2}$ or $\frac{3}{4}$ *grivna,* the Russian unit of weight (the original meaning of the word *grivna* was in fact neck-ring). They were probably used as jewellery as well as ring-money, like arm-rings in Scotland. As neck-rings they are particularly common in the areas of Perm and Kirov, north of the bend of the Volga.

From *c.* 875 to 900 the influx of Islamic coins into Russia, and hence into Scandinavia, ceased, probably because the trading patterns between the Caliphate and Russia broke down. When new links were established after the turn of the century the picture had totally altered: until around 970 the coins used in transactions were struck in the Islamic Samanide realm in central Asia, north of the river Oxus, often in Samarkand and Tashkent. Here there were large silver mines and the good silver coins found their way by the million to Russia as payment for luxury goods. A number of them reached Scandinavia. It was at this time that Bulgar became the main centre for distributing the highly prized silver as well as the centre of the fur trade.

Shortly after 965 this stream of silver came to an abrupt end, possibly because of a scarcity of silver in the Islamic realms. The effects were acute. The lack of silver in Scandinavia may have led to Birka being abandoned *c.* 975 and to Harald Bluetooth's balance of power in relation to the German realm breaking down in 974. It was also presumably why many people from now on turned their attention westward, to wealthy England. When Islamic silver again started to arrive in Scandinavia at the end of the tenth century it was only in small amounts and around 1015 it stopped completely.

The large amounts of silver in Scandinavia cannot simply be the payments made by Muslim merchants in return for goods from Scandinavia or for Western European transit wares, because the things that the Vikings could supply and the Muslims desired were available in abundance much closer in Eastern Europe: furs, walrus tusks ('fish teeth'), slaves, wax, honey, amber. Moreover the Scandinavians were only one of many trading peoples and Western European luxury goods also reached Russia, Byzantium and the Caliphate either via the Mediterranean or across central Europe, along the great trade route from Mainz via Prague and Cracow to Kiev and on to the east or the south.

The Scandinavians may, however, have sold swords of their own or of Western European manufacture in Russia, and it appears from written sources that the Scandinavians imposed tribute on the local population in various parts of Russia, to be paid in silver or in goods, and that they also went on looting expeditions. In 860 they even attempted to capture Byzantium, while the emperor was away, and are said to have tried again later. Furthermore there are accounts of expeditions across the Caspian Sea. As in Western Europe, the income from tribute and the booty from successful raids may well have been exchanged for silver on the great markets. Throughout the tenth and eleventh centuries many Vikings were employed as mercenaries by princes in Russia or the emperor in Byzantium and their wages were another source of the silver which ended up in Scandinavia. It was most probably one or more of these mercenaries who scratched runes on a marble balustrade in Hagia Sophia, the main church of Byzantium and of the Orthodox Church; the name Halfdan can be distinguished among the scribbles.

The Arabs called the Scandinavians *rus*, as did the people of the Byzantine Empire. The origin of the word is uncertain and it was sometimes applied to quite different peoples. The earliest mention of *rus* occurs in the Western European Annals of St Bertin. Under the year 839 it relates that some *rus* were of the Svear people; emissaries had been sent by their kings to the Emperor of Byzantium but could not return home the way they had come, because of barbarians and wild peoples. Instead they accompanied an emissary from Byzantium to the Emperor Louis the Pious in Ingelheim. Louis' realm was subject to violent Viking attacks at this time so before he complied with the Byzantine emperor's request to send them home, he wished to discover whether they were spies. If they were, they would be packed off back to Byzantium. Other sources more generally identify the *rus* with people from Scandinavia.

The term *rus* is also used in the Russian *Primary Chronicle*, in connection with the three brothers Riurik, Sineus and Truvor, who are said to have been chosen to rule over tribal groups in northern Russia and Estonia in 862. Sineus and Truvor are said to have died two years later, whereupon Riurik assumed power over their areas too. He is said to have been the ancestor of the old Russian royal dynasty and that after his death his kinsman Oleg, who was the guardian of Riurik's young son Igor, seized power in Kiev too in 882. Kiev became the capital of this realm, which soon expanded and became a major power.

The famous and much discussed 'Legend of the Calling of the Princes' from *The Russian Primary Chronicle* says of the year 6367 (i.e. after the creation of the world; Byzantine and Old Russian chronology started with this event and 6367 corresponds to our year AD 859):

The Varangians [i.e. Scandinavians] from beyond the sea imposed tribute upon the Chuds, the Slavs, the Merians, the Ves', and the Krivichians ... Year 6368–6370 [860–862]. The tributaries of the Varangians drove them back beyond the sea and, refusing them further tribute, set out to govern themselves. There was no law among them, but tribe rose against tribe. Discord thus ensued among them, and they began to war one against another. They said to themselves, 'Let us seek a prince who may rule over us and judge us according to the Law.' They accordingly went overseas to the Varangian Russes: these particular Varangians were known as Russes, just as some are called Swedes, and others Normans, English and Gotlanders, for they were thus named. The Chuds, the Slavs, the Krivichians, and the Ves' then said to the people of Rus', 'Our land is great and rich, but there is no order in it. Come to rule and reign over us.' They thus selected three brothers, with their kinsfolk, who took with them all the Russes and migrated. The oldest, Rurik, located himself in Novgorod [one of the manuscripts says Ladoga, i.e. Staraja Ladoga, and this could be right, but Gorodishche on the Volchov river, 2 km south of Novgorod, is also a possibility; Novgorod itself does not appear to be so old]; the second, Sineus, at Beloozero; and the third, Truvor, in Izborsk. On account of these Varangians, the district of Novgorod became known as the land of Rus. The present inhabitants of Novgorod are descended from the Varangian race, but aforetime they were Slavs.

These events in the ninth century are naturally of a legendary nature, for the *Primary Chronicle* was not compiled in Kiev until the beginning of the twelfth century. But this version would have been acceptable there at that time and the names of the earliest members of the dynasty must mean that they were of Scandinavian descent: Riurik (the Danish Viking chieftain by the name of Rurik, who operated at the same time in Frisia, can hardly be the same person), Oleg (Helgi), Igor (Ingvar) and his wife Olga (Helga). Oleg, Igor and Olga are known from reliable historical sources. Igor's and Olga's son Sviatoslav (957–73) was the first ruler to have a Slav name. In 988 his son Vladimir adopted Orthodox Christianity, and he was the first Russian ruler to have coins struck. In the reign of his son Yaroslav the Wise (1014–54) the connections with Scandinavia were sealed by royal marriages. Yaroslav himself married Ingegerd, the daughter of the Swedish king Olof Skötkonung, and his daughter was married to King Harald Harðráði of Norway, who had done great services and gained huge wealth at the court in Byzantium. It was with Yaroslav that King Olaf and his son Magnus sought refuge from Cnut the Great in 1028.

From the end of the ninth century there were close contacts between the realm of Kiev and Byzantium. Treaties, recorded in the *Primary Chronicle*, were made in the years 907, 912, 945 and 971, which regulated military and mercantile matters. After the introduction of Christianity the connections were further strengthened. The strong Byzantine and Eastern influences which reached eastern Sweden and Gotland were probably mainly the result of contact with Kiev, rather than the direct influence of Byzantium and the Caliphate. The many imported goods and the fashions among Birka's upper class have been mentioned in earlier chapters; a fine example of the influence of the Eastern Church has survived in the form of coloured glazed clay eggs, symbols of the resurrection and made near Kiev, which have been found in several places in Sweden.

A number of Scandinavians other than princes lived in Russia. Scandinavian names are mentioned in written sources about Russia, for example in the treaties mentioned above, and the Slav language absorbed a certain number of loan-words, some of which are still in use, for example *lar'* (box, casket) from Scandinavian *lár*. Many Viking graves have been found in Russia, the women's containing oval brooches, among other things. The Vikings were normally buried in cemeteries among the local people, which indicates that the relationship was often good. Cemeteries, with one or more Scandinavian graves, have been found in several places along rivers in the heart of Russia, often by town, or trading stations, for example near Staraja Ladoga and a little south east of Lake Ladoga; at Yaroslav on the upper Volga, near Bulgar; at Gnezdovo on the upper Dniepr, only a short distance from the Dvina; at Černigov on the Desna, a tributary of the Dniepr; and in Kiev.

Other Scandinavian finds from these areas, and from all the way down to southern Russia, include hoards and twelve Islamic coins with incised runes and at least five other runic inscriptions. One found in Staraja Ladoga is a complicated verse, while the inscription on a stone raised on the small island of Berezani in the Black Sea, by the mouth of the Dniepr, reads: 'Grane made this sarcophagus after Karl, his partner', who was presumably buried there. The stone is now in the museum at Odessa.

The Scandinavian finds in Russia are numerous. At least 187 oval brooches are known, for example, far more than from the whole of Western Europe. It is reasonable to assume that some Vikings became farmers in Russia as in Western Europe, especially where conditions were similar to the Mälar region and where the distance to the homeland was not too great, such as on Lake Ladoga. However, many Scandinavian settlements in Russia were presumably only a temporary base for individuals. There were permanent trading stations where merchants would stay while goods were acquired in the district, before departing for the great markets, and stopping there again on their way home. Other settlements may have been a mixture of a permanent trading station and military base, rather like in Ireland, where women too would have lived. A number of Scandinavians must have lived permanently in Russia.

Left and right: silver pendants in Borre style from a large hoard found in Gnezdovo near Smolensk, USSR, tenth century. Height 3.7 cm and 3.4 cm. Center: bronze disc decorated in Ringerike style from Carwitz, Germany, eleventh century. Diameter 4.8 cm.

In art, the Borre and Jellinge styles were predominant and they were also used by craftsmen in Russia. As elsewhere, a mixed art came into being, but the idioms of Scandinavian and Slav art were so different that when combined, the results were often fantastic and almost grotesque in their strength and imaginativeness, as in the case of the large silver brooch from Elec.

THE GREAT RIVERWAYS AND THE MEMORIALS

No Scandinavian place-names are in use in Russia today, but the Scandinavians in the Viking Age had their own names for the large towns and, significantly, for the rapids on the lower Dniepr south of Kiev, which many passed on their way to Byzantium. The name of the most dangerous of these, *Aifur*, was mentioned on a Gotland rune stone: 'they went far to Aifur' and by the Emperor Constantine in his work *De Administrando Imperio* (*On the Administration of the Empire*) written *c.* 950, where he tells of the journeys of the *rus* from Kiev to Byzantium: in the month of June (when the waters had sunk to a reasonable level after the thawing of the winter snows) they gathered from many places in Kiev and moved off in a party. South of Kiev the river Dniepr flowed wide and calm but seven rapids had to be passed before they reached the Black Sea. Through some they dragged the ships carefully. In other places, among them *Aifur*, the ships had to be dragged or carried over land. On many sections of the route there was the risk of attack. After the last rapid they halted on an island and made sacrifices of, among other things, live cocks, and cast lots in order to make various decisions. On their arrival at the Black Sea they halted again at Berezani and then continued to Byzantium past the Danube delta.

What goods they brought, apart from slaves, is not recorded, but the account ends with a passage which relates that the *rus* from Kiev travelled out in November to collect tribute from their dominions and that they returned in April. They no doubt sold this tribute, but we are not told what they acquired in Byzantium, although one of the treaties recorded in the *Primary Chronicle* gives the *rus* the right to buy silk there for a stipulated sum. Much of the silk which reached Scandinavia in the Viking

Age presumably came from Byzantium. This coveted commodity was subject to export restrictions and the goods which were taken north were no doubt taxed both in Kiev and in other places where trade could be controlled.

The route from Byzantium to the Baltic is briefly described in the *Primary Chronicle*: across the Black Sea and up the Dniepr; in the upper reaches of the Dniepr by portage to the river Lovat, which flows into Lake Ilmen; along the Volchov, which flows into Lake Ladoga, and from there along the river Neva into the Baltic, 'the Varangian Sea'. This route passed Kiev, as well as Novgorod and Staraja Ladoga. It was also possible to cross from the Dniepr to the Dvina and from there into the Gulf of Riga and the Baltic. The more easterly route to the Volga and Bulgar would have gone from Lake Ladoga along the river Svir to Lake Onega and from there a little way south and then a distance overland to the river which led to Lake Beloozero and the town of the same name. It was in this area that Riurik's brother, Sineus, settled in 862 according to the legend. From Beloozero a river provided a route southwards to the Volga, already almost 1 km wide at this point. Another route to the Volga, which also entailed portage, started from Lake Ilmen.

Some of those who won wealth and glory in the East in the eleventh century were commemorated on rune stones, especially in eastern Sweden. Some returned home with rich booty and used it sensibly, as is related on a stone near Veda in Uppland: 'Torsten made it in memory of Ärnmund, his son, and bought this farm, and made the money east in Garðariki' (Russia). Other inscriptions speak of fallen heroes, like the stanza on the Turinge stone in Södermanland, in memory of the chieftain Þorstein and his brother:

> The brothers were
> among the best men
> on land
> and out in the host,
> treated their
> retainers well.
> He fell in action
> east in Garðariki,
> the host's captain,
> of 'land-men' the best

Novgorod (Hólmgarð) is also mentioned on a couple of rune stones (see page 15), but not Staraja Ladoga or Kiev. The Byzantine Empire (Grίkland), however, is often mentioned, for example on a stone at Ed, north of Stockholm, which says:

> Ragnvald had the runes cut in memory
> of Fastvi, his mother,
> Onäm's daughter. She died in Ed. God
> help her soul.

> Ragnvald let
> the runes be cut.
> He was in Greece,
> was leader of the host.

The returned hero may have been in the imperial guard. Ingvar's unfortunate expedition in *c*. 1040 to Serkland, probably the Caliphate, has been mentioned on page 190. Probably none of its members returned home, but twenty-five rune stones in Sweden and romantic tales in later Icelandic literature are reminders of Ingvar and his men.

The Gotlander Rodfos met a particularly lamentable end and his parents raised a stone in Sjonhem in his memory. Its inscription ends:

> Wallachians betrayed him on an
> expedition. God help Rodfos's soul. God
> betray those who betrayed him.

The Wallachians probably lived in present-day Romania. The most splendid runic monument to Viking deeds in the romantic East is a large marble lion. For many centuries it had guarded the harbour of Athens, Porto Leone in Piraeus, when a Swede carved an inscription on its shoulder, shaped like a writhing snake, as on the rune stones back home. Unfortunately wind and weather and battles in the harbour have made the inscription illegible. Today the lion stands at the Arsenal in Venice, where it was taken as a victory trophy in 1687.

Conclusion

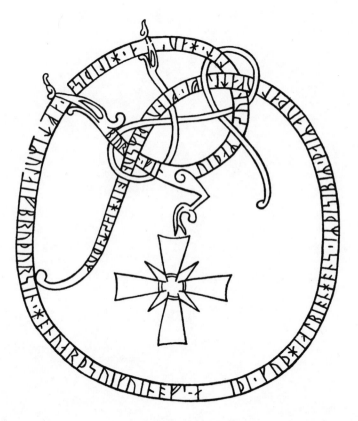

Runic inscription and Urnes-style ornament on a memorial stone
from the late Viking Age in Nora in Uppland, Sweden. The
inscription begins on the neck of the larger animal. It reads: 'Björn,
Finnvid's son, had this rock carved in memory of Olav, his brother.
He was betrayed on Finnveden. God help his soul. This farm is their
odal [allodium] and family inheritance, the sons of Finnvid at Älgesta.'
Finnveden is in the south-western part of Småland.

The World of the Vikings

The world of the Vikings was extensive. It stretched round the whole of Europe: from Scandinavia to the Mediterranean, along both easterly and westerly routes, and to the north-west to Iceland, Greenland and America. Throughout the Viking Age many sought their fortune in distant lands. Some remained there, others returned home and the tough life took its toll. Never before or since have so many Scandinavians been commemorated at home for exploits abroad – on rune stones, in poems and later on in the sagas. Many played out great roles on the European stage: the chieftain Hasting, who operated in the Loire, in the Mediterranean and in England; Godfred, who took land in Frisia and married the emperor's daughter, but did not get half the kingdom; Olaf Godfredsson, who sought to unite the kingdoms of Dublin and York; Cnut the Great, who became king of all England as well as of Denmark and Norway and part of the Swedes; Ingolf, who took land in Reykjavík; Erik the Red, who took farmers to Greenland; Riurik, Oleg and Igor in Russia. Others, like Ingvar in the land of the Saracens and Rodfos from Gotland, who was so outrageously betrayed by the Wallachians in the south – what parts did they play?

The many foreign cultures which the Vikings encountered meant that a multitude of new influences and enormous riches came to Scandinavia. Cultural change and development had never been so fast. By the end of the Viking Age the Scandinavian communities were quite unlike those that had existed around the year 800, when bands of men had first set out for Lindisfarne, Ireland, France and across the Baltic. Now there were three large kingdoms each with growing, centralized power, several towns and increasing specialization of occupations. Norway and

Denmark were Christian, and Sweden almost Christian; the standard-bearers of the new faith sought energetically to change the old life-style and introduce new ideals.

Europe too had been subject to great changes. New powerful realms had been created and others had foundered, and in Russia and Normandy there were ruling dynasties of Scandinavian origin. South-west Greenland, Iceland, the Faroes, Shetlands and Orkney, the Hebrides and the Isle of Man were Scandinavian. There were Scandinavian enclaves in Ireland, and Scandinavian people also lived in several places along the southern and eastern coast of the Baltic and in Russia. Many descendants of Scandinavian immigrants lived in England and Normandy and it was not long since England and Denmark had been ruled by one king.

If one date has to be chosen to mark the end of the Viking Age it has to be 1066. The Scandinavian era was far from over everywhere, but by then the expeditions on the Continent were long since past and almost a century had elapsed since the stream of Islamic silver had dried up. In 1051 English silver also ceased to flow into Scandinavia. The last mercenaries were sent home and no similar sources of income were available elsewhere. The last major Viking expedition, which took place in 1066, decided the fate of England and England's relationship with Scandinavia; in two great battles Vikings and Viking descendants from completely different regions and backgrounds met and fought.

The Norwegians were on one side under the command of Harald Harðráði, half-brother of Saint Olaf, son-in-law of Yaroslav the Wise of Russia, brother-in-law of kings of Hungary and France. He had played a dramatic part as an imperial officer in the Byzantine Empire, fighting in Sicily and serving in the emperor's bodyguard. He had brought great riches from the East when he returned home in 1045, and twenty-one years later he sailed with an immense fleet to attempt the conquest of England. The English Earl Tostig joined forces with him and the earldom of Orkney and others also lent assistance. Harald Harðráði was killed in the battle of Stamford Bridge in 1066. According to Snorri Sturluson he declaimed a poem before the battle in good Viking fashion, first one with which he was dissatisfied, then a stanza in scaldic style:

We do not creep in battle under the shelter of shields,
before the crash of weapons;
this is what the loyal goddess
of the hawk's land [woman] commanded us.
The bearer of the necklace told me long ago
to hold the prop of the helmet [head] high in the din
  of weapons,
when the valkyrie's ice [sword]
met the skulls of men.

The victor at Stamford Bridge was the king of England, Harold Godwinsson, brother of Earl Tostig. They were the scions of an English family which had enjoyed great advancement while Danish kings ruled the country, and Scandinavian blood coursed in their veins too.

The third protagonist was Duke William of Normandy, a descendant of Rollo, who had laid the foundation of the dukedom c. 911 and, according to the saga, was of the same family as the earls of Orkney. He landed in southern England three days after the Battle of Stamford Bridge, and defeated Harold Godwinsson.

Harald Harðráði's successors in Norway were his sons Magnus and Olaf. In 1069 Olaf, who was later known as Olaf Kyrre, 'the Quiet', became sole king. The expansionist policy was abandoned and Norway's foreign policy was now primarily concerned with exercising their power over the Norse islands – the Faroes, the Orkney earldom, the Isle of Man and the Hebrides – and with protecting their interests in Iceland.

Denmark and Sweden saw a new period of expansion in the twelfth and thirteenth centuries, with expeditions and conquests on the south and east coasts of the Baltic and in Finland. Some of these were Crusades. The vanquished were converted by force and Sweden gained a firm foothold in Finland. The Danish conquests in the West Slav area and in Estonia did not lead to any Danish settlements nor to any lasting Danish cultural influence.

The enormous energy which characterized the Viking Age and which had sent waves of people across many parts of Europe had now dwindled, but the deeds of the Viking Age inspired Scandinavian literature, history and politics, and enhanced national pride and identity.

Notes on the Translation

———

Personal names are generally given in their Old Norse normalized forms, the nominative endings omitted. However, in cases where an accepted English form exists, such as Cnut, this has been used. Place-names are given in their modern forms, whenever they exist.

Quotations are taken or translated from the following works.

I WORKS REFERRED TO *PASSIM*

RUNIC INSCRIPTIONS
(unless specified in II below)

Denmark (including Skåne): E. Moltke, *Runes and their Origin: Denmark and elsewhere*, Copenhagen, 1985.

Norway: Magnus Olsen *et al.*, *Norges innskrifter med de yngre runer*, Oslo, 1941 ff.

Sweden: S. B. F. Jansson, *Runes in Sweden*, Gidlunds, Stockholm, 1987.

THE ANGLO-SAXON CHRONICLE

English Historical Documents vol. 1 (ed. D. Whitelock), rev. ed. London, 1979.

ADAM OF BREMEN

History of the Archbishops of Hamburg-Bremen (trans. F. J. Tschan), New York, 1959.

AT-TARTUSHI AND IBN FADHLAN AND OTHER ARAB
TRAVELLERS
(unless specified in II below)

H. Birkeland, *Nordens historie i middelalderen etter arabiske kilder*,
Oslo, 1954.

The translations from Ibn Fadhlan have also used S. Wikander:
Araber Vikingar Väringar, Svenska Humanistiska Forbundet, 90,
Lund, 1978.

II INDIVIDUAL QUOTATIONS

p. 13   Snorri Sturluson on Ari: *Heimskringla*, Part 2, *Sagas of the
Norse Kings*, (trans. S. Laing, rev. P. Foote), London, New
York, 1975, p. 6.

p. 13   Snorri Sturluson on Harald Finehair: ibid., p. 4.

p. 17   Regino's Chronicle AD 892: *Quellen zur Karolingischen
Reichsgeschichte* Vol. 3 (rev. R. Rau), Darmstadt, 1969, p. 296 ff.

p. 30   *Rígsþula: Edda: Die Lieder des Codex Regius* I (ed. H. Kuhn),
Heidelberg, 1962, p. 280 ff.

p. 32   Danish fashions: *English Historical Documents* Vol. 1 (ed.
D. Whitelock), rev. ed. London, 1979, p. 895 ff.

p. 37   *Rígsþula:* op. cit.

p. 49   Ansgar AD 831: *Proceedings of the Sixth Viking Congress,
Uppsala 1969*, Uppsala, 1971, p. 74.

p. 53   Annals of Xanten AD 837: *Quellen zur Karolingischen
Reichsgeschichte* Vol. 2 (ed. R. Rau), Darmstadt, 1972, p. 324 ff.

p. 59   Dynna stone: Trans. R. I. Page in J. Graham-Campbell,
The Viking World, rev. ed. London, 1989, p. 158.

p. 62   *Hávamál: The Elder Edda: A Selection* (trans. P. B. Taylor
and W. H. Auden), London, 1969, p. 47 ff.

p. 69   Ansgar and King Olaf: *Rimbert: Ansgars levned* (trans. P. A.
Fenger, rev. H. Olrik), 5th ed. Copenhagen, 1926, p. 141.

p. 72   Magnus Barefoot: *Heimskringla*, op. cit., p. 275.

p. 74   Cnut's letter: *English Historical Documents* Vol. 1 (ed. D.
Whitelock), rev. ed. London, 1979, p. 476.

p. 88   Monk of St Omer: *Encomium Emmae Reginae* (ed. and
trans. A. Campbell), *Camden Third Series* vol. 72, London,
1949, p. 12 ff.

p. 105 Ohthere: *Two Voyagers to the Court of King Alfred* (ed. N. Lund, trans. C. Fell), York, 1984, p. 18 ff.

p. 117 At-Tartūshi on Hedeby: J. Graham-Campbell, *The Viking World*, rev. ed. London, 1989, p. 92.

p. 118 Annals of Fulda AD 873: *Quellen zur Karolingischen Reichsgeschichte* Vol. 3 (rev. R. Rau), Darmstadt, 1969, p. 88 ff.

p. 145 Egil Skallagrímsson: *Egil's saga* (ed. and trans. C. Fell, poems trans. J. Lucas), London, 1975, p. 70.

p. 162 Widukind: *Quellen zur Geschichte der sächsischen Kaiserzeit* (rev. A. Bauer and R. Rau), Darmstadt, 1971, p. 168 ff.

p. 178 Hällestad stone: Sven B. F. Jansson, *Runes in Sweden*, (trans. Peter Foote), Stockholm, 1987, p. 86.

p. 181 *Vǫluspá: The Elder Edda*, op. cit., p. 145

p. 182 *Hávamál: The Elder Edda*, op. cit., p. 47

p. 182 Egil Skallagrímsson: *Egil's saga*, op. cit., pp. xxiii ff, 84 ff.

p. 187 Dudo: *Dudo: Normandiets historie under de første Hertuger* (trans. E. Albrectsen), Odense, 1979, p. 23.

p. 190 Senja ring: R. I. Page, *'A most vile people': Early English historians on the Vikings*, Dorothea Coke Memorial Lecture 1986, London, 1987, p. 6.

p. 197 Annals of St Bertin AD 841: *Quellen zur Karolingischen Reichsgeschichte* Vol. 2 (rev. R. Rau), Darmstadt, 1972, p. 54 ff.

p. 198 Attack on Paris AD 845: ibid., p. 66 ff.

p. 199 Ermentarius of Noirmoutier: J. Graham-Campbell, *The Viking World*, rev. ed. London, 1989, p. 31 ff.

p. 199 Settlement in Aquitaine: *Quellen zur Karolingischen Reichsgeschichte*, Vol. 2, p. 66 ff.

p. 200 Lothar and Rurik: ibid., p. 76 ff.

p. 201 Regino Chronicle: op. cit., p. 268 ff.

p. 216 Iona stone: A. Liestøl, 'An Iona Rune Stone', *The Viking Age in the Isle of Man*, Select papers from the Ninth Viking Congress, Isle of Man, 4–14 July 1981 (ed. C. Fell et al.), London, 1983, p. 85.

p. 218 Kirk Michael stone: H. Shetelig, *Viking Antiquities in Great Britain and Ireland* Part 4, Oslo, 1954, p. 209.

p. 253 Óttar: *Knytlinga saga* (ed. and trans. Hermann Pálsson and P. Edwards), Odense, 1986, p. 28.

p. 256 Cnut: ibid., p. 43.

p. 259   St Paul's stone: E. Moltke, *Runes and their Origin: Denmark and Elsewhere*, Copenhagen, 1985, p. 325.

p. 266   Ari: 'The Book of the Icelanders (Íslendingabók)' (ed. and trans. Halldórr Hermansson), *Islandica* Vol. 20, Cornell, 1930, p. 60.

p. 287   'The Legend of the Calling of the Princes': *The Russian Primary Chronicle: Laurentian Text* (ed. and trans. S. H. Cross and O. P. Sherbowitz-Wetzor), Cambridge MA, 1953?, p. 59.

p. 289   Berezani inscription: S. B. F. Jansson, *Runes in Sweden*, Gidlunds, Stockholm, 1987, p. 61.

p. 297   Harald Harðráði: E. O. G. Turville-Petre, *Harald the Hard-ruler and his Poets*, Dorothea Coke Memorial Lecture 1966, London, 1968, p. 20.

BIBLIOGRAPHY

This bibliography is intended as an introduction to the extensive literature about the Viking Age and to the documentary sources. Most of the works cited contain further references.

Whenever an English translation of a foreign work has been published, the English edition is given. Editions of documentary sources are given in their modern translations (English wherever possible) and nearly all contain extensive commentaries. Quotations are taken from these and from other editions. A full list of the sources of quotations can be found in the section Notes on the Translation.

1 GENERAL WORKS

B. Almgren et al., *The Viking*, Gothenburg, 1967.

H. Arbman, *The Vikings*, London, 1961; rev. 1962; Boulder CO, 1961.

P. G. Foote and D. M. Wilson, *The Viking Achievement*, London, 1970; rev. 1980; New York, 1970.

J. Graham-Campbell, *Viking Artefacts: A select catalogue*, London, 1980.

J. Graham-Campbell, *The Viking World*, London, 1980; rev. 1989.

J. Graham-Campbell and D. Kidd, *The Vikings*, London, New York, 1980.

E. Haugen, *The Scandinavian Languages: An Introduction to their History*, London, 1976.

G. Jones, *A History of the Vikings*, Oxford, New York, 1968; rev. 1984.

M. Magnusson, *Vikings!*, London, 1980.

The Northern World (ed. D. M. Wilson), London, 1980.

R. I. Page, *Runes*, London, 1987.

P. H. Sawyer, *The Age of the Vikings*, London, 1962; rev. 1971.

P. H. Sawyer, *Kings and Vikings*, London, 1982.

H. Zettel, *Das Bild der Normannen und der Normanneneinfälle in westfränkischen, ostfränkischen und angelsächsischen Quellen des 8. bis 11. Jahrhunderts*, Munich, 1977.

2   LEXICA AND CURRENT CONGRESS REPORTS

Beretning fra første (*ff.*) *tværfaglige vikingesymposium* (published by Forlaget Hikuin and Afdeling for middelalder-arkæologi), Århus, 1983 ff.

Kulturhistorisk Leksikon for Nordisk Middelalder I–XXII, Copenhagen, 1956–78; reprinted 1980–82.

Reallexikon der Germanischen Altertumskunde (ed. H. Beck et al.), 1 ff., Berlin, New York, 1973 ff.

Vikingatidens ABC (ed. L. Thunmark-Nylen et al.), Stockholm, 1981.

Proceedings of the First (*ff.*) *Viking Congress* (proceedings of interdisciplinary Viking congresses held every four years since 1949, published in English in a Scandinavian or British country under slightly varying titles).

3   SELECTED DOCUMENTARY SOURCES

SCANDINAVIAN

Danmarks Runeindskrifter (ed. L. Jacobsen and E. Moltke), Copenhagen, 1941–2.

Norges innskrifter med de yngre runer 1–5 (ed. M. Olsen and A. Liestøl), Oslo, 1941–60.

Sveriges Runinskrifter, Stockholm, 1900 ff.

S. B. F. Jansson, *Runes in Sweden*, Gidlunds, Stockholm, 1987.

E. Moltke, *Runes and their Origin: Denmark and elsewhere*, Copenhagen, 1985.

The Elder Edda: A Selection (trans. P. B. Taylor and W. H. Auden), London, 1969.

The Poetic Edda (trans. and introd. Lee M. Hollander), University of Texas Press, 2nd rev. ed. 1969.

Snorri Sturluson, *Edda* (trans. and introd. A. Faulkes), London and Melbourne, 1987.

Finnur Jónsson, *Den norsk-islandske skjaldedigtning* 1–4, Copenhagen, 1912–15.

G. Jones, *The Norse Atlantic Saga*, London, New York, Toronto, 1964; rev. 1986.

Orkneyinga Saga (trans. Hermann Pálsson and P. Edwards), London, 1978.

Snorri Sturluson, *Heimskringla: The Olaf Sagas* 1–2 (trans. S. Laing, rev. J. Simpson), London, New York, 1964 (and later eds).

Snorri Sturluson, *Heimskringla: Sagas of the Norse Kings*, (trans. S. Laing, rev. P. Foote), London, New York, 1961 (and later eds).

Two voyagers at the Court of King Alfred: The ventures of Ohthere and Wulfstan (ed. N. Lund, trans. C. Fell), York, 1984.

FROM THE MAINLAND OF WESTERN EUROPE

Abbon. *Le siège de Paris par les Normands: Poème du IXe siècle* (trans. and ed. H. Waquet), *Les classiques de l'histoire de France au moyen age*, Paris, 1942; 2nd ed. 1964.

Adam of Bremen. *History of the Archbishops of Hamburg-Bremen*, (trans. F. J. Tschan), New York, 1975.

Dudo. *Normandiets Historie under de første Hertuger* (trans. and commentary E. Albrectsen), Odense, 1979.

Quellen zur Karolingischen Reichsgeschichte I, Die Reichsannalen, Einhard Leben Karls des Grossen, Zwei 'Leben' Ludwigs, Nithard Geschichten (rev. R. Rau), Berlin, 1955.

Quellen zur Karolingischen Reichsgeschichte II, Jahrbücher von St Bertin, Jahrbücher von St Vaast, Xantener Jahrbücher (rev. R. Rau), Darmstadt, 1972.

Quellen zur Karolingischen Reichsgeschichte III, Jahrbücher von Fulda, Regino Chronik, Notker Taten Karls (rev. R. Rau), Darmstadt, 1969.

Rimbert. 'Leben Ansgars', *Quellen des 9. und 11. Jahrhunderts zur Geschichte der Hamburgischen Kirche und des Reiches* (ed. W. Trillmich and R. Buchner), Darmstadt, 1973.

B. W. Scholtz, *Carolingian Chronicles*, Ann Arbor MI, 1970.

Vikingerne i Franken: Skriftlige Kilder fra det 9. Århundrede (trans. E. Albrectsen), Odense, 1976. (Extracts from annals and chronicles which mention Vikings.)

Vikingerne i Paris: Beretninger fra 9. århundrede (trans. and commentary N. Skyum-Nielsen), 2nd rev. ed. Copenhagen, 1967.

Widukind. 'Sachsengeschichte', *Quellen zur Geschichte der sächsischen Kaiserzeit* (rev. A. Bauer and R. Rau), Darmstadt, 1971.

ANGLO-SAXON

Encomium Emmae Reginae (ed. and trans. A. Campbell), London, 1949. (Written in Flanders.)

English Historical Documents I, *c.* 500–1042 (ed. D. Whitelock), London, 1955; rev. ed. 1979. (This is the best modern English translation of the various editions of the Anglo-Saxon Chronicle; it also includes a number of other sources which mention Vikings.)

EASTERN EUROPEAN AND ISLAMIC

H. Birkeland, *Nordens historie i middelalderen etter arabiske kilder*, Oslo, 1954.

M. Canard, 'La relation du voyage d'Ibn Fadlan chez les Bulgares de la Volga', *Annales de l'Institut d'études orientales*, Alger 16, 1958.

Constantine Porphyrogenitus de Administrando Imperio (ed. Gy. Moravcsik, trans. R. J. H. Jenkins), Dumbarton Oaks Texts I, Columbia, 1967.

G. Jacob, 'Arabische Berichte von Gesandten an germanische Fürstenhöfe aus dem 9. und 10. Jahrhundert', *Quellen zur Deutschen Volkskunde* I (trans. and notes V. von Geramb et al.), Berlin, Leipzig, 1927.

The Russian Primary Chronicle: Laurentian Text (trans. and ed. S. H. Cross and O. P. Sherbowitz-Wetzor), Cambridge MA, 1953?

4 SCANDINAVIA

A   SURVEYS AND GENERAL WORKS

G. Fellows-Jensen, 'Place-name research in Scandinavia 1960–82', *Names*, Vol. 32, No. 3, 1984.

Hus, Gård og Bebyggelse (ed. G. Ólafsson), Reykjavik, 1983.

L. Weibull, *Nordisk historia I. Forskningar och undersökningar*, Lund, 1948. (A collection of articles written over a number of years.)

Denmark

Archäologische und naturwissenschaftlische Untersuchungen an ländlischen und frühstädtischen Siedlungen im deutschen Küstengebiet, Vol. 2, *Händelsplätze* (ed. H. Jankuhn et al.), Bonn, 1984.

Berichte über die Ausgrabungen in Haithabu, 1 ff. (ed. K. Schietzel), Neumünster, 1969 ff.

A. E. Christensen, *Vikingetidens Danmark*, Copenhagen, 1969; reprinted 1977.

N. Lund and K. Hørby, 'Samfundet i vikingetid og middelalder 800–1500', *Dansk social historie 2*, Copenhagen, 1980.

E. Moltke, *Runes and their Origin: Denmark and elsewhere*, Copenhagen, 1985.

E. Roesdahl, *Viking Age Denmark*, London, 1982.

P. Sawyer, 'Da Danmark blev Danmark', *Gyldendals og Politikens Danmarkshistorie 3* (ed. O. Olsen), Copenhagen, 1988.

I. Skovgaard-Petersen, 'Oldtid og vikingetid', *Danmarks Historie I* (I. Skovgaard-Petersen et al.), Copenhagen, 1977.

Norway

P. S. Andersen, *Samlingen av Norge og kristningen av landet 800–1130*, Oslo, 1977.

A. W. Brøgger, H. Falk, H. Shetelig, *Osebergfundet I–V*, Oslo, 1917–28.

B. Magnus and B. Myhre, *Norges Historie* Vol. 1, Oslo, 1976; rev. 1986.

Norwegian Archaeological Review Vol. 15, 1–2, 1982.

Proceedings of the Tenth Viking Congress, Universitetets Oldsaksamlings Skrifter, Ny Rekke nr. 9, Festskrift for Charlotte Blindheim (ed. J. E. Knirk), Oslo, 1987.

T. Sjøvold, *The Iron Age Settlement of Arctic Norway* II, Oslo, 1977.

Vikingtog og Vikingtid (with contributions by C. Blindheim et al.), Schipsteds Forlag, Oslo, 1977.

Sweden

H. Arbman, *Birka I: Die Gräber, Tafeln*, Stockholm, 1940; *Text*, Uppsala, 1943.

Birka II (1–3): Systematische Analysen der Gräberfunde (ed. G. Arwidsson), Stockholm, 1984, 1986, 1989.

Gutar och vikingar (ed. I. Jansson), Stockholm, 1983.

S. B. F. Jansson, *Runes in Sweden*, Stockholm, 1987.

E. Lønnroth, 'Administration och samhälle i 1000-talets Sverige', *Bebyggelseshistorisk Tidsskrift* 4, 1982.

E. Nylen and J. P. Lamm, *Stones, Ships and Symbols*, Stockholm, 1988.

P. Sawyer, *The Making of Sweden*, Occasional papers on Medieval Topics 3, Alingsås, 1988.

M. Stenberger, *Det forntida Sverige*, Uppsala, 1964; reprinted 1971.

H. Wideen, *Västsvenska vikingatidsstudier*, Gothenburg, 1955.

I. Zahrisson, *Lapps and Scandinavians*, Stockholm, 1976.

B SUPPLEMENTARY WORKS

The people (pp. 30–45)

I. Hägg, *Kvinnodräkten i Birka*, Uppsala, 1974.

I. Hägg, 'Birkas orientalska praktplagg', *Fornvännen* 78, 3–4, 1983.

I. Hägg, 'Die Textilfunde aus dem Hafen von Haithabu', *Berichte über die Ausgrabungen in Haithabu* 20 (ed. K. Schietzel), Neumünster, 1984.

B. J. Sellevold, U. Lund Hansen, J. Balslev Jørgensen, *Iron Age Man in Denmark*, Copenhagen, 1984.

Kings and kingdoms (pp. 64–77)

A. W. Brøgger, *Borrefundet og Vestfoldkongernes grave*, Videnskapsselskapets Skrifter 2, Christiania, 1916.

J. Kornerup, *Kongehøiene i Jellinge*, Copenhagen, 1875.

K. J. Krogh, 'The Royal Viking-Age Monuments in Jelling in

the Light of Recent Archaeological Excavations', *Acta Archaeologica* 53, 1982.

Travel, transport and ships (pp. 78–93)

A. Binns, *Viking Voyagers: Then and Now*, London, 1980.

A. W. Brøgger and H. Shetelig, *The Viking Ships*, Oslo, 1951.

O. Crumlin-Pedersen, 'Viking shipbuilding and seamanship', *Proceedings of the Eighth Viking Congress 1977* (ed. H. Bekker-Nielsen et al.), Odense, 1981.

O. Crumlin-Pedersen, 'Cargo ships of Northern Europe AD 800–1300', *Conference on Waterfront Archaeology in North European Towns* No. 2 (ed. A. Herteig), Bergen, 1985.

D. Ellmers, *Frühmittelalterliche Handelsschiffart in Mittel- und Nordeuropa*, Neumünster, 1972.

R. Malmros, 'Leding og skjaldekvad', *Aarbøger for nordisk Oldkyndighed og Historie*, 1985.

O. Olsen and O. Crumlin-Pedersen, *Five Viking Ships from Roskilde Fjord*, Copenhagen, 1978.

Sailing into the Past (ed. O. Crumlin-Pedersen and M. Winner), Roskilde, 1986.

Livelihood and settlement (pp. 94–107)

B. Ambrosiani, *Fornlämningar och bebyggelse*, Uppsala, 1964.

S. Hvass, 'Vorbasse – Eine Dorfsiedlung während des 1. Jahrhunderts n. Chr. in Mitteljütland, Dänemark', *Von der Eisenzeit zum Mittelalter: Bericht der Römisch-Germanischen Kommission* 67, Frankfurt am Main, 1986.

Iron and Man in Prehistoric Sweden (ed. H. Clarke), Stockholm, 1979.

G. S. Munch and O. S. Johansen, 'Borg in Lofoten: An Inter-Scandinavian Research Project', *Norwegian Archaeological Review* Vol. 21, No. 2, 1988.

A. Skjølsvold, *Klebersteinsindustrien i Vikingetiden*, Oslo, 1961.

Exchange, silver and merchandise (pp. 108–16), *Trade and towns* (pp. 117–28)

B. Ambrosiani, *Birka*, Svenska Kulturminnen 2, Uddevalla, 1988.

H. H. Andersen, P. J. Crabb, H. J. Madsen, *Århus Søndervold: En byarkæologisk undersøgelse*, Højbjerg, 1971.

C. Blindheim and R. Tollnes, *Kaupang: Vikingernes handelsplass*, Oslo, 1972.

A. Christophersen, 'Royal authority and early urbanization in Trondheim during the transition to the historical period', *Arkeologiske Skrifter Historisk Museum* Vol. 5, 1989.

R. H. M. Dolley, *Viking Coins of the Danelaw and Dublin*, London, 1969.

L. B. Frandsen and S. Jensen, 'Pre-Viking and Early Viking Age Ribe', *Journal of Danish Archaeology* 6, 1987.

B. Hårdh, 'Trade and Money in Scandinavia in the Viking Age', *Meddelanden från Lunds Universitets Historiska Museum*, 1977–8.

H. Jankuhn, *Haithabu*, 8th ed., Neumünster, 1986.

B. Malmer, *Mynt och människor*, Stockholm, 1968.

U. Näsman, 'Om fjärrhandel i Sydskandinaviens ynge järnålder', *Hikuin* 16, 1990.

Ribe Excavations 1970–76 (ed. M. Bencard), 1 ff., Esbjerg, 1981 ff.

Society and Trade in the Baltic during the Viking Age, Visbysymposiet 1983 (ed. S.-O. Lindquist), Visby, 1985.

Untersuchungen zu Handel und Verkehr der vor- und frühgeschichtlichen Zeit in Mittel- und Nordeuropa IV (ed. K. Düwel et al.), Göttingen, 1987.

Viking-Age Coinage in the Northern Lands (ed. M. A. S. Blackburn and D. M. Metcalf), Oxford, 1981.

V. Vogel, *Schleswig im Mittelalter: Archäeologie einer Stadt*, Neumünster, 1989.

Fortifications, weapons and warfare (pp. 129–46)

H. H. Andersen, H. J. Madsen, O. Voss, *Danevirke* I–II, Copenhagen, 1976.

Eketorp: Fortification and Settlement on Öland/Sweden: The Monument (ed. K. Borg, U. Näsman, E. Wegræus), Stockholm, 1976.

N. Lund, 'The armies of Swein Forkbeard and Cnut: *leding* or *lið*?', *Anglo-Saxon England* 15, 1986.

O. Olsen and H. Schmidt, *Fyrkat I: Borgen og bebyggelsen*, Copenhagen, 1977.

E. Roesdahl, *Fyrkat II: Oldsagerne og gravpladsen*, Copenhagen, 1977.

E. Roesdahl, 'The Danish geometrical Viking fortresses and their Context', *Anglo-Norman Studies* IX, 1987.

The old and the new religion (pp. 147–67)

The Christianization of Scandinavia (ed. B. Sawyer, P. Sawyer, I. Wood), Alingsås, 1987.

A. S. Gräslund, *Birka IV: The Burial Customs*, Uppsala, 1980.

K. J. Krogh, 'The Royal Viking-Age Monuments in Jelling in the Light of Recent Archaeological Excavations', *Acta Archaeologica* 53, 1982.

M. Müller-Wille, 'Opferplätze der Wikingerzeit', *Frühmittelalterliche Studien* 18, 1984.

O. Olsen, *Hørg, hov og kirke*, Copenhagen, 1966.

R. I. Page, *Norse Myths*, London, 1990.

E. O. G. Turville-Petre, *Myth and Religion of the North*, London, 1964.

Art and poetry (pp. 168–84)

Egil's Saga (trans. and ed. C. Fell, poems trans. by J. Lucas), London, 1975; paperback ed. 1985.

P. Foote, 'Scandinavische Dichtung der Wikingerzeit', *Europäisches Frühmittelalter* (ed. K. von See), *Neues Handbuch der Litteraturwissenschaft* Vol. 6, Wiesbaden, 1985.

S. H. Fuglesang, 'Vikingetidens kunst', *Norges Kunsthistorie* I (ed. K. Berg et al.), Oslo, 1981.

S. H. Fuglesang, 'Stylistic Groups in Late Viking and Early Romanesque Art': 'Early Viking Art', *Acta ad Archaeologicam et Artium Historiam Pertinentia* (ser. alt. in 8), Vols. I–II, 1981, 1982.

J. Graham-Campbell, 'From Scandinavia to the Irish Sea: Viking art reviewed', *Ireland and Insular Art* (ed. M. Ryan), Dublin, 1987.

J. Kristjánsson, *Eddas and Sagas. Iceland's Medieval Literature* (trans. P. Foote), Reykjavik, 1988.

E. O. G. Turville-Petre, *Scaldic Poetry*, Oxford, 1976.

D. M. Wilson and O. Klindt-Jensen, *Viking Art*, London, 1966; 2nd edition 1980.

5 THE EXPANSION

A number of the works listed in 1, 2 and 4 A above also deal with the expansion or aspects of it. The sources listed under 3, most of which are accompanied by extensive commentaries, are of vital importance for the understanding of the expansion in the individual regions.

N. P. Brooks, 'England in the Ninth Century: The Crucible of Defeat', *Transactions of the Royal Historical Society* 5th series, vol. 29, London, 1979.

R. Frank, 'Viking Atrocity and Scaldic Verse: The Rite of the Blood-Eagle', *English Historical Review* XCIX, 1984.

R. I. Page, *'A most vile people': Early English historians on the Vikings*, Dorothea Coke Memorial Lecture 1986, London, 1987.

The mainland of Western Europe (pp. 195–209)

J. Adigard des Gautries, *Les noms de personnes scandinaves en Normandie de 911 à 1066*, Lund, 1954.

D. Bates, *Normandy before 1066*, London, 1982.

F.-X. Dillmann, 'Les vikings dans l'Empire franc: Bibliographie', *Revue du Nord* LVI, No. 220, 1974.

G. Fellows-Jensen, 'Scandinavian place-names and Viking settlements in Normandy: a review', *Namn och Bygd* 76, 1988.

A. d'Haenens, *Les invasions normandes en Belgique au IXe siècle: Le phénomène de sa répercussion dans l'histoire médievale*, Louvain-Paris, 1967.

M. Müller-Wille, 'Das Schiffsgrab von der Ile de Groix (Bretagne)', *Berichte über die Ausgrabungen in Haithabu* 12 (ed. K. Schietzel), Neumünster, 1978.

L. Musset, 'Naissance de la Normandie', *Histoire de la Normandie*, (ed. M. de Bouard), Toulouse, 1970.

H. H. van Regteren Altena and H. A. Heidinga, 'The North Sea region in the Early Medieval period (400–950)', *Ex Horreo*, 1977.

W. Vogel, *Die Normannen und das fränkische Reich bis zur Gründung der Normandie (799–911)*, Heidelberg, 1906.

Scotland and the Isle of Man (pp. 210–20)

C. E. Batey, *Freswick Links, Caithness: a re-appraisal of the Late Norse site in its context*, BAR, Oxford, 1987.

B. Crawford, *Scandinavian Scotland*, Leicester, 1987.

J. A. Graham-Campbell, 'The Viking-Age silver and gold hoards of Scandinavian character from Scotland', *Proceedings of the Society of Antiquaries of Scotland* Vol. 107, 1975–6.

C. D. Morris, 'Viking Orkney: A Survey', *The Prehistory of Orkney* (ed. C. Renfrew), Edinburgh, 1985.

W. F. H. Nicolaisen, *Scottish Place-names*, London, 1976.

The Northern Isles (ed. F. T. Wainwright), Edinburgh, 1962.

The Northern and Western Isles in the Viking World: Survival, continuity and change (ed. A. Fenton and H. Pálsson), Edinburgh, 1984.

Orkney Heritage Vol. 2, Birsay, Kirkwall, 1983.

The Viking Age in the Isle of Man, Select papers from the Ninth Viking Congress, Isle of Man (ed. C. Fell et al.), London, 1983.

D. M. Wilson, *The Viking Age in the Isle of Man: The archaeological evidence*, Odense, 1974.

D. M. Wilson, 'Scandinavian settlement in the North and West of the British Isles: an archaeological point-of-view', *Transactions of the Royal Historical Society*, 5th series, Vol. 26, 1976.

Ireland (pp. 221–32)

T. Fanning, 'The Archaeology of the Vikings in Ireland', *A Survey of Irish Archaeology to 1600 AD* (ed. J. Bradley et al.), Dublin, 1990.

D. Ó Corráin, *Ireland before the Normans*, Dublin, 1972 (and later eds).

M. and L. de Paor, *Early Christian Ireland*, London, 1958.

Proceedings of the Seventh Viking Congress: Dublin (ed. B. Almqvist et al.), Dublin, 1976.

A. P. Smyth, *Scandinavian York and Dublin*, Dublin, 1975; 1979.

Viking Dublin exposed: The Wood Quay saga (ed. J. Bradley), Dublin, 1984.

P. Wallace, 'The Archaeology of Viking Dublin', *The Comparative History of Urban Origins in Non-Roman Europe* (ed. H. B. Clarke et al.), Oxford, 1985.

P. Wallace, 'The Economy and Commerce of Viking Age Dublin', *Untersuchungen zu Handel und Verkehr der vor- und frühgeschichtlichen Zeit* IV (ed. K. Düvel et al.), Göttingen, 1987.

England (pp. 233–61)

R. Bailey, *Viking Age Sculpture in Northern England*, London, 1980.

G. Fellows-Jensen, 'Anglo-Saxons and Vikings in the British Isles: the place-name evidence', *Angli e sassone al di qua e al di là del mare* 2, Spoleto, 1986.

S. H. Fuglesang, 'The Relationship between Scandinavian and English Art from the Late Eighth to the Mid-Twelfth Century', *Sources of Anglo-Saxon Culture* (ed. P. E. Szarmach), Kalamazoo MI, 1986.

J. Graham-Campbell, 'The Archaeology of the Danelaw: An Introduction', *Les Mondes Normands* (ed. H. Galinié), Caen, 1989.

R. Hall, *The Viking Dig: The excavations at York*, London, 1984.

S. Keynes, 'A Tale of Two Kings: Alfred the Great and Æthelred the Unready', *Transactions of the Royal Historical Society* 5th ser., Vol. 36, 1986.

T. Kisbye, *Vikingerne i England. Sproglige spor*, Århus, 1982.

L. M. Larson, *Cnut the Great*, New York, 1912.

H. R. Loyn, *The Vikings in Britain*, London, 1977.

N. Lund, 'The armies of Swein Forkbeard and Cnut: *leding* or *lið*?', *Anglo-Saxon England* 15, 1986.

K. Mack, 'Changing Thegns: Cnut's Conquest and the English Aristocracy', *Albion* 16, 4, 1984.

C. D. Morris, 'The Vikings in the British Isles: some aspects of their settlement and economy', *The Vikings* (ed. R. T. Farrell), London, 1982.

F. M. Stenton, *Anglo-Saxon England*, 3rd ed., London, 1971.

Viking Age York and the North (ed. R. Hall), London, 1978.

The Vikings in England (ed. E. Roesdahl et al.), London, 1981.

D. M. Wilson, 'The Scandinavians in England', *The Archaeology of Anglo-Saxon England* (ed. D. M. Wilson), London, 1976.

D. M. Wilson, *The Bayeux Tapestry*, London, 1985.

Iceland, the Faroes, Greenland and America (pp. 262–76)

S. V. Arge, 'Om landnamet på Færøerne', *Beretning fra sjette tværfaglige vikingesymposium* (ed. G. Fellows-Jensen and N. Lund), Århus, 1987.

S. Dahl, 'The Norse Settlement of the Faroe Islands', *Medieval Archaeology* XIV, 1970.

K. Eldjárn, *Kuml og haugfé ur heiðnum sið á Íslandi*, Akureyri, 1956.

K. Eldjárn, *Skriftlige og arkæologiske vidnesbyrd om Islands ældste bebyggelse*, Nyt fra Odense Universitet, Særnummer, August 1974.

F. Gad, *History of Greenland*, Vol. 1 ff, London, 1970 ff.

Grønland, Nos. 5–9 (published by Det grønlandske Selskab), 1982.

K. Hastrup, *Culture and History in Medieval Iceland: An Anthropological Analysis of Structure and Change*, Oxford, 1985.

A. S. Ingstad, *The Discovery of a Norse Settlement in America*, Oslo, 1977; reprinted with corrections under the title *The Norse Discovery of America* vol. I, *Excavations of a Norse Settlement at l'Anse aux Meadows, New Foundland, 1961–1968*, Oslo, 1985.

G. Jones, *The Norse Atlantic Saga*, 2nd ed. Oxford, New York, 1986 (with appendices by B. Wallace, T. McGovern, R. McGhee).

K. J. Krogh, *Viking Greenland*, Copenhagen, 1967; revised and extended Danish ed. *Erik den Rødes Grønland* (sagatekster ved H. Bekker-Nielsen), Copenhagen, 1982.

P. Meulengracht Sørensen, *Saga og Samfund*, Copenhagen, 1977.

B. Thorsteinsson, 'Island', *Politikens Danmarkshistorie*, Copenhagen, 1985.

The Vinland Sagas: The Norse Discovery of America (trans. and introd. M. Magnusson and H. Pálsson), Penguin Books, Harmondsworth, 1965.

The Baltic region, Russia, Byzantium and the Caliphate (pp. 277–92)

Only works in West European languages have been cited.

H. Arbman, *Svear i Österviking*, Stockholm, 1955.

T. J. Arne, *La Suède et l'Orient*, Uppsala, 1914.

Gutar och vikingar (ed. I. Jansson), Stockholm, 1983.

I. Jansson, 'Communications between Scandinavia and Eastern Europe in the Viking Age', *Untersuchungen zu Handel und Verkehr der vor- und frühgeschichtlichen Zeit* IV (ed. K. Düvel et al.), Göttingen, 1987.

E. N. Nosov, 'New data on the Ryurik Gorodishche near Novgorod', *Fennoscandia archeologica* IV, 1987.

Oldenburg—Wolin—Staraja Ladoga—Novgorod—Kiev: Handel und Handelsverbindungen im südlichen und östlichen Ostseeraum während des frühen Mittelalters, Bericht der Römisch-Germanischen Kommission 69, Frankfurt, 1988.

H. Paszkiewicz, *The Origin of Russia*, London, 1954.

Les Pays du Nord et Byzance (ed. R. Zeitler), Uppsala, 1981.

The Russian Primary Chronicle: Laurentian Text (ed. and trans. S. H. Cross and O. P. Sherbowitz-Wetzor), The Medieval Academy of America, No. 60, Cambridge MA, 1953?

Society and Trade in the Baltic during the Viking Age, Visbysymposiet 1983 (ed. S.-O. Lindquist), Visby, 1985.

A. Stalsberg, 'Scandinavian relations with North-western Russia during the Viking Age: the archaeological evidence', *Journal of Baltic Studies* 13/3, 1982.

Untersuchungen zu Handel und Verkehr der vor- und frühgeschichtlichen Zeit in Mittel- und Nordeuropa IV (ed. K. Düvel et al.), Göttingen, 1987.

Varangian Problems (ed. K. Hannestad et al.), *Scando-Slavica*, Supplementum I, Copenhagen, 1970.

Wikinger und Slawen (ed. J. Herrmann), Berlin, 1982.

INDEXES

GENERAL INDEX

Page numbers in bold type indicate multiple references to the entry; page numbers in italic indicate illustrations

INDEX OF PERSONAL NAMES

INDEX OF PLACES